Gods and Goddesses

IN THE GARDEN

Gods and Goddesses

IN THE GARDEN

Greco-Roman Mythology
and the Scientific Names of Plants

PETER BERNHARDT

RUTGERS UNIVERSITY PRESS

NEW BRUNSWICK, NEW JERSEY, AND LONDON

Library of Congress Cataloging-in-Publication Data

Bernhardt, Peter, 1952–
Gods and goddesses in the garden : Greco-Roman mythology and the
scientific names of plants / Peter Bernhardt.
p. cm.
Includes bibliographical references and index.
ISBN 978–0-8135–4266–9 (hardcover : alk. paper)
1. Plants—Nomenclature. 2. Plants—Mythology. 3. Plants—Forklore.
I. Title.
QK96.B27 2008
580.1′4—dc22
2007024985

A British Cataloging-in-Publication record for this book is available
from the British Library.

Visit our Web site: http://rutgerspress.rutgers.edu

Manufactured in the United States of America

DEDICATED TO THE MEMORY OF MY GRANDFATHER,

Harold Bernhardt.

He was so embarrassed by his lack of education, yet he
ran his own florist's shop and enjoyed introducing his customers
to the scientific names of plants.

Contents

PREFACE

The Face in the Flower

Thou still unravished bride of quietness!
Thou foster-child of Silence and slow Time,
Sylvan historian, who canst thus express
A flowery tale more sweetly than our rhyme:
What leaf-fringed legend haunts about thy shape
Of deities or mortals, or of both,
In Tempe or the dales of Arcady?

—JOHN KEATS, "Ode on a Grecian Urn"

Is it better for gardeners, professional horticulturists, conservationists, and naturalists to learn the common names of plants or their scientific names? Readers of my past books know I emphasize the importance of common names, as they offer a royal road to world folklore and economic botany. The more common names a plant receives, both regionally and in different languages, the easier it is to discern how different cultures have viewed it and used it over time. Perennial herbs sold under the name of monkshood or troll's hat reflect nothing more than a whimsical interpretation of a flower's shape. When the same plants are called wolfsbane or badger's bane, they take us back to darker times when roots were rendered to make poison baits to lure and kill wild animals.

Unfortunately, when common names are employed exclusively to make identifications, we are often forced to contend with three equally frustrating problems. First, many plants lack common names, or their common names were lost. It is estimated that there are more than a quarter of a million plant species on this planet. Natural variation defies human imagination and verbal creativity. Traditional cultures often fail to name plants that have no immediate use. Thousands of wild orchid species cling to the limbs of trees from southern Mexico to Panama, for example, but local people, if questioned, are likely to refer to almost all of them as *parasitas* (parasites), or to their flowers as *conchitas* (little shells). The famous ethnobotanist and conservationist Paul Cox warns that as "weedy, European languages" (especially English and Spanish) infiltrate the few remaining indigenous cultures around the world, common names of plants are lost after a single generation. This is a tragedy, as the aboriginal name of a tree often tells you its specific use as a tool, medicine, or recreational drug.

The second problem is that common names are too imprecise for identification purposes because very different species often have the exact same name. Some of us make bad choices when we try to use a common name to match up a source of bulbs or seeds in insufficiently illustrated catalogs. For example, in the United States, Sweet William is a name given to a popular bedding plant (*Dianthus barbatus*), but it is also applied to some native *Phlox* species now in cultivation. Moreover, the same common name is often applied to many closely related plants, making it harder to select the one you really want. Do you like basil in pesto and tomato sauces? There are at least a 150 wild species of plants called basil in English and an additional four or five of these species are domesticated plants in cultivation. Their foliage produces essential oils, but fragrances vary in composition and concentration from species to species. One of these herbs (*Ocimum basilcium*) tastes best on a pizza, whereas another serves in Hindu rituals (*O. sanctum*). If a woman is offered basil (*O. selloi*) while visiting Uruguay, it may be an unsubtle hint that she needs a traditional remedy to curb her fertility, not an invitation to dinner.

That leads to the third problem. Common names do not respect natural alliances based on shared genes. Rockroses (*Cistus* spp.), the rose bay (*Nerium oleander*), the guelder rose (*Viburnum opulus*), native roses (*Boronia* spp.), and the rose pink (*Sabatia angularis*) all share one thing in common. None of them belong to the rose family (Rosaceae). In contrast, such different-sounding names as old goose, Noah's Ark, moccasin flower, sparrow's egg, *flor de pelicano*, and hare's lip are applied to thirteen closely related species of North American orchids in the genus *Cypripedium*.

You cannot assemble a collection of closely related plants if you do not know the classification rules and terminology that assure you that these plants belong to the same "family tree." You cannot protect any endangered species until everyone agrees that all remaining small, isolated populations are composed of the same thing.

I apologize for opening with a trick question. The honest answer is that we need both common *and* scientific names if we want to verify scientific research, keep a greenhouse for business or pleasure, design herb gardens, enjoy walks in the woods, participate in eco-tourism, and vote on pressing environmental issues. Many English-speaking residents of Britain, South Africa, Australia, and New Zealand store lots of common and scientific names in their memories, much as we keep shovels and rakes in garden sheds. You cannot do the job right without the right tool. Many Australians have modified scientific names to fit the vernacular. They take you for a nice walk in the bush, introducing you to their "eucalypts, banksias, and acacias" before they remember to tell you that these plants are called gum trees (*Eucalyptus* spp.), native honeysuckles (*Banksia* spp.), and wattles (*Acacia* spp.).

Americans tend to resist scientific names, employing much the same passive-aggressive technique that we have used so successfully to resist national implementation of the metric system. I have written elsewhere (*The Rose's Kiss*, 2002) how public schools avoid teaching the basics of botany from primary grades through high school biology courses. Well, scientific names are one of the first tools every instructor needs in order to teach the overlapping branches of the life sciences. When classes about the composition and use of scientific names are replaced with lessons about how to recycle trash, plant trees, and turn off the faucet while brushing one's teeth, we are replacing access to a scientific tool with lessons in environmental stewardship. Both subjects are important, but, as they have different goals, environmental protocols are never adequate replacements for the principles of biology. Substitute a different topic for science, and you deaden youthful interests in plant conservation and future careers in intense but objective research. I teach four plant science courses to biology majors at Saint Louis University. Every semester someone whines, "Do we have to know all these names?"

Of course, it is my responsibility to make classification and the translations of scientific names relevant and entertaining, but I have never been alone. Every five or six years some botanist or professional horticulturist writes a book meant to explain the ground rules and attempts to lead home gardeners through the jungle of plant names. Some would nominate *How Plants Get Their Names*, by L. H. Bailey, as the short and sweet granddaddy of such reference books. Many more have followed and will continue to follow. I think these well-written books have limited impact, because most are conceived as lexicons or dictionaries, turning the definitions of scientific names into disconnected sound bites. We prefer narratives and want to be convinced that there is an overarching story behind centuries of botanical classification. One of Howard Ensign Evans's last books, *Pioneer Naturalists* (1993), explained why so many American plants and animals were named after explorers and collectors. Evans offered brief biographies to show why these men and women deserved the honor of having a genus or species named after them. The author showed that *Lewisia* (bitterroot) and *Clarkia* (ragged robin, farewell-to-spring) celebrate the expedition of Meriwether Lewis and William Clark.

That makes a fine start, but will enthusiasm for scientific names increase if the stories take on a fantastic twist? One aspect of Western civilization has not changed in more than two millennia. We still prefer stories about potent drugs, bizarre sex, and violent crimes. Most of us still enjoy a good yarn featuring drugs made from plants. Unfortunately, it is hard to turn floral sex or the smothering violence of vines competing for sunlight into salacious gossip (heaven knows, I've tried; see my *Natural Affairs: A Botanist Looks at the Attachments between Plants and People* [New York: Villard Books, 1993] and *Wily Violets and Underground Orchids: Revelations of a Botanist* [1989; repr., Chicago: University of Chicago Press, 2003]). Fortunately, we need only revisit the Greco-Roman myths to locate the archetypes of perversity and outrageous cruelty. Western art and science share the same fascination with classical celebrities. Every century, the protagonists in these myths are invited to repeat their unnatural acts in new poems, novels, dramas, films, paintings, and sculptures. Likewise, biologists have used them as sources of scientific names since the second half of the eighteenth century. I encountered them in college courses in botany but awarded them little significance for almost three decades. What changed my attitude?

In 1997, the Stanley Smith Horticultural Society gave me a grant to study the breeding system of mandrakes (*Mandragora officinarum*) in northern Israel. This wayside weed bears fragrant berries, used to scent a novel liqueur. Investigation of the natural sex life of the mandrake ultimately helped determine how the grower might increase fruit yield. My Israeli mentor, Dr. Amots Dafni at the University of Haifa, was determined that my weekends would not pass exclusively in muddy fields kneeling over to pollinate mandrake flowers. Amots is a proud sabra, and he was determined I would see wonders beyond the Kishon valley. Please pardon the classical allusion, but this book's odyssey began precisely on the first of January 1998 when Amots and his daughter took me to the archaeological dig, or Tel, at Bet She'an. Several civilizations settled there over thousands of years, but it was now part of a long-term project to excavate and reconstruct the town established by conquering Romans. We walked by resurrected sections of an amphitheater, bathhouse, goldsmith shop, and a temple to the goddess Nysa. A sign said she was a nursemaid of Bacchus. I thought I knew my Greco-Roman mythology rather well, but who was Nysa? How did she come to nurture the god of wine, and why did her name sound so . . . well, botanical? It brought back odd memories of a stroll in a swamp in Louisiana.

Upon my return to St. Louis I purchased an old paperback copy of the *Dictionary of Classical Mythology* by J. E. Zimmerman (1971). This gave me a proper introduction to Nysa, or Nyssa (as her name is most often spelled in English). However, like most dictionaries, it did not give me a full story, so I treated myself to both volumes of *The Greek Myths,* by Robert Graves (1957). Botanical lexicons cleared up the last mystery. *Nyssa* is the name of a genus that the Swedish plant taxonomist Carl von Linnaeus gave to the genus of tupelos. *Nyssa aquatica* was the sour gum tupelo I saw, years earlier, in a park outside New Orleans. At that time the tree limbs cradled local snakes, not baby deities, and the image of sleeping cottonmouths coiled around branches was hard to forget.

It did not stop there. Leafing through the lexicons, I discovered that my own garden harbored gods, goddesses, nymphs, and heroes. Smilax continued to disdain the mortal boy, Crocus, as she grew in backyard shade while he needed the sunny front rock garden. Paeonius dispensed flowers instead of medical remedies. Iris and Hermes waited to take messages from the King of the Gods, but he was too busy dropping walnuts on my roof. I just had to share this information with others, but how? I considered writing another specialized dictionary or lexicon, to follow a noble tradition, but then I ran into Dr. Ghillean Prance, who was visiting the Missouri Botanical Gardens. Dr. Prance had spent years working at the Bronx Botanical Gardens (I was one of his technicians back in 1977) before he became the director of Kew Gardens in England. He liked the idea of the book but said that most Americans were unfamiliar with the classical myths so I must retell the stories.

Showing the connection between false gods and real plants seemed entertaining and innovative. After all, most books of Greek mythology are presented as pseudohistories. They start with creation tales of Mother Earth and her Titan children; pass on to Zeus, his Olympian family, and the deeds of their half-mortal bastards; and then finish with the Trojan War and the wanderings of Odysseus. I learned that some botanists honored characters in the most obscure myths. It gave me confidence that even the residents of the British Commonwealth might also be unfamiliar with Nyssa.

Because stories are superior to glossaries, it seemed logical to borrow the format preferred by Robert Graves. Tell each myth separately, but organize them to show how they interconnect with each other. Follow each tale with itemized interpretations. However, readers are warned that I do not subscribe to any of Graves's theories about the origins of Mediterranean religions. The history of the worship of an immortal, triple-faced goddess and her more vulnerable sons is best left to the pertinent criticisms of serious scholars. I prefer to parallel each myth with more relevant commentary on plants named after the protagonists and how the plot line enriched the language of botany. It is a modest goal. Owing to space limitations, the names discussed and explained must be limited to seed plants. Someone else can have the pleasure of introducing the myths that inspired the scientific names of other members of the plant kingdom (mosses, liverworts, ferns, and their allies), as well as the associated kingdoms of fungi and algae.

Even if I cannot convince you to use scientific names on a regular basis, perhaps this book will improve social events. The quickest way to kill party conversation in Missouri these days is for someone to say, "Gardening is such a challenge in the Midwest." Silence falls as we stare into our cocktail glasses, remembering bulbs eaten by squirrels and bills paid to remove trees toppled by tornados. Discussing plants named after centaurs sounds far more amusing and fitting (especially over wine). Sometimes the most magnificent garden is the one you keep in your head.

ACKNOWLEDGMENTS

Some books must be written during periods of extended trouble and sadness. Some Greeks believed that Death, Misery, and Vexation are children of Night but so are Joy and Friendship. My wife, Linda, is thanked first for her support and kindness. The tolerant administration of Saint Louis University continues to stick by my odder projects. That is why I am particularly grateful to biology chairperson Rick Mayden and Dean Donald Brennan of the School of Arts and Sciences.

Dr. Ghillean Prance, of the Royal Botanic Gardens at Kew, deserves the credit for suggesting how to present the information in the following text. A Kenan Fellowship spent at the National Tropical Botanical Garden in Hawaii permitted special instruction from its then-director, Dr. Paul Cox, on the fate of plant names. I also thank Dr. Cox for showing me a copy of an illustration in a Lapland notebook of Carl von Linnaeus. Permission to use this drawing came from the Linnean Society of London.

It is my good fortune that both the Missouri Botanical Garden (St. Louis) and the Royal Botanic Gardens of Sydney (New South Wales, Australia) continue to allow me to work at both institutions as a research associate. This gives me access to live plants, preserved specimens, and superior libraries in two hemispheres. I would like to thank the library staff at both gardens for their time and patience. In particular, I must thank curator Karen Wilson at Sydney for helping me with the history and interpretation of the scientific names of some Australian plants. Dr. Peter Weston introduced me to a living grove of *Eidothea hardenensis* and helped obtain some of the illustrations. Director Peter Raven and curator Peter Goldblatt at the Missouri Botanical Garden provided lively exchanges of ideas and interpretations.

DISCLAIMER

Over thousands of years, herbalists and scientists gave some plants either common or scientific names that identified them as sources of food, fiber, medicine, or as murder weapons. Some of these uses are discussed in this book but only within their historical context. The author and publishers do not encourage or support the traditional medicinal, recreational, or criminal use of any species for any reason. In light of modern advances in the study of allergies, diabetes, and other ailments related to plant products, we do not advocate the use of any species in this book as a safe source of food, beverages, clothing, construction materials, infant care, and so forth. Although personal experiences of the author with plants and plant products are related in this text, the reader is not encouraged to take any of the same risks.

The ancient Greeks believed that different gods made and remade humanity at various intervals. The first human beings created lived in the Golden Age. Upon their extinction, they were replaced subsequently by the lesser races of the Silver, Bronze, and Iron Ages. Some poets added a stone race that repopulated the world following Deucalion's Flood. Each age differed, and all scrolls and books agreed that the quality of mankind declined severely with each replacement. If these authors could read this disclaimer, they would understand the need to protect ourselves in this Age of Litigation.

Gods and Goddesses

IN THE GARDEN

CHAPTER I

❧ ❧ ❧

In the Cyclop's Orchard

The Why and How
of Scientific Names

> . . . Apples I have
> Loading the boughs, and I have golden grapes
> And purple in my vineyards—all for you.
> Your hands shall gather luscious strawberries
> In woodland shade; in autumn you shall pick
> Cherries and plums, not only dusky black,
> But yellow fat and waxen in the sun
> And chestnuts shall be yours, if I am yours,
> And every tree shall bear its fruit for you.
>
> —OVID, *Metamorphoses* (translation by A. D. Melville)

The Roman poet Ovid (43 B.C.E.–17 C.E.) put these honeyed words into the mouth of a one-eyed, lovesick monster, Polyphemus the Cyclops. Considering the period in which this passage was written, we know that Polyphemus must have cultivated plants associated with the walled orchards and wild, hilly countryside around imperial Rome. The imaginary monster had some apple trees (*Malus* ×*domestica*) and two breeds of grapes (*Vitis vinifera*; purple and yellow varieties had the same wild ancestor). There were alpine strawberries (*Fragaria vesca*), sweet cherries (*Prunus avium*), and European chestnuts (*Castanea sativa*). These plants are so familiar to most readers and have been in domestication for such a long time that adding scientific names seems superfluous.

Plums are a different matter. Were those dusky black fruits European plums (*Prunus domestica*) or damsons (*P. damascena*)? The twigs of bullaces (*P. insititia*) or gages (*P. italica*) might have produced the waxy yellow plums. In Ovid's poem, the Cyclops offered his favorite possessions to court the sea nymph Galatea. The nymph had a handsome young lover, so she hid herself from Polyphemus and refused to reply. Perhaps the Cyclops would have

I

endured a more gentle and courteous rejection had Ovid lived much later (say, during the eighteenth century) when you could identify all the contents in a fruit basket with clarity and precision.

Have you noticed how the two parts of each scientific name, written above, cluster similar species together? At the same time, each double name (binomial) also preserves the unique identity of each species. How is this possible? The genus name, *Prunus*, unites sweet cherries (*P. avium*) with European plums (*P. domestica*), damsons (*P. damascena*), bullaces (*P. insititia*), and gages (*P. italica*). Had the Cyclops access to a modern nursery catalog he could have added peaches (*P. persica*) to his *Prunus* collection.

All six species of *Prunus* trees have more things in common with each other than any of them have in common with apples (*Malus*), grapes (*Vitis*), strawberries (*Fragaria*), or chestnuts (*Castanea*). *Prunus* species bear branches wearing simple leaves with toothed or serrated margins. Each flower has five green sepals and five white-pink petals. Each flower can make only one fruit. Each fruit can make only one seed. The fruit wall always locks up the lone seed within a stony layer of tissue, known as the endocarp. The edible flesh (mesocarp) covering the hard endocarp becomes soft and juicy when ripe. A *Vitis* vine, a *Fragaria* herb, and *Malus* and *Castanea* tree species may share one to three of these same characteristics in common, but not all of them. The second name of each *Prunus* tree (*avium, damascena, domestica, insititia, italica* and *persica*) is the species name. This name tells you that, although these different trees share features in common, there is always something unique about each one. The fruit of the *persica* (peach) contains a deeply ridged to pitted endocarp and a velvety-hairy skin. The fruit of the *avium* (sweet cherry) contains a smooth endocarp and a smooth, thin skin. If you hold the *italica* (gage) fruit to a light, the skin is so transparent that the modestly wrinkled endocarp is visible as a dark shadow within the mesocarp.

The double, scientific name (binomial) is simple, specific, and, in my opinion, elegant. Some people who spend their careers identifying and naming new species turn them into a lyrical art form, shorter and more pointed than any epigram or haiku. What would we do without the binomial system? I can show you. Join me in the herbarium of the Missouri Botanical Garden (MOBOT) in St. Louis, Missouri.

1.1 INSIDE THE HERBARIUM

A herbarium is a plant museum consisting, primarily, of specimens requiring special preservation after they are pressed and dried. Each flattened specimen is attached to a large, stiff, paper rectangle and is given a label identifying it to species. The label will also give you the place and date where the plant was collected. Labels may also record living characteristics that could not survive drying, such as odors and the colors of flowers, sap, and leaves. Herbarium sheets stay in numbered and cataloged metal cabinets. They are well fumigated to protect against attacks by cigarette beetles, fungi, and other pests. As of January 2007, the Missouri Botanical Garden owned close to six million mounted plant sheets.

Most specimen sheets stay in these cool, dry, dark cabinets until someone needs to examine them. Some may not be studied for decades. The "celebrity sheets" displayed on a tabletop on the second floor of the MOBOT herbarium are important exceptions. Each one is placed in its own transparent, rectangular, sealed bag and may be handled and viewed by any visitor who is willing to pick up a sheet and endure the faint odor of mothballs while reading the label. These special sheets are exhibited to help educate tour groups, as they tell special stories about scientific progress. Some specimens may even enjoy snob appeal.

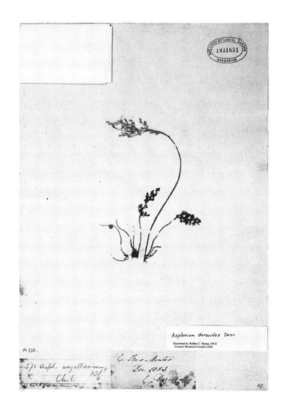

1. This pressed and mounted specimen of a necklace fern, collected by Charles Darwin in Chile during his voyage on the H.M.S. *Beagle*, remains on display at the herbarium of the Missouri Botanical Garden. Note there are two scientific names on the same specimen sheet. The old label in the right-hand corner shows that a nineteenth-century botanist identified the specimen as *Asplenium magellanicum*. By the close of the twentieth century, Dr. Robbin Moran reidentified it as *Asplenium dareoides*, fixing a new determination slip to the sheet.

For example, that simple little *Asplenium dareoides* (a necklace fern) was collected in Chile by Charles Darwin in 1834. The label even bears his signature. Those stems of *Solanum paniculatum* (a tropical nightshade) were picked in Brazil in 1768 by botanists accompanying Captain James Cook on his voyage to the South Pacific. The branch of *Ancistrocladus korupensis* came from a tree growing in Cameroon, Africa, in 1994. Traditional healers boil the roots to treat dysentery, and this tree may have future potential as a source of drugs to treat fevers and other forms of inflammation.

In my opinion, though, the most important sheet is the first one on the left. Georg Rudolph Boehmer (1723–1803) a botanist at the University of Wittenberg, Germany, collected it around 1740. The specimen came from a blackberry or bramble. Looking at the identification label, you will see there is no double name. All it says is "Rubus foliis ternatis et quinatis, costa spinosa, fructu nigro et laeui." *Rubus* is an old Latin word for blackberry or bramble. The remainder of the sentence gives you a brief description of the twig's leaves, prickles, and fruits. The translation runs, "bramble with each leaf subdivided into three or five leaflets, leaf midrib prickly, and the fruit is black and shiny." This was the standard method of publishing information on new plant or animal specimens, from the time of the first scrolls of the Greek naturalist Theophrastus (370–287 B.C.E.), until the first half of the eighteenth century. Living things were given general (generic) names in Latin or Greek. If you wanted to be specific about the exact "kind" of bramble you picked up in the woods, you had to attach a long descriptive phrase.

What's easier to remember? Would you prefer to memorize a name consisting of two words (the binomial), or a descriptive phrase that lacks an obvious word limit? Boehmer collected the bramble to write a book recording all the native plants found in one corner of eastern Germany. When it was published in 1750, his *Flora Lipsiae Indigena* was behind the times. The first revolution in the classification of living things had appeared, in print, a good fifteen years earlier.

1.2 ENTER THE LINNAEAN SYSTEM

This earlier work was the *Systema Naturae* of 1735. It was written by a Swedish naturalist, botanist, and physician named Carl Linne. Among its virtues, the book popularized the concept of giving each species two names. Linne or Linnaeus, as he would be called, did not invent the binomial system, but he certainly made it acceptable to an audience who felt they were drowning in a wordy sea of descriptions.

By the eighteenth century, the small but growing community of scientists who describe and classify living things (we call them taxonomists) understood they were overwhelmed by natural diversity. The process of collecting and discovering new species was centuries old. Significant opportunities and difficulties really started after 1492, as Europe enjoyed the "Great Colombian Exchange." Plants and animals collected in the western hemisphere arrived in western Europe to be admired, traded, and exploited. As the chance that a new species would make its way to fashionable London, Paris, or Vienna was often limited to its immediate potential as a source of food, fiber, medicine, or living ornament, one could still use the ancient descriptive system to catalog a few dozen novel garden varieties.

By the eighteenth century, though, European governments were funding long-term expeditions to unmapped parts of the world. These voyages ultimately added thousands of unnamed and preserved specimens to new museums and private collections. Furthermore, microscopes invented in the seventeenth century were much improved a hundred years later. Under magnification the world of insects, spiders, tiny crustaceans, and worms, once easily ignored, proved to be far richer than anyone imagined. Publishing a book on the plants and animals of a region was a laudable, and often profitable, venture, but paper, ink, and binding were still expensive. You could absorb the cost of describing and publishing a new species once, but not if it meant printing the same descriptive lines over and over again.

It was time to usher in a different system to better catalog the earth's diversity, and Linne came from a culture ready to appreciate it. Robbin Moran, a curator of ferns at the New York Botanical Gardens, made an important point to me during a recent conversation. Carl Linne came from a country that, only a generation or so before, gave up the traditional, "Erick-son-of-Olaf" system of names. The Linnes were a comparatively progressive family of farmers. They took their new surname from a big linden tree on their property. Linne also understood that even the best ideas suffer neglect unless spread by enthusiastic converts. By 1742, he was teaching at the University of Uppsala. By then known as Carolus Linnaeus, he filled the chair of medicine and, later, of botany. The enrollment at Uppsala rose from five hundred to fifteen hundred during his tenure. Young men came from all over Europe to learn the Linnaean system of nomenclature and classification. Some classes were closer to what we now think of as learning workshops. Student groups were expected to take excursions in the Swedish countryside to collect specimens.

1.3 Naming a New Species

When a new species is discovered, it receives its official name upon valid publication. The system enforced today for naming, describing, and publishing descends directly from Linnaeus, his trusted contemporaries, and his "apostles." Consequently, the procedure has not changed much since the end of the eighteenth century. There is no need to go through every rule but it is important to understand some of the inherent checks and balances in the system.

Description must start with a single specimen (fresh or preserved), solid evidence of the find. You cannot base a name on the memory of something glimpsed during a pleasant walk in the woods. In addition, the specimen used must be sexually mature. It must bear its adult foliage and it must be in a reproductive state (flowers and/or fruit) at the time of collection. Linnaeus understood that complete plant identification to the species level was almost impossible without reproductive structures. Those structures must be visible on the pressed, dried specimen.

I have been studying the pollination biology of flowering plants since 1974, so I have taken a lot of walks in the woods of five countries. I carry a notebook and a plant press to record and obtain vouchers of plants, whose blossoms are under observation. I also bring insect-collecting equipment (nets and killing jars). Most plants are insect-pollinated. To prove that an insect species is a true pollinator, I must take bug specimens when I see them inside the flower foraging on pollen and nectar while they touch the tips of receptive female organs (stigmas). The pressed plants go to a herbarium and are identified by botanists if I cannot identify them myself. The pinned insects go to natural history museums where they are identified by entomologists.

It is my impression that it is easier for a botanist to select a plant specimen to describe a new species than it is for a zoologist to select an animal specimen for the same procedure. A zoologist needs the whole animal for description. A botanist can make do with a nice branch or stem, providing it offers mature growth, flowers, and/or fruit and some leaves. Furthermore, most plants are bisexual. When male and female organs occur in the same flower, botanical terminology classifies the flower as "perfect." In other plants, male flowers (pollen makers) are found on the same branches as female flowers (seed makers). Botanists say the plant is monoecious (literally, "husbands and wives" live in different rooms in the same house).

In contrast, most zoologists must make a choice. Will they describe a new species using a male specimen or a female? Many zoologists are forced to practice gender bias because they require a specimen that shows the greatest number of visible structures and convincing characteristics. Ornithologists, for example, need birds in their breeding plumage, and males are usually more extravagant than females. Taxonomists describing tiny, parasitic wasps want females because they come equipped with an exaggerated device, the ovipositor, to puncture a host victim. Curators of fish collections can go either way depending on the groups they study. Some want a male resplendent in his spawning dress. In other cases, the male is such a tiny thing that the ichthyologist is far better off with the larger female. In all cases, absence of the appropriate sex can delay description of a new animal species.

Back in 2002, I was part of a consortium of scientists studying the primitive bitter leaf vine (*Trimenia moorei*) in the mountains of northeastern Australia. As usual, I dutifully netted, killed, and pinned the insects I found on the flowers. Kenneth Walker, an entomologist working in Melbourne, was particularly interested in one of the miner bees (*Lasioglossum*) I sent him. "It's a new species," Ken said. "Would you mind if I named it after you?" Of course, I was flattered and agreed immediately. Unfortunately, I am still waiting to read the formal publication of *Lasioglossum bernhardti*. What's the problem? My specimen is undamaged, colorful, and well-pinned, but it is a female. Bee taxonomists prefer to describe new species from the males. Why? The genitals of a male insect are usually more distinct and well-sculptured than the female's. To put it in simple terms, it is easier and less destructive to describe the key instead of the keyhole. Entomologists have returned to my bitter leaf site looking for the male bee, on two separate occasions. We now have an additional five or six females of Bernhardt's miner bee but still no males. I think I am in for a long wait.

Let's say you do have a flowering or fruiting specimen and you want to write up a paper and describe it as a new species. As we have seen, a new species has one name made out of two words. The genus word (capitalized) always precedes the species word (lowercased). The full name is always written in taxonomic Latin, but taxonomic Latin actually consists of two tongues. There is the true Latin, descended from the Roman Empire, and then there is a form of Greek written with a Western (Latinized) alphabet.

If two words are going to be linked together to form a double name, they must agree with each other in language and gender. If you select a Greek genus, you must follow through with a Greek species. We forget that Latin and Greek nouns are either masculine or feminine. For several centuries, it was almost a tradition for botanists to treat plant names as feminine, whereas zoologists often preferred masculine-sounding names for animals. This explains why plant genera named after classical heroes and male deities such as Achilles, Cecrops, Paeon, Proteus, and Romulus were feminized as *Achillea, Cecropia, Paeonia, Protea,* and *Romulea.* In contrast, plant genera honoring mythical princesses and goddesses—Iphigenia, Iris, Lycaste, Polyxena— remained almost unmodified by taxonomic Latin.

You may derive your scientific name from virtually any language, provided that it is a real word in a foreign tongue and you Latinize it. Did you find your plant in Ladysmith, South Africa, and want to name the new species after the collection site? You may publish it as *ladysmithensis* or *ladysmithense,* depending on the preferred gender. No wonder that the British science fiction writer, John Wyndham, once mocked the language of taxonomy as dog Greek and dog Latin. Nevertheless, the Creole tongue of classification shows every sign of outlasting the novels of John Wyndham.

A popular language often splits into dialects. Botanists often use Latinized Greek, in part, because most of the classical herbalists and physicians wrote their treatises on medicinal plants in that language. However, paleontologists who name new species from animal fossils also favor the speech of ancient Athens and Sparta. Consequently, the Australian orchid genus, *Pterostylis* (the pistil neck, or style, has wings) sounds like *Pterodactylus* (a genus of flying dinosaurs with winged fingers).

The history of zoologists classifying living animals often shows greater flexibility. The names of animal genera with backbones often reflect the vernacular of Roman hunters, farmers, and fishermen. The frog you probably dissected in high school biology class belonged, and still belongs, to the Latin genus, *Rana.* Botanists have been known to agree with zoologists on the use of true Latin. As wild buttercups often adopt an amphibious lifestyle, and live in the same wet places as frogs, we place these shiny, yellow flowers in the Latin genus, *Ranunculus.*

Therefore, Linnaeus was well aware of the terrible confusion that could ensue when the same word was used over and over. Consequently, the oldest published name of a species is always the valid name. Linnaeus and his students regularly went "fishing" for the oldest names of plants in ancient herbals, medical treatises, and even in great epic poems. After all, they were written in Greek, and some were in Latin. Why not use *Artemisia, Paeonia, Prunus, Rubus,* and so forth as building blocks for genus names? By making the oldest name the only valid name, taxonomists avoid the embarrassment of giving different species of plants the same name and also of assigning different names to the same species. This is very tempting when you want to give a pretty new plant an appropriately pretty name from Greek mythology. The genus *Chelone* (see §5.3), refers specifically to half a dozen species producing flowers that resemble white and pink snapdragons. No other genus in the kingdom of plants has exactly that name, spelled the same way. There are over fourteen hundred wild species in the genus *Solanum* (nightshades, potatoes, eggplants, buffalo burs, and others), but only one species is named *Solanum oedipus* (§6.1).

On the other hand, it is perfectly acceptable to use the same or a similar name if the species is found in a completely different kingdom of organisms. Plants and animals often share the same genus or species name. For example, *Chelone glabra* is a wildflower known as turtlehead. *Chelonia mydas* is the scientific name of the green sea turtle, once savored in soups. There is not much chance anyone will confuse a plant with a reptile. There are other rules, but they consist of finer points and are of greatest interest to professional taxonomists. In any case, it is now time to write up the description and submit the manuscript. Some descriptions are short and some are long, but they must all contain the same, five basic components.

1. The new name. The new binomial (genus and species) is presented and the author adds his or her name after the new combination. The new name is now permanently associated with the person or persons (authorities) who first described the species.

2. Diagnosis. The plant is described, from top to bottom, using botanical Latin terminology. Most authors start with the growth form (habit) of the plant, for example, whether it is a tree, shrub, or herb. Next, the taxonomist progresses through the vegetative organs. This includes the roots (when available), stems, the arrangement of leaves on the stem, and the shapes taken by leaf margins. Reproductive organs, including the architecture of the flowering stems, the kind and number of organs in flowers, fruits, and seeds are saved for last. It is perfectly acceptable to write a diagnosis and lack a plant organ, provided the organ is not an essential characteristic used to discriminate between closely related species. For example, most dried and pressed tree specimens lack roots. However, some diagnoses demand underground organs. It is most important to have the thin, papery coat (tunic) worn by the bulb (corm) of a new *Crocus*, as the coat's "weave" often varies between species.

3. Deposition of specimens. The specimen used to describe the species becomes the type specimen. Potential challengers of your description should be able to compare your type against their own collections. Therefore, you must tell the reader where the type is stored. Did you collect more than one specimen

of the new species on the same day? If so, you must tell your readers where they can examine these extra specimens. You never know when they might be needed. The original type, called the holotype, may be lost to pests, fires, floods, theft, or misfiling. Types were lost during World War II when European herbaria were bombed. When a type is destroyed, a second preserved specimen, taken on the same day of the original collection is elevated to the status of new holotype. Different museums have different policies concerning the protection of types. When I worked at the New York Botanical Garden in the Bronx, all types went into a special, separate covey of cabinets isolated from the main collection. There is no special location at the Missouri Botanical Garden. A type is dressed in a bright orange file and is shelved in the general "sea of specimens." A type specimen of a new South American specimen of coral tree (*Erythrina*) goes into the cabinets hosting the sheets of dozens of other species of South American coral trees. Alphabetizing both the names on the "common sheets" and the name on the new, garish, orange cover makes it easy to find any type.

4. Etymology. What does the name mean? Curiously, although taxonomists must define the word or words in a binomial, they are never required to explain or defend the choice of words. Books, monographs, and scientific journals are chock full of descriptions of new genera and species, but we do not always know what was on the scientist's mind when the words were chosen. The older generation of botanists, in particular, enjoyed classical educations. Many loved naming plants after figures in Greco-Roman mythology. As we will see, some of these taxonomists never bothered to explain why the name of a particular deity, hero, sacred site, or monster took their fancy. These botanists assumed anyone interested in scientific names had the same education they did and would immediately catch on to the allusion, pretty comparison, or joke. Alas, sometimes the reference is so obscure we are forced to speculate.

5. Distribution. The botanist should tell the reader where the specimen was found. Locations are often deplorably broad and vague in old publications. Eighteenth- and nineteenth-century authors often refer to a country (Brazil), the banks of a river (Orinoco), or even an unexplored continent (a specimen from Van Diemen's Land refers to an old Dutch name for the west coast of Australia). Modern technology has made this part of a publication quite precise. Satellite tracking gives you latitude, longitude, and elevation. Some far-thinking scientists now add conservation status to their section on distribution. Did the specimen come from a tiny population? Does it grow in a protected, national park or was the land sold and leveled to put in a housing development or extend a road?

It is not compulsory to include a photograph or illustration of the new species in its first documented description. However, most reputable taxonomists are happy to include pictures of the new species and, when they are not on a tight budget, employ trained artists. The best modern diagnoses, in my opinion, still offer fine line drawings, illustrating the unique shapes of leaves and the architecture of organs inside flowers. This clears up any ambiguities in the text.

Other authors embellish their publications with other useful features. Some provide tables or graphs to compare the new species to look-alikes in the same genus. Others publish superior photos of microscopic characteristics, like the sculptures on a seed or the hairs on a leaf. Some describe the habitat in which the specimen grew. They identify the geological strata and test the soil's chemistry to see if it is acidic or basic. Others describe the plant communities, listing the other species found growing in concert with the new species.

1.4 RAFINESQUE: A CAUTIONARY TALE

What happens if you flout any of these orderly rules of nomenclature? Frankly, it would have been better if you had not wasted your time describing a new species at all. Students of taxonomy who are lax with Latin, or think they know a shortcut, are often told the story of Constantine Samuel Rafinesque (1783–1840). This sad sack of a scientist is treated as the equivalent of the foolish humans and beasts populating Aesop's Fables. Think of him as the boy who cried wolf or the overconfident hare.

The son of a French father and a Greek-German mother, Rafinesque grew up in southern France and amused himself collecting seashells around the harbors and shores of Marseille. When he emigrated to the United States at the age of nineteen, the young naturalist found his true calling. He would spend most of his life visiting virgin territories collecting and describing new species. Rafinesque is remembered primarily as a botanist, but he was also happy to describe new fish, bats, and other animals. He published more than nine hundred descriptions in his lifetime. Few of his binomials survive intact to this day. Rafinesque's contemporaries found his obsession with novelty exasperating, at best. "His passion for establishing new genera and species appears to have become a complete monomania," said Asa Gray (1810–1888), Harvard's first professor of botany. Even Rafinesque's wife's tolerance was limited. She ran off with an actor.

The man had an almost preternatural talent for invalidating his own work. This is particularly astonishing in taxonomy, as people laboring in this field of science take malicious delight in discrediting both their contemporaries and predecessors. Some historians find a pathological element in Rafinesque's publications. They argue he was in such a frenzy to publish first that his hurried, sloppy approach generated more errors, thus leaving him vulnerable to enemies with more formal training.

Like most taxonomists, Rafinesque built the names of new genera and species by joining together either Greek or Latin words. When he united these words, his abbreviations were often compounded improperly. Bad grammar and syntax invalidated his publications. Like most plant taxonomists, Rafinesque enjoyed naming new plants with pretty flowers after nymphs in Greco-Roman mythology (see §3.4–3.6). He erected the genera *Adipe, Enothera, Cordula,* and *Lysimnia.* No one has ever found these nymphs in the classic poems, plays, or books of mythology. He made up those names out of thin air. This invalidated his publications, because a scientific name must always be based on a real word used in a real language. In at least one famous case, his description was flawless, but he chose a binomial used previously by another scientist, who published years earlier. Of course, this invalidated Rafinesque's publication.

Sterner historians of taxonomy close Rafinesque's chapter by mentioning that he died poverty-stricken in a garret at the age of fifty-seven. I take a gentler view, because the law of averages was on the poor man's side. It is impossible to be 100 percent wrong if you do the same job more than nine hundred times. To wit: if you visit the hardwood forests growing on lime-rich soils from eastern Canada south though North Carolina and as far west as Oklahoma from April to July, you may be lucky enough to find an orchid blooming in the leaf litter. It has two broad, paired leaves. Each pink-purple flower has a broad lip and wears a "helmet" of overlapping petals and sepals. This is the purple-hooded orchid (*Galearis spectabilis*). The name means good-looking (*spectabilis*) helmet (*Galearis*). Rafinesque erected the genus.

Linnaeus received the first dried specimens of this American orchid and named it *Orchis spectabilis* in 1753. Eighty years later, Rafinesque took a second look at the organs that made up each flower. He realized that the shapes of the flower organs and their overlapping positions made this Yankee species different from the *Orchis* species of Europe (see §5.7). The top of the flower of the purple-hooded orchid does resemble the helmet worn by a Spanish conquistador. Changing *Orchis* to *Galearis* was a timely and appropriate revision. Even Rafinesque understood the value of critically reexamining the work of his forefathers. Yes, this time his revised taxonomy endured.

1.5 A Hierarchy Based on Sex

Returning to Linnaeus, we can see the benefits of the binomial system. It is much easier to recognize and catalog species once you understand that alliances are based on shared physical characteristics. If several different-looking trees in the Cyclops's orchard all produce fruit containing soft flesh and one large, protective pit or stone, you could cluster dozens, even hundreds of species within the genus *Prunus.*

Earlier authors writing plant books prior to the Linnaean method did not have this option. Once again, we visit the herbarium of the Missouri Botanical Garden. This time, though, we head for the fourth-floor library. We need admission to its wonderful rare book room. The display tables feature tomes from the sixteenth and seventeenth centuries. Most are herbals, interested in the medicinal "virtues" of plants. Others incorporate the arrival and uses of plants from the New World. Here are some of the earliest botanical depictions of such exotic crops as Indian maize and tomatoes.

The books are as thick as bricks and often much larger. Most lack an index, and you almost need a sixth sense to find a particular species. Some older authors grouped plants together on the basis of growth habit. Cucumbers, pumpkins, beans, and peas are clustered together in one herbal for no other reason than their fruits grow on twining but short-lived vines. Other plants are grouped according to their primary uses. Plants with edible underground portions (onions, leeks, radishes, parsnips) form their own section. With the invention of hand lenses, the better authors start aligning plants with similar leaf and floral structures. *The Herball; or, Generall Historie of Plants* (1597) by John Gerard remains an amazing work. It has an index. Shared plant anatomy takes precedence over medical virtues. Lilylike flowers that rise from bulbs and have leafless stems (lilies, hyacinths, crocuses etc.) have their own section. Orchids get a separate corner, but so do nightshades and their relatives (henbanes and mandrakes). A more natural and logical system of classification developed by the end of the seventeenth century, but it was not possible to construct an overarching system of classification based on long, inconsistent descriptions.

More than 135 years later, Linnaeus showed that once a scientific description became a binomial, you were left with two useful categories: genera and species. Linnaeus thought, "Why not expand classification beyond the genus level? Let's ally plants in different genera that happen to share one characteristic in common." This made it far easier to group and locate plant specimens within herbarium cabinets. More important, hierarchies made it far easier to find and identify unfamiliar plants within the same pages of a big, thick book. Linnaeus's attempt at higher classification was simple and sexual. Hand lenses made it possible to look into the heart of the smallest blossom. Our great Swedish taxonomist knew that the number and arrangement of organs in any flower was fixed and self-consistent. The Linnaean classification system made two minor demands on a botanist. First, you had to know how to count. Second, you had to own a good lens or microscope, strong enough to see how floral organs attached themselves to each other.

Read Linnaeus, and you will see how he compares the flower to a wedding bed. A flower can contain as many as four different kinds of organs. Those that make up the outer protective bud case are known as sepals. The ring of sepals in the flower is called the calyx (the husk or container). Linnaeus compared it to a bed. The next circle of organs consists of the colorful, often perfumed, petals. They constitute the corolla (the little crown). In the eighteenth century all the finest poster beds offered extra privacy to wealthier newlyweds because they had thick, beautiful, often perfumed curtains. Who are the husbands in a flower? Part the petal bed curtains and see the lollipoplike organs called stamens. The lobed and swollen tip of each stamen produces pollen, and these grains fertilize young seeds developing inside the flower. Surely, it is appropriate to refer to the ring, or rings, of stamens as the androecium (the men's quarters). And which structures represent the wives? These are the carpels, and each one has its own ovary to nurture one or more developing seeds (ovules). Sometimes the carpels fuse together to make one fertile organ known as the pistil. In either case, the pistil or the cluster of carpels must be called the gynoecium (the women's quarters). Note how many stamens encircle the pistil in each flower. Linnaeus noted that floral husbands often outnumbered their prospective brides.

This scheme made it possible for our Swedish taxonomist to divide all the known genera of flowering plants into twenty-four categories he called classes. Each class was determined by the limited natural variation of pollen-making stamens to seed-making carpels inside a flower. The sheer number of bed slats and curtains were not important. If Polyphemus, for example, owned his own giant magnifying glass, he would note that each plum blossom (*Prunus*) contains more than a dozen stamens, and they surround the pistil by fusing themselves to the surface of a cup-like structure called the hypanthium. Linnaeus placed the genus *Prunus* in the class Polyandria (Poly = many; andria = males).

In contrast, most orchids have only one stamen in a flower, and it is fused to the pistil. Orchids went into the class Gynandria (Gyn = female; andria = male). A pumpkin (*Cucurbita pepo*) bears male flowers (stamens present, pistil absent) and female flowers (pistil present, stamens absent) on the same vine. Pumpkins, gourds, squashes, and all plants with similar floral arrangements went into the class Monoecia. The Linnaean system of classification is telling us that the husbands (stamens) and wives (pistils) are found in the same house (the same vine) but they occupy different beds (separate flowers).

1.6 SEX IS NOT ENOUGH

Classification is far more sophisticated today than it was in the second half of the eighteenth century. The sexual systems of plants continue to yield fixed, dependable characteristics for classification and identification, but stamens and pistils do not supply enough features required to pigeonhole an estimated quarter of a million species of flowering plants. Moreover, the quaint days of the animal and vegetable kingdoms are long gone. As we learn more about cell and gene structure, we understand that there are important and fundamental differences between major groups of living things. These days, many modern biologists (myself included) feel far more comfortable thinking about half a dozen, or more, kingdoms.

A taxonomist must divide and conquer to classify all the living things on this planet. Some people think we divide too much. Some divisions are recent and some take us back to Linnaeus and his cronies. Here is how it works within the first decade of the twenty-first century. Species are still clustered within a genus. Since the early nineteenth century we have clustered genera within families. In turn, families belong inside orders. Orders sink into classes, and classes are arranged within phyla. Phyla fit within six, or more, kingdoms. Kingdoms currently rest within three domains.

Let's return to the Cyclops's orchard and explain the modern classification system based on *Prunus insititia* (the domesticated bullace). You will see that many characteristics are used at different levels in the hierarchy. We will work backward, from the individual to the general. Note also how we go from very specific shape and architecture-driven characteristics to the broader biochemical and cellular attributes. To save time and some page space, I will not itemize all the features used in each level of the hierarchy. If you read carefully, you will see that some characteristics employed by Linnaeus remain important, but they are now embedded within a much larger matrix.

> Species: *insititia*. It is a large, thorny shrub or small tree. The underside of the leaves tends to be hairy. Only one to three flowers (about two centimeters in width) bloom together in leafy clusters on twigs in spring.

Genus: *Prunus.* All species are woody plants with simple toothed or serrated leaves. Their flowers have a low cup- or urn-shaped hypanthium. The five, pink-white petals on a flower are very short-lived. Each fleshy fruit contains a single seed. The seed is locked inside a thick and hard layer of fruit tissue known as the endocarp. The genus also includes at least four hundred species, including peaches (*Prunus persica*), apricots (*Prunus armeniaca*), and almonds (*Prunus dulcis*).

Family: Rosaceae. Each flower, in every genus, should produce a total of five sepals (calyx), five petals (corolla), many stamens (androecium) and one to many pistils (gynoecium). The sepals fuse to the bases of the petals, which in turn fuse to the bases of the stamens. This forms a tubular sleeve or cup known as the hypanthium. The family contains more than a hundred genera, including garden roses (*Rosa*), apples (*Malus*), strawberries (*Fragaria*), and pears (*Pyrus*).

Order: Rosales. The families nesting together tend to consist of species rich in tannin compounds, but the cells lack betalain (true beet-red) pigments. Each flower usually has no more than five petals in each corolla (if petals are present at all). Some flowers contain more than ten stamens. Pistils are never buried under or fused to extra tissues produced by the sepals, petals, or stamens. There are nine to twenty-three families in the order, depending on how closely one accepts the recent and additional evidence from genetic analyses. This includes the Rhamnaceae (buckthorns) and Hydrangeaceae (hydrangeas), but there may be a far stronger alliance between the rose family and the Ulmaceae (elms) and Cannabaceae (hemp and marijuana).

Class: Eudicotyledones. The allied orders consist of plants bearing flowers that have only four or five organs in the calyx and the corolla (e.g., five sepals and five petals *or* four sepals and four petals). Each flower contains four or five stamens or multiples of four or five (e.g., ten, fifteen, twenty . . . one hundred). The veins in the flat leaf blades form multibranching nets. Veins in the stem usually form a ring. Each pollen grain wears a minimum of three pores and/or three furrows. Each embryo inside the seed is attached to two embryonic leaves (cotyledons), but they usually dry up soon after the seedling sprouts. The class contains about thirty orders, including the Rosales, Ranunculales (buttercups and their allies), Geraniales (geraniums and their allies), and Eriacles (northern and southern heaths).

Phylum: Anthophyta. Seeds belonging to plants in these classes must develop inside a leaf bump that closes up to form a chambered vessel (the carpel or pistil). Pollen grains contain a maximum of two sperm cells. When pollen lands on the receptive tip of the pistil (known as the stigma) the grains produce sperm-filled tubes. The pollen tubes penetrate the pistil, grow down to the ovary chamber(s), enter the young seed, and discharge their sperm. One sperm cell fertilizes the egg (destined to become the embryo). The second sperm fertilizes the polar cells (destined to become storage tissue; endosperm). We once recognized only two classes in this phylum (monocotyledons and dicotyledons). The dicotyledons are now subdivided into the eudicotyledones and a series of smaller classes featuring plants with magnolialike flowers and primitive water-tissues (xylem) that often lack big, efficient vessel cells.

Kingdom: Plantae. All phyla consist of organisms in which most cell walls contain tiny, coiled fibers made of cellulose and its by-products. Most organisms have specialized cells containing chlorophyll, allowing them to make their own food in the presence of sunlight, water, and carbon dioxide. Sugars produced are stored as starch granules. Cells join to make specialized tissues that unite to form organs. Following the unification of a sperm and an egg there will always be true, embryonic development within a protective structure. Flowering plants share this kingdom with cone-bearing plants (gynosperms), ferns, and mosses.

Domain: Eucarya. Organisms in these kingdoms are made of one to many cells. A special envelope surrounds the cell's nucleus. Each nucleus is made of more than one chromosome. When the chromosomes are ready to divide, they separate into distinctive lines (linear). The interior of the cell has its own biochemical skeleton and contains smaller organelles (plastids, mitochondria) wrapped in membranes. We currently recognize that the fungus kingdom is more closely related to the animal kingdom than either is to the plant kingdom. Algae, seaweeds, and all the unicellular creatures that make up marine and pond plankton have been split up and comprise several unique kingdoms of their own.

Historically, the names of most plant families and orders are derived from a prominent genus. There is no such thing as the Prunaceae or Prunales. Plums are placed in the same family as garden roses (*Rosa*), so we have the Rosaceae and Rosales. That is why a number of field guides and wildflower books attempt to simplify classification and will refer to the rose family (Rosaceae) or the buttercup family (Ranunculaceae). Buttercups are placed in the genus *Ranunculus*.

Although the family Rosaceae is named after the most favored of garden flowers in Europe and North America, it contains most of our economically important, sweet, fleshy fruits. Returning to Polyphemus's property in early spring, we pick a strawberry flower and examine it with a hand lens. It has five sepals, five petals, and many stamens that fuse to form an urn-shaped cup around many tiny carpels. The genus, *Fragaria*, belongs to the Rosaceae and is allied to cherries, apples, peaches, and all plums.

Our Cyclops was no fan of pears (*Pyrus*) or quinces (*Cydonia*). He did not grow cultivated raspberries, loganberries, boysenberries, dewberries, or salmonberries, all placed in the same genus as Boehmer's bramble (*Rubus*). Nevertheless, these core fruits and thimble fruits also belong to the Rosaceae. The internal structure and maturation rates of pistils in the rose family is so variable that closely related species continue to offer us fruit with remarkably different ranges of flesh textures, seed numbers, and skin colors and surfaces.

1.7 CAN YOU SUBDIVIDE A SPECIES?

The hierarchy employed by taxonomists appears to focus on the "widest view" of plant classification. There is also a smaller and much narrower hierarchy of some importance to conservationists, plant breeders, and scientists who study the natural distribution of plants and animals. People who study the relation of species to varying degrees of latitude, longitude, and elevation are known as biogeographers. If you check some of the better field guides to the woody plants and wildflowers in your area, you may see the impact made by biogeographers. The distribution of your favorite plants has been well mapped or check-listed county by county. You may also find that some plants appear to have three scientific names. Why would anyone want to replace the dependable binomial with a trinomial?

Let's consider the American species of yellow lady's-slipper orchid (*Cypripedium parviflorum*). I am using a wild orchid as an example of variation because the genus name (*Cypripedium*) is of particular interest to this book. The word *Cypripedium* incorporates one of the names of the Greek goddess of love (see §5.8). If you check a field guide or a modern orchid book specializing in plants native to the U.S. Midwest, you will see that these publications insist there are three "varieties" of *C. parviflorum*: *Cypripedium parviflorum* var. *parviflorum* is found throughout much of the undisturbed heartland, but you must look for it on acid soils. You are more likely to encounter *C. parviflorum* var. *makasin* in cooler, alkaline prairies of the Great Plains. Within the Midwest, *makasin* is more common in Iowa and Minnesota, although it gets into Illinois. *Cypripedium parviflorum* var. *pubescens* is, once again, distributed through most midwestern states, as far south as Arkansas, but it also likes alkaline soils growing over limestone slabs.

Plant taxonomists carve this perfectly good species into three varieties because they see small physical differences between plants isolated in different populations over its North American range. The *makasin* variety has the smallest flowers with the darkest sepals and lateral petals. When a plant of *pubescens* comes into bloom, the leaflike organ (bract) found behind the flower wears a coat of dense, white hairs. Plain old variety *parviflorum* has flowers larger and lighter colored than *makasin* but lacks the "furry collar" worn by *pubescens.* Zoologists do much the same thing with animals, but they seem uncomfortable with the word *variety.* They are more likely to break a species into smaller subspecies. Whatever the case, you may think that characteristics used to establish varieties or subspecies are rather trivial. Most taxonomists will agree with you. If the flower size, color, and leaf hairs of the three varieties were more self-consistent and exaggerated, they would probably be reclassified as three separate and discrete species. In fact, all plants of *C. parviflorum* display at least a few hairs on their bracts. We call one variety *pubescens* throughout its natural range because it has the densest, thickest coat of hairs. Attributes expressed by varieties are simply a matter of degree, and they are not genetically "fixed." When the distributions of different varieties overlap, the plants interbreed. The offspring produced between two different varieties are completely fertile, and this second generation inherits blended or intermediate characteristics from their two parent varieties.

Stephen Jay Gould (1941–2002), that great American historian of evolutionary biology, felt that the names of varieties and subspecies were holdovers from the nineteenth century. They reflected a more restricted time when taxonomists wanted to draw attention to some minor novelty expressed by an obscure population within a species. Varieties and subspecies came from an era before modern mapping techniques. They belong to eras before the scientific community understood the boundaries of Earth's topography. Cumbersome attempts to anchor *makasin, parviflorum,* and *pubescens* to *C. parviflorum* proper were supposed to fade away as satellite tracking and computer-recorded collections became more precise and sophisticated. If you read recent monographs, treatises, and field guides that revise the classification of plants and animals, you know that varieties refuse to go gently into that good night. Frankly, it is still far easier to use a variety name than it is to describe minor differences over and over again and then relegate the individuals that have them to a bunch of scattered quadrants.

Yes, the characteristics that define a variety are minor, but consider how important they are to people searching for rare or threatened species. What about the needs of the conservationist, trying to establish protected reserves for surviving populations with unusually fragmented distributions? Only *parviflorum* thrives on acid soil. You will not find it on the limestone ridges of the Flint Hills of Kansas. If you prefer the relatively mild winters of Arkansas, you had better forget about ever finding the cold-loving *makasin*. If we are going to save a species, we must consider preserving as much of its genetic variability as possible. That means being able to recognize and identify populations in which certain features are well expressed or almost absent. Would you not prefer to protect sites accommodating clumps of *parviflorum, makasin,* and *pubescens*?

In fact, many biologists are convinced that some populations of varieties and subspecies retain the genetic luggage required for the evolution of new species. As climate and geology change over time, the natural distribution (the biogeography) of varieties expands and contracts. As stress levels in different areas change, some varieties or subspecies contract or even become extinct. Others thrive and expand under new conditions. If the distribution of a thriving variety of slipper orchid remains isolated from declining (less fit) varieties, it may expand to become a new, separate species.

Some botanists add one more division to the taxonomic hierarchy. They refer to a form or *forma* within the plant species. They acknowledge that, whenever you survey a species, a few striking individuals appear. These individuals offer one or two attributes atypical to the original description of the original species. Some forms are really mutants. Although they represent rare genetic accidents, they still repeat themselves with a good deal of mathematical predictability. One out of every thousand seeds of a wild rose grows into a bush in which each flower produces ten or more petals instead of the usual five.

Other forms occur when parents mate with their own offspring or siblings mate with each other. This increases the possibility that two halves of a recessive gene will link up in the embryo. The scarlet pimpernel (*Anagallis arvensis*) gets the best publicity owing to its role in an old novel, some Hollywood movies, and, at least one musical comedy. In fact, the red-flowered pimpernels often share the same meadows and roadsides with a high frequency of blue-flowered pimpernels classified, simply, as *forma caerulea*.

Finding both hardy varieties and uncommon forms are often the secrets of success in the plant breeding industry. To domesticate wild trees, bushes, or wildflowers horticulturists look for the varieties that thrive best in the chemically mixed, much cultivated soils of gardens. After all, as concrete weathers and leaches, acid soils grow increasingly alkaline. When new varieties are placed on the market, it is the rare forms that attract the wealthiest clientele. Snob value is so profitable in the garden industry. In the nineteenth century, hobbyists wanted the white-flowered forms of the species of tropical orchids that usually produced purple flowers. The plant on sale in a catalog or at an auction sold quickly if the species name ended with the epithet *forma alba*.

1.8 But What Is a Species?

Families, varieties, and forms are interesting concepts in different ways. They reflect a useful form of cataloging and, when properly studied, tell us something about evolutionary history and genealogy on a planetwide scale. However, no taxonomist believes that families, orders, classes, kingdoms, and domains actually exist in nature. For all biologists, the earth's living diversity consists exclusively of its described and undescribed species. In print, each described species is represented by its binomial.

Here's a potentially embarrassing question. How do we know that species are real? Why do we not treat them as hierarchical divisions as artificial as families or orders? Linnaeus and his students would have dismissed such a question. It was obvious to them that species represented real units in nature. Each species is made of a limited suite of fixed and unique characteristics. Those qualities give a species its credentials. Bullace plums always come from thorny trees, bearing simple leaves with only one to three flowers produced per twig cluster. The fruit contains a single, wrinkled stone and a purple or yellow skin. Of course, oddities occur from time to time. A plum blossom may develop ten petals instead of five. A plum seed may sprout and grow into a thornless tree. These "sports of nature" have their charms and may be valuable under domestication, but what of it? The vast majority of individuals in the same species were identical at maturity, producing the same sort of growth habits, foliage shapes, floral architecture, and fruit interiors.

Charles Darwin (1809–1882) also believed in the reality of natural species. However, he did not accept that species consisted of immutable units. Simple measurements and observations showed that plants grown from seeds taken from the same pod matured to show slight but consistent differences in size, leaf dimensions, height, flower color, seed shape, and many other attributes. Those differences persisted even when the plants were grown under exactly the same conditions. Sometimes these differences blended or intergraded; sometimes they were fixed and distinctive, forming stereotyped forms or morphs.

When exposed to different levels of environmental stress (drought, low temperatures, inadequate levels of sunlight, plant-eating pests) some members of the same species fail to survive long enough to produce the next generation of healthy, sprouting seeds. Levels of genetic variation within a species when coupled with environmental stress levels (natural selection) are the building blocks of evolution. Some species exist for long, stable periods. Some become extinct. Under certain circumstances, populations fragment and become isolated for long periods. These isolated groups may be exposed to different forms of environmental stress. Over time these populations vary so much that one species subdivides into two or more new species.

Species do exist. That means that every binomial represents one or more distinct populations. Because natural selection changes the survival value of certain traits over time, it is best to compare and measure important characteristics between and within populations. Essentially, every living species (even those under threat of extinction) consists of two or more individuals sharing the same life cycle. The generation following Darwin understood that, in most cases, plant species have a past history of changing and modifying genes and gene frequencies. This occurred as their ancestors exchanged or received sperm locked up in microscopic boxes called pollen grains.

That fact puts an ironic twist on the identification, description, and classification of new species. Whereas species are based on varying populations (Darwin), describing a new species is dependent on a solitary specimen (Linnaeus). Concepts and research techniques that were initiated in the nineteenth century coexist with, but contradict, a protocol developed in the eighteenth century. Every month new issues of scientific journals appear describing dozens of new species. Hundreds are described annually (especially in entomological journals). Descriptions, as always, are based on a single specimen. Additional specimens taken with the type specimen are put into storage. Some species are based on the results of only one lucky day of collection. Or consider the richness of rainforests, which have a high diversity of woody species but a low density of individuals in each species. There may be more than a hundred different trees, shrubs, and woody vine species in a single acre of land. However, you may only find one or two trees that belong to the same species per acre. The arrangement of plants in a rainforest is often at random. Therefore, if you stick to the same narrow, meandering trail you may see the same species only once every ten or twenty miles.

The ratio of botanists to plants is always skewed in favor of the plants. What are we to make of the contents of those herbarium cabinets? Some cabinet shelves are stuffed with sheets. Others are so bare that pigeons could use them as nesting boxes. Does the presence of a solitary species attached to a solitary sheet reflect natural rarity, a freakish form posing as a "good species," a lack of professional interest, insufficient funds to mount a significant expedition, or all four concerns? Do type specimens represent real species or the possibility of new species?

1.9 A Curse on Your Synonyms

Competent taxonomists spend their lives answering these questions, and that often means changing scientific names. Many binomials have a limited shelf life. Most private plant collectors, members of plant societies, people in the nursery industry, home gardeners, forest rangers, and conservationists share the same opinion when it comes to changing nomenclature. They hate to see changes in scientific names, and they often hate the taxonomists who make those changes.

I don't blame them. If your greenhouses contain a wonderful living collection of passionflower vines (*Passiflora*), you do not want to be told that you own ninety-nine species instead of a hundred. Are you are trying to protect a beautiful forest from land developers because some wooded glade is a refuge for a rare species? You certainly do not want to be told that your precious plants are nothing more than infrequent color forms of some common and thriving species distributed naturally throughout the United States. Firms preparing expensive seed catalogs do not want to be reminded that their supply of the rare and choice is neither very rare, nor very choice.

Some names must change as the result of invalid publications. We have already visited the "dark side" of this problem in the extreme case of Constantine Rafinesque. In fact, plenty of odd, innocent errors afflict the careers of the most meticulous taxonomists. It is suspected that lots of species have been named more than once. That means that one species may be represented by more than one holotype in more than one museum around the world. The taxonomist who named a previously described species a second time is often unaware of the error. Perhaps he or she lacked access to an important, earlier publication. More likely, the taxonomist did not have a full set of specimens of every described and published species belonging to the same genus.

There are an estimated 250 species of beardtongues (*Penstemon*) in North America. Although found through much of the continent, these beautiful wildflowers are most diverse in the western half of the United States. Some rare species are confined to isolated canyons or hard-to-reach slopes on a restricted number of mountainsides. I have read books explaining beard-tongue diversity and the evolution of new species. I have gazed longingly on photographs of their magnificent flowers and studied the drawings of dissected flowers. Minute differences in petal, stamen, and pistil sculptur-ing make each species unique. My professional response reflects suspicion. If all of those mountains and obscure canyons interconnected would not four or five of the rarer, blue-flowered species be reduced to one? That is heresy to many members of the American Penstemon Society.

Back in 1981, the great orchid taxonomist Robert Dressler subdivided his fellow taxonomists into splitters, lumpers, and splimpers. Splitters see vast differences between specimens and may divide a solitary species into two or more new species. Lumpers find certain characteristics overrated and are more likely to "sink" several preexisting species into one large species. The curious splimpers splits the species that interest and obsess them most while lumping the species with which they are less familiar. It does not mat-ter if you make little ones out of big ones or unite the little ones into one superspecies. The results are the same. One, or both, of the words in the original binomial must change. If the genus, or the species, or both genus and species names change, then the original, older name becomes a syn-onym. This change in status is not a tragedy. Synonyms are important for history's sake, and they give people a chance to compare and make their own decisions.

Just because a scientist changes the names of a group of species, and the work is published as a revision, does not mean that the new treatment will be immune to challenges or criticism. Generally speaking, the more recent a revision, the greater the number of critiques it will receive from compet-ing botanists. This is especially true if the taxonomist works on a group of plants dear to private collectors and/or the agricultural, home gardening, or medical industries. Taxonomy is no place for the passive.

As a case in point, let's reconsider the yellow lady's-slipper. Yes, it's correct to call it *Cypripedium parviflorum*. Nevertheless, since 1753 until almost the end of the twentieth century, it was also known as *C. calceolus, C. flavescens, C. aureum, C. undatum, C. hirsutum, C. veganum, C. bulbosum,* and even *Calceolus hirsutus*. Only *Cypripedium calceolus* survives, because that is the original and official name Linnaeus gave to the yellow slipper native to western Europe. For more than three and a half centuries most botanists insisted that the yellow slipper of North America was the same species as the yellow slipper of Sweden, Britain, and Italy. We now treat them as two separate species: *C. parviflorum* of North America and *C. calceolus* of Eurasia.

If the preceding paragraphs have left you with the impression that plant taxonomists change names capriciously and plant classification is comparable to astrology, then I must apologize. The vast majority of modern taxonomists take the status of species seriously even when they are forced to wear the clothes of an eighteenth-century "typologist." The great taxonomists—and I have been fortunate enough to meet some—gather a lot of data before they come to the serious conclusion that a binomial must be reduced to a synonym. This means a long-term commitment to measurements followed by statistical calculations, chemical tests, field observations, and greenhouse experiments.

There are all sorts of procedures required to establish whether you are looking at a population of interbreeding organisms that share the same life cycle. When the great taxonomists revise a lineage or "flock" of interrelated species, they ultimately give us fresh, important information regarding the basic definition of the word *species*. These days, computers count, define, and compare variation in DNA, gene by gene. Before this can occur, the taxonomist is sent on a scavenger hunt, taking tissue samples from dozens (or hundreds) of organisms to use in analyses. There are plenty of other important techniques. One of my colleagues carefully germinated seeds of hundreds of different South African bulbs, squashed the young roots, and counted the chromosomes in the dividing cells. Another analyzed the enzymes made in the leaves of different citrus trees. Others grow different plants en masse, in protected, isolated greenhouses. They wait until they bloom and then perform hundreds of hand cross-pollinations to determine whether species A accepts or rejects the pollen of species B, C, or D.

The results are very interesting. Some rare species turn out to be recurrent hybrids. This occurs when the birds and the bees get careless. One or more strange new plants pop up where two members of the same genus have overlapping distributions. Hybrids occur naturally in a number of wild American sedges, grasses, violets, Louisiana irises, prickly pear cacti, columbines, sunflowers, and oaks. Many were collected by field botanists and described as new species. A later generation of taxonomists performed controlled crosses, raised the offspring to maturity, and realized that some rare species were really first generation combinations between two common and distinct species. Hybrids do not, as a rule, become new species. The first generation of hybrids often have major fertility problems, such as the production of lots of sterile pollen or difficulties forming significant numbers of healthy seeds. The chromosomes from both of the parents often fail to "match up" in the hybrid offspring. There is also the basic principle of genetic stability and frequency. You cannot fool the mathematical laws of Gregor Mendel (1822–1884). Even when hybrids cross with hybrids, they do not breed true. Parental combinations of genes reappear in the next generation.

Let's consider the apples in the Cyclops's orchard. Note that the scientific name of the domesticated apple, *Malus ×domestica*, is not a true species, although it is written in italics. The × separating the genus from the species indicates its hybrid origin. Studies suggest that three wild species exchanged pollen over time, contributing to the bewildering variety of apples for fruit, cider, and ornamental spring blossoms. The heirloom tree in your garden may have such wild ancestors as the European crab apple (*Malus sylvestris*) and two Asian species, *M. sieversii* and *M. orientalis*.

During the nineteenth century there was quite a fad in Europe to collect the glorious *Cattleya* orchids of Central and South America. The flowers of *Cattleya guatemalensis* were prized for their delicate, waxy, pink petals and their pleasant aroma. By the early twentieth century technology caught up with orchid culture. It became much easier to grow and germinate the plants using lab techniques that would cosset and culture their microscopic seeds. Different species were crossed to make bigger corsage flowers and to change color patterns found in the wild. Hybridization of two Guatemalan cattleyas, *C. aurantiaca* and *C. skinneri*, produced offspring identical to the rare, wild, pink "species." *Cattleya guatemalensis* is now written *Cattleya ×guatemalensis*.

Hybrids represent glamorous puzzles. Most taxonomists, though, are left with the basic question of where one species stops and another one begins. Leaf size, flower color, the density and forms of hairs, bark sculpture, and branch architecture are variable characteristics. Variation in each feature is presented as a bell-shaped curve. If the bell curves for leaf length of two species overlap by more than 50 percent, are we still justified in referring to them as two separate species? Probably. But what happens when the bell curves for all the other characteristics overlap as well?

On the other hand, big differences in form between populations may be deceptive. They can represent nurture instead of nature. Does species A have leaves five times larger than species B because it has different dominant genes or because it grows on richer, moister soils that stimulate more seasonal growth? The taxonomist may have to grow questionable species in test plot gardens, subjecting them to different amounts of fertilizer or substrates like sand and gravel.

Just how much weight should a scientist give to characteristics that are too small to be seen with the naked eye? Some American oaks (*Quercus*) have hairy leaves, but there are hairs and then there are hairs. Under a scanning electron microscope the hairs of one species look like beautiful little stars. The hairs of a second species are shaped like smooth whips, whereas others are stalked and resemble fuzzy brushes. Some leaves of some species bear only one kind of hair. Other species produce several different kinds of hairs on the same leaf. Other oaks bear leaves that grow bald as they age. The hair falls off the plant's skin within a few days after the blade uncurls. This leaves a scar pattern quite distinctive under a strong microscope.

At the molecular level, some plant species look alike but make flowers that smell different from each other. Fragrance analyses of some wild orchids show that different species produce certain alcohols, esters, and terpene molecules in different quantities. In fact, some molecules are unique to the odors of certain flowers. If different odors attract different insect pollinators, then different plants may not cross with each other even if they grow right next to each other and bloom at exactly the same time. Does that not make the two orchids distinct and separate species even though their flowers, leaves, and swollen stems look so much alike? We may not be able to tell them apart with ease, but their bees can and do.

You cannot appreciate all of these unique features just by staring at a type specimen on a sheet. The field collector does not have time to observe all these differences while cutting specimens and pressing them. Collection is often a matter of urgency. Within less than an hour after cutting, important characteristics can be lost as you hike through a tropical forest with a sack of wilting specimens slung over your shoulder. Petals fall off flowers. Special structures and sculptures deflate or blacken or turn into slimy ooze. A plant specimen in a hot, humid sack is at the mercy of hungry, invasive fungi sprouting from invisible spores. No, the field is no place to worry about fine details. It is the place to worry about fast and efficient preservation of specimens. Taxonomists working near the equator often take portable driers with them. Taking clunky equipment into the jungle is preferable to changing wet newspapers and blotting paper every day before a sample turns into a motel for molds. It also explains why so many revisions go beyond changing the species name within the binomial. Genera are not immune to taxonomic recombination. Just as species characteristics are plotted along a bell-shaped curve, the taxonomist must also consider where one genus begins and another ends. As we will see in the next chapter, some of the most charming genus names are now stored in the dusty attic of synonyms.

❧ § ❧

CHAPTER 2

Constructing a Centaur

The Informative Art of
Scientific Names

Yesterday I cut an orchid, for my buttonhole. It was a marvelous spotted thing, as effective as the seven deadly sins. In a thoughtless moment I asked one of the gardeners what it was called. He told me it was a fine specimen of *Robinsoniana*, or something dreadful of that kind. It is a sad truth. But we have lost the faculty of giving lovely names to things. Names are everything.

—OSCAR WILDE, *The Picture of Dorian Gray*

The Greco-Roman myths offered habitats for creatures far uglier than Polyphemus the Cyclops. Many members of this monstrous menagerie had multiple heads or an odd number of limbs. Most were hodge-podges of unrelated animal parts, with snakes sprouting from their heads instead of hair. Centaurs were exceptions to the rule "ugly is as ugly does." Although the majority of centaurs were depicted as stupid, untrustworthy, and dangerous, classical sculptors gave them a sort of rude nobility. Greek culture regarded young men and horses as the most beautiful of living things. A centaur had a human face and torso but his waist was connected to a stallion's body. The Greeks were happy to contradict themselves and regarded centaurs as "harmonious monsters."

Many scientific names are harmonious monsters. The genus word may have an origin and focus differing completely from the species word. Taxonomists may choose from five word categories in order to erect the perfect binomial. Check the identification tag on that nice bush or perennial you brought home from the nursery. Its binomial may derive from two distinct categories.

2.1 CLASSICAL NAMES

When Linnaeus decided that the oldest names in Greek or Latin were always the valid names, he forever connected taxonomy to scrolls and texts written long before the invention of the printing press. Ancient herbals, medical treatises, and epic poems offered the names of plants found in the Mediterranean or imported from Asian and African trading partners. I have noted, previously, that *Rubus* was an old Mediterranean name for blackberry. There are many more examples. For instance, five hundred plant names appear in *History of Plants,* a book written by Theophrastus (370–287 B.C.E.), a student of Plato and Aristotle. Pliny the Elder (23–79 C.E.) wrote sixteen books on plants in his encyclopedia of natural history, *Historia Naturalis.* These manuscripts offered rich grazing for Linnaeus and his disciples, who used them as sources for many genus names.

Fruit and timber were important to the survival of all Mediterranean civilizations. That explains why the modern genus names of so many trees including *Quercus* (oaks), *Fraxinus* (ash trees), *Prunus* (plums), *Malus* (apples), and *Ficus* (figs) derive from ancient sources. A nearly forgotten line of Ovid's, "Dedicat at nuper vile fuistus Acer," gave taxonomists the name for the modern genus of maples (*Acer*). Some of the oldest names for trees and medicinal herbs also allude to divinities and mortal kings. In later chapters, I will explain such generic names as *Centaurea* (see §3.7), *Diospyros* and *Juglans* (§4.1), and *Mentha* (§5.2). For now, it is enough to say that hungry people may think of tasty fruits and nuts as gifts of the gods. Herbs believed to contain powerful medicines, such as *Gentiana* (§3.7) or *Achillea* (§7.3), may be associated with powerful heroes or wise kings.

With some important exceptions, Linnaeus and his intellectual descendents turned most of the classical names into genus names. Sometimes they would comb an old text and find a fascinating name that could not be attached to a living member of the Mediterranean vegetation. The old herbals and poems often lacked adequate descriptions to make a scholarly identification. Rather than waste a word, the taxonomists used it to name a new genus of plants found on some distant continent, never seen by ancient Greeks or Romans.

2.2 Descriptive Names

Many classical names must be older than their Greek or Latin alphabets. Descriptive names, in contrast, are rarely older than the eighteenth century. Some classical names are so old that we are not sure we know the root meaning of the word. For example, the words *narcissus* and *narcotic* may have a common origin (see §3.6). On the other hand, we always know the precise meaning of a comparatively modern, descriptive name. Most classical names are applied to genera; descriptive names are assigned to both genera and species.

Descriptive names always tell us something about the physical nature of the plant. The genus name *Campanula* means "little bell." The petals (corolla) in a *Campanula* flower fuse together to form a continuous nodding bell. That is why gardeners and wildflower guides call them bellflowers. *Campanula rapunculus* is the rampion plant mentioned in the story of Rapunzel. In English, this binomial means bellflower with a swollen (turniplike) root. No wonder Rapunzel's mother wanted to eat it. Other descriptive names tell us about a plant's past uses. *Calluna* means broom. The Scottish heather (*Calluna vulgaris*) is a rather common (*vulgaris*) little shrub throughout Europe and Turkey. Its young shoots were baled and used as broom straws. Descriptive names are the most commonly used names for species. The same word may be used over and over again, throughout the plant kingdom, provided it is used only once in the same genus. Here are some common names for species with distinctive stems. You have probably read the same names on identification tags in garden shops and hardware stores.

amplectans. The base of each leaf clasps the stem.
bulbosus. The underground stem forms one or more bulbs.
nudicaulis. The flowering stem is nude because it lacks leaves.
ramulosus. The stem divides into many smaller twigs.

Descriptive names are the most commonly used names in plant taxonomy; many binomials consist of both a descriptive genus and a descriptive species.

2.3 GEOGRAPHIC NAMES

The majority of geographic names are used to describe species. Genera with geographic names remain rare. Some geographic names give rather vague directions instead of precise locations. If the species is named *hesperius*, it was found in the west. If it is named *borealis*, it had a northerly distribution. How far west or north do we have to go to find these plants today? Obviously, the name of the species does not tell us. In most cases, the taxonomist who described the new species was alluding to some region west or north of his or her herbarium.

Other names try to attach a species to a particular continent or country. Any plant named *europaeus* grew wild somewhere in Europe. The taxonomist who named a plant *pacificus* was stating that the type specimen came from a location on the western coast of North or South America. Some botanists tried to enclose plant distribution within distinct political boundaries. If you buy a tropical plant and the species is named *salvadorensis*, that usually means it was discovered in the Central American country of El Salvador. The country, in turn was named after Jesus, "the Savior." In reality, of course, plant species show contempt for political boundaries. Remember, a new species is always described from a single type specimen. The botanist, working only on a limited number of herbarium specimens, often has little idea of the full and natural range of the new plant. Expeditions will not provide the full distribution of a species unless they are designed to hunt for the same thing over a period of decades.

The first collections of North American plants for the herbarium cabinets of Europe began in the sixteenth and seventeenth centuries. The earliest expeditions to what is now eastern Canada and the United States were rather restricted. Most would-be botanists stayed within the narrow radius of a few European settlements. Consequently, your shopping trip to a modern nursery in search of domesticated forms of native American plants is often a trip back to the old Virginia colony. If you do not want to buy that pot of *Fragaria virginiana,* please consider a nice *Clematis virginiana* or a *Tradescantia virginiana.* If there is space on your property for a big tree or bush, what about a *Juniperus virginiana* or a *Hamamelis virginiana*?

For various reasons, taxonomists have from time to time scrambled plant geography. Most of the large-flowered cyclamens sold as winter-blooming houseplants, for instance, are derived from the wild species, *Cyclamen persicum.* The scientific name means Persian cyclamen. It is a relatively common plant through much of the Middle East, growing as far west as Tunisia and eastward through Israel and Jordan. There is one minor point to consider, however: it is not a native wildflower of Persia (Iran).

2.4 Honorifics

Modern taxonomists are not permitted to name new species after themselves anymore. However, there is nothing to prevent the same scientist from naming a new plant after someone else. You do not even have to know the individual you lionize in botanical Latin. The only rule is that the name must belong to someone who exists or existed. That is the only thing that really separates an honorific from a classical name given to a purely mythical figure.

Linnaeus, for example, decided to name the genus of true yams (*Dioscorea*) after Dioscorides, the first-century (c.e.) physician who wrote the *Materia Medica.* This ancient manuscript introduced generations of botanists to the medicinal plants of the Mediterranean. Using yams to honor the memory of a father of medical botany turned out to be sound judgment, in hindsight. The tubers of some African and tropical American species are rich in molecules that resemble the building blocks of estrogen and cortisone. Many people have benefited from yam-based medicines.

Back in those early and innocent days of plant taxonomy, Linnaeus was allowed to honor himself. Twinflower (*Linnaea borealis*) is a little creeper in the honeysuckle family (Caprifoliaceae). It grows around the Arctic Circle (borealis). Another botanist mistook it for a bluebell (*Campanula borealis*), but Linnaeus noted that the sexual organs in a twinflower did not follow the usual bluebell pattern. In an era of astonishing botanical discoveries, Linnaeus could have named something big and spectacular after himself (a mighty tree or a lily with gaudy flowers). Instead, he succumbed to sentimentality, choosing the twinflower he collected during his student days in Lapland. He insisted on giving the new genus his name because it was so "lowly, insignificant, disregarded, flowering for a brief space—from Linnaeus who resembles it."

Physicians, naturalists, nursery growers, and scientists are not the only people whose names survive in binomials. They may honor a person who signed the Declaration of Independence (*Franklinia* and *Jeffersonia*), a famous concubine (*Aspasia*), a beloved monarch known for her love of flowers (*Victoria*), a wealthy and influential patron known to support botanical expeditions (*Lapageria* and *Phelipaea*), or a devoted spouse (*wilsoniae*).

Whatever the inspiration for honorific names, there should be some sort of thread to tie the genus or species to an actual person. These associations are often vague, at best. President Thomas Jefferson promoted the introduction of useful and exotic plants on American farms. Rheumatism root (*Jeffersonia diphylla*) grows in Jefferson's home state of Virginia and also in many forests once part of the original thirteen colonies. No one has ever found an economically significant use for the herb. As mentioned in the previous chapter, entomologists traditionally named a species after the person who first collected the new insect. In the nineteenth century, many orchid plants ripped from tropical forests, exported to Europe, and sold at auction could not be identified unless they survived long enough to bloom. A few orchid taxonomists honored hobbyists who imported unknown specimens or provided plants from their own private collections (*Barkeria, Cattleya, Nageliellia*, and *Ponthieva*).

Honorifics receive more negative criticism than any of the other four categories serving as name sources. Consider the aesthetics: should we name a pretty, and potentially popular, plant after an ugly, and often obscure, human? How can you justify a scientific name that turns a new genus or species into a rude-sounding or hard-to-spell tongue twister (*hookeri, Loiseleuria,*

Macleaya, Stranvaesia, or *tabernaemontanus,* for example)? If you believe that the history of biology is all about scientists interacting and helping each other, then there is no argument at all. Naming new species reflects fashions in history, and naming them after people is as valid as using any other word. Who says that applying botanical Latin to a person's last name condemns new species to an eternity of bad jokes? We buy expensive corsages based on wild *Cattleya* species, treasure the *Magnolia* tree in the backyard, and weep at an opera about a lady devoted to flowers in the genus *Camellia.* All three genera were named after people. That did not hurt sales of the plants and flowers or stop authors from popularizing the scientific names and popping them into poems, plays, and lyrics.

There are ways of making honorifics more palatable to purists. Take the last name of the individual, and translate it into botanical Latin. Peter Raven, director of the Missouri Botanical Garden, has been a big name in botany for decades. Among his many contributions to the plant sciences, he is regarded as an international authority on the evening primrose family (Onagraceae). Colleagues decided to honor him with a new genus of wildflowers. The genus was published under the name *Megacorax* (*Mega* means big and *corax* means raven).

2.5 MYTHOLOGICAL AND LITERARY ALLUSIONS

Cynics may argue that a scientific name based on a figure in a Greco-Roman myth represents nothing more than a quaint subdivision within the honorific category. Of course, there is some overlap. I argue, though, that genus and species names based on classical allusions confer special benefits within plant taxonomy. Unlike pure honorifics, when the name of a mythical figure is used properly, no one can accuse the botanist of either toadying to the wealthy or inflating a minor reputation. Classical allusions are neither bland nor overly nationalistic, unlike geographic names. When a descriptive name is used, the taxonomist must attend to matters of conjugation, tenses, and the use of appropriate syllables. The name of a deity or hero is always correct as it stands.

When you think about it, scientific names based on mythological figures or characters found in poems and stories represent a pleasant and logical extension of classical names. The early Greeks and Romans named several of their native trees and wildflowers after favorite heroes, monarchs, and gods. Scientists revived and modernized the tradition. These names derive from long-dead religions. It is impossible to cause real offense when a taxonomist uses them.

Giving newly discovered plants names derived from Greco-Roman myths began, as usual, with Linnaeus. He embellished the tradition he found in the works of Theophrastus, Dioscorides, and their unnamed contemporaries. The remaining chapters in this book testify to his taste, imagination, and classical education. Using Greco-Roman myths, though, did not stop Linnaeus from drawing on other sources for appropriate names. As we will see, he was equally adept in all four categories and thought nothing of making one word do the work of three. However, it is also obvious that his use of myths inspired colleagues and future generations of taxonomists.

Why do botanists use classical allusions when devising binomials? Is it merely a matter of giving a lovely thing a lovely name or damning a monstrous specimen with a name of the damned? That line of logic plays a large part in this story. Many taxonomists believed, and still believe, that plants are entitled to fantastic names if the specimen offers exaggerated growth forms, organs, colors, and odors. After all, when we enter the world of Greco-Roman myth voluntarily we are expected to leave our common sense on the doorstep. Therefore, use art when life imitates art.

2.6 LINDLEY'S LOGIC

There is a second reason for dressing up scientific names in mythical robes. The English taxonomist John Lindley (1799–1865) was one of the greatest proponents of using classical allusions when naming new genera. I regard Lindley as one of the most brilliant botanists of his day. He classified orchids according to how sex organs in the flower constructed, dispersed, and accepted pollen. In 1862, Charles Darwin used Lindley's classification to better explain how orchid flowers manipulated insect pollinators. Lindley worked tirelessly with greenhouse architects and horticulturists to make botany accessible and useful to professional and amateur gardeners. Few professional botanists, then and now, could claim their work served as a bridge uniting scientific and practical concerns.

Lindley lived in a great era of expeditions. In particular, preserved and living collections of plants, all new to science, came to European herbaria and greenhouses from the diverse vegetation of South America and China. There were plenty of new species, and many were so unique that they deserved new genus names. Lindley believed that a new genus was served best if it received a name that was lyrical and easy to remember. He did not quite trust a genus name based exclusively on any descriptive characteristic.

After all, every type specimen used to describe a new genus usually shows several unique physical characteristics. That is why it deserves the rank of new genus. When we decide to give the type a wholly descriptive name, we are forced to concentrate on only one of these unique characteristics when we construct a new genus name. How can anyone guess which attribute (flower color, leaf shape, stem architecture, hairiness, or fruit anatomy) best represents the defining feature of a new genus? But stringing too many Latin syllables together in order to accommodate all the possibilities makes a genus name too long and cumbersome. In the meantime, expeditions continue. Collectors do their jobs well, and more new species are added to this original genus. What happens, though, if someone finds a new plant species that obviously belongs to this genus, but the new type specimen lacks the "definitive" characteristic we Latinized to establish the genus's name? We are now forced to either ignore the deficiency (all of our colleagues will notice, unfortunately) or erect a new genus name for the new specimen that lacks only this one trait.

Classical allusions were Lindley's alternative to clumsy, descriptive, and potentially embarrassing descriptive names. A name based on a mythical figure is always neutral. It tells us nothing specific about the plant's form or organs. It offers a lyrical word that is easy to remember. During Lindley's lifetime, educated Europeans knew their classical myths. They could not escape them. Plots and characters based on Greco-Roman stories were employed constantly by contemporary poets, performed in operas, painted on canvasses, and exhibited as public sculptures. When a well-spoken person used an expression like "Herculean effort" or "the judgment of Paris," every educated individual knew immediately what the allusion meant

Lindley practiced what he preached. In particular, he liked giving the names of mythological figures to new orchid genera. As we will soon see, there is nothing like an unidentified orchid to bring out the romanticist in an otherwise dour and meticulous taxonomist. It is a shame that some of his most intriguing names for new genera, such as *Empusa* (see §4.7) and *Ate* were reduced to synonyms. Lindley knew how to fish for words in the deep ocean of European literature as well. He searched for allusions outside the body of Greco-Roman fantasies, with considerable success. He named a genus of orchids after Shakespeare's king of the fairies. There are more than three hundred *Oberonia* species distributed through the African and Asian tropics. Most are small plants that spend their lives clinging to tree branches. Lindley saw at least one living plant in bloom. The cluster of curved leaves suggested the outline of an open carriage. The flowers reminded him of tiny horses connected to the carriage by individual reins (the flower stalks). Here was Oberon, driving his chariot through the branches of the forest.

2.7 SCIENTISTS CONCEAL MEANINGS IN CLASSICAL ALLUSIONS

That fact is a big part of the appeal of scientific names based on literary and classical allusions. The most thoughtful taxonomists allow you to enjoy their dry wit, refined over centuries. The best of these names are little puzzles. Remember, although every published description of a new species must contain definitions explaining the new combination of words, the author is never required to tell you why such words were chosen in the first place. If you can figure out the rationale behind a scientific name based on a mythical figure, you become entitled to an unusual reward. For a brief moment you are allowed to live in the botanist's mind.

I suspect it was far easier for educated readers to solve the word puzzles one or two centuries ago. Most of our larger public schools offered Latin. The privately educated student was expected to translate Ovid and Virgil. Popular books, written for children, simplified the myths of Homer and usually introduced the characters under their Roman names. Our society no longer emphasizes classical languages. We do not look on Greek or Latin as unifying or even entertaining tools. When was the last time you planted a new shrub and became enchanted by the binomial on the identification tag?

Although the ancient tradition of naming plants after deities and monarchs began with the specialized language of rural root collectors (the *rhizotomi*) of prehistoric Greece, Linnaeus and his followers modernized and formalized the procedure until it spread far beyond the Mediterranean basin. Consequently, you are now assured of finding plants named after gods and goddesses if you start at the Arctic Circle and walk south. It does not matter whether you stop at the tip of South America, the Cape of Good Hope, or the shores of Tasmania. Binomials bearing the name of a nymph or hero represent a recurrent trend spanning almost three centuries.

This trend always started with expeditions to poorly explored lands. While collecting plants in Lapland for his doctoral dissertation, the young Linnaeus fell in love with a bush in a bog and decided to name it after the Princess Andromeda (6.6). Linnaeus never left Europe, but by the time he became a professor, collectors sent him specimens from all over the world. By the end of the eighteenth century, many genera native to North America were named after mythological figures thanks to Linnaeus and his students. Most plant collectors traveling abroad did not name the specimens they found in the field. That activity was reserved for the taxonomist seated in the herbarium. I personally find it amazing that piles of flat, discolored, desiccated stems and blossoms (often smelling like common hay) retained enough power to trigger nostalgic memories of schoolroom stories and old poems.

2.8 BUT WHAT WERE THOSE RHIZOTOMI THINKING?

One thing is certain: it is much easier to solve the riddles left by taxonomists over the past three centuries than it is to explain the aboriginal names left by the earliest root collectors, or rhizotomi. Remember, they were the first to apply the names of some mythical characters to wild plants. The later herbalists and physicians who preserved the folklore in manuscript form were not interested in how these plants got their names. They wanted to record each plant's "virtues" to treat a variety of ills.

The real gift of the rhizotomi was their protocol for identifying plants in the absence of magnifying lenses. The naked eye, after all, is barred from the easy recognition cues concealed within small flowers. When the ancient, preliterate root collectors picked or dug wild plants for sale, they were confined to circumscribed territories by their own two feet or, at best, the four hooves of a beast of burden. Nevertheless, the Mediterranean basin remains a center of plant diversity, and even small islands like Crete still boast hundreds of species. Skim the pages of the oldest herbals and illustrated compendia, and you will understand how these men and women operated in the field. They trained themselves, or were trained by mentors, to recognize a plant's habit. That is, when possible, they concentrated on the form taken by plant once it reached reproductive maturity.

We continue to follow these rules. Mature plants have either a woody or herbaceous habit (growth form). Woody plants offer stems reinforced internally with water-conducting cells (xylem) deposited in rings. Rings of wood form an internal skeleton, and that permits the growth of two major kinds of natural architecture. Trees have only one major, erect stem, but that trunk supports several lateral, secondary branches. Shrubs, in contrast, lack a central stem. Several smaller, woody shoots emerge from the plant's crown. These shoots appear to bud and branch into smaller, new stems almost indefinitely.

Herbs also contain water-conducting tissues, but they fail to deposit this tissue in rings over the long term. Consequently, their aerial stems usually fail to survive more than one growing season. The rhizotomi were particularly observant of variation in growth patterns, as the stems often yielded the medicines they needed. The herbals show that collectors were expected to recognize the shape of leaves and how they attached to the stems. The architecture of the stem in bloom was of primary importance, as well. Did it develop into a stiff, straight spike, with blossoms arranged from base to tip, or did it unfurl like the spokes of an umbrella? Did the plant die after it bloomed and set seed, or did a portion survive underground as part of its annual cycle of regeneration? The rhizotomi were adept at recognizing specialized stems that sent up tufts of leaves and flowering stalks following seasonal changes in climate. We have inherited their vocabulary for bulbs, tubers, corms, and rhizomes, all underground stems with different shapes and coats. Did the flowers and foliage appear on the same stem? If so, the herb was caulescent. Some stalks bolted upward but bore only flowers. Their green leaves formed a pretty, flattened rosette, lying flush with the earth. The flowering stalk stood in the center of the rosette like a maypole. These herbs were acaulescent.

2.9 TAXONOMISTS CONTINUE TO EXPAND THE TRADITIONS OF THE RHIZOTOMI

The rhizotomi left scientists more than the terminology for growth habits. Ancient Greeks and Italians named a number of common plants after divinities, monarchs, and heroes. Linnaeus and his students eagerly received the "torch" passed by these herbalists. The modern, taxonomic logic for basing the names of new species on classical allusions often follows tales known by extinct plant collectors. This explains why some groups of flowering plants appear to enjoy a surfeit of classical allusions whereas other groups are more likely to reflect fashions in honorific, geographical, and descriptive names.

Some binomials reflect literary and mythological allusions because the plants were obviously related to species with classical names. For example, the rhizotomi first honored the myth of the wise centaur, Chiron, by referring to some medicinal herbs as centaur plants. Eighteenth-century techniques for plant classification showed that the flowers of the original centaur herbs resembled those of gentians and daisies. Linnaean taxonomists extended the work of the rhizotomi, playing with the classical themes and figures. These botanists named newly discovered genera in the gentian family (Gentianceae) after Chiron (see §3.7) and other characters that appeared in the body of myths about centaurs (§6.8–6.10). A South American member of the daisy family (Asteraceae) was named after Chiron's daughter (§3.7).

Botanists also honor the intellectual whims of botanists past. In the eighteenth century, Linnaeus named the genus of slipper orchids, *Cypripedium*, after the goddess of love (see §5.9). In the nineteenth, the German orchid taxonomist E. Pfitzer took a second look at these gorgeous wildflowers and concluded that there were four genera of lady's slippers instead of one. Pfitzer showed his loyalty to the memory of Linnaeus. The love goddess has so many names that it was easy to name one new genus *Paphiopedilum* (§5.8). A second genus honored Selene, a rather amorous goddess of the moon (§5.11).

Did these taxonomists ever feel that some type specimens had characteristics that almost predestined them to names based on classical and literary allusions? I suspect so. While collecting names for this book I noticed a few recurrent trends. First, several genera named after mythological figures were all restricted to the islands of Macronesia. The travel industry refers to these islands as the Azores and Canaries. Why should gods and princesses play together on Tenerife or Madeira (see §5.4, 5.7, 7.4)? Although Greeks and Romans believed that many gods controlled the maturation of crops and the earth's fertility, few of their deities actually owned private gardens. Hades had his Elysian Fields, but that piece of real estate, as we will see, symbolized fallow land and a few unloved flowers of starvation (§4.7). No, the Canaries have nothing to do with the land of the dead. Queen Hera (Roman, Juno) was the only goddess in the pantheon who kept a private garden. Where was it? All poets agreed it was far to the west. Possible locations included Spain, a mountain in Morocco, or two islands out in the Atlantic. For the botanists of the eighteenth and nineteenth centuries, the Canaries became the de facto Garden of the Hesperides. The islands provided a unique flora, well-fitted to take the names of the children of Zeus and his lovers.

Second, the unusual life histories of some plants lent themselves to obvious comparisons with mythological figures. Aquatic vegetation, both freshwater and marine, encouraged taxonomists to invoke the names of sea gods (see §4.6) and water nymphs (§3.4, 3.5). A few carnivorous plants were associated with the unsavory reputations of females who loved thoroughly but unscrupulously (§5.9, 6.2, 7.4). Were male botanists suggesting that these herbs deceived and trapped insects, just as their namesakes seduced and ruined men? I think so, but we can never be certain.

Third, some botanists looked at the folklore of many other cultures and judged some plants by their reputations. An extravagantly praised medicinal herb (still sold in health food stores) from China was named after a daughter of the god of medicine (see §5.5). The genus of suicide trees (still causing tragedies in India) was supposed to remind us of the hound of hell (§6.8).

Fourth, some new plants seemed entitled to names based on myths because they reminded botanists of the economy or culture of classical civilization. I note that the names of several genera and species in the grass family (Poaceae) are based on classical allusions (see §3.2, 5.2, 7.5, 7.7). Ancient Greece was grass-fed. Breads based on several grains were the staff of life for all members of society. Both private wealth and ritual sacrifices depended on pasture-grazed flocks and herds.

Finally, we must remind ourselves that all Greco-Roman myths were based on the most beautiful exaggerations. No wonder that generations of botanists used classical allusions to name newly discovered members of the orchid family (Orchidaceae). Most tropical orchids spend their lives clinging to twigs and branches favored by wood nymphs (see §3.4). Evolution has exaggerated orchid flowers so magnificently that they seem tailor-made to honor old tales. Like gods and mythical kings, the greatest orchid taxonomists and private collectors were obsessed by the need to possess both the grotesque (§4.2, 5.8) and the sublime (§3.4, 5.9, 7.2).

2.10 But Is This a Book about Myths or a Book about Plants?

Don't take my word for it. Read the myths that follow, and see if you can spot any of these five overlapping trends. As promised in my preface, the organization of the stories follows the usual outline offered in most modern books retelling Greco-Roman myths. I start with the standard Creation tales and end with the fates of warriors coming home after the decade-long Trojan War.

I have made only one change to the common format. Ovid's epic *Metamorphoses* contained an outline for myth cycles still preferred by most authors. As usual, Ovid began with the Greek tales and ended his book with legends unique to the religions of Rome and the assimilated Etruscans, who inhabited the Italian region we now call Tuscany. I decided to break tradition and preferred to incorporate the Latin stories within the greater body of Greek myth. This made it easier to cluster plants from the same family or the same part of the world, even though their namesakes came from different pantheons. The Romans borrowed much of their theology from the Greeks. They modified their Latin deities and heroes to fit into Greek lineages and stories. I do not think my mix makes much of a difference from the botanical side of things.

After all, this is really a book about plant names. Some of the narratives that follow remain incomplete or reduced because some plots, while beautiful or exciting, have not inspired botanists to erect new genera or species. If you want the complete tales of the loves of Zeus, all twelve labors of Heracles, or the death of every Trojan warrior, you should read any of the good, modern translations of the classics or consult some of the fine compendia of myths in print (see the selected and annotated bibliography).

2.11 And What about Synonyms?

I also had to make a decision about whether to include many botanical synonyms (see §1.9) based on literary and classical allusions. Plant names based on mythical characters are not given preferential treatment by taxonomists. There are many intriguing and pretty plant names (such as *Cybele, Castalia, Dryadea, Ione,* and *Juno*) honoring gods and heroes, but those names were reduced to synonyms decades or centuries ago. Should any synonyms be used in this book? I think that I must be flexible. As discussed in the previous chapter, many scientific names have a limited shelf life. Even if I resolved to be completely up to date and to discard every synonym from the eighteenth century up to the year when this book was published, my work still would age rapidly. Many species are under scientific scrutiny, so their names are always in danger of partial or complete disintegration. Consequently, I've retained some synonyms for two important reasons.

First, I kept some synonyms if they represented name changes made recently, within about the past twenty years. Even the most recent gardening books, manuals on herbal medicines, and the majority of seed and bulb catalogs are often taxonomic attics. These publications tend to retain the old scientific names of plants long after professional botanists dispose of them. I keep the synonym in the appropriate myth and then introduce the reader to the new name in the botanical section that follows. I hope it will give some of you a chance to catch up with important changes in the classification of some of your favorite plants.

Second, as mentioned above, some plant names based on Greco-Roman myths represent a combination of sly jokes and serious homage to earlier generations of taxonomists. Sometimes you cannot understand the meaning of a valid scientific name without looking at older names for closely related plants, now reduced to synonym status. Helen of Troy (see §7.2) keeps her proud status as an American genus in the daisy family. Her Trojan mother-in-law, Queen Hecuba (§7.1), also lent her name to an American genus in the daisy family, but it did not endure. Hecuba was reduced to synonym status. The fates of characters in myths and botany are rarely fair.

Here are the myths that inspired botanists. It is time to read some familiar—and unfamiliar—old stories.

2. Chiron is surrounded by herbs and a sculpture of the molecule of morphine (a product of the opium poppy). A knapweed, *Centaurea solsitalis*, sets seed above the centaur's tail. A bachelor button (*Centaurea stoebe*) blooms in the upper right-hand corner. The lower right-hand corner depicts both the flower and flowering stem of the showy centaury plant (*Centaurium pulchellum*). Beneath Chiron's hooves we see a monkey fiddle flower (*Hesperochiron californicum*). Illustration by John Myers.

CHAPTER 3

෴

Mother Earth and Her Children

> But Gaia's first born was one
> who matched her every dimension,
> Ouranos, the starry sky,
> to cover her all over,
> to be an unshakable standing-place
> for the blessed immortals.
> Then she brought forth the tall Hills,
> those wild haunts that are beloved
> by the goddess Nymphs who live on the hills
> and in their forests.

—HESIOD, *Theogony*
    (translation by Richard Lattimore)

3.1 EARTH'S ORIGIN AND NIGHT'S CHILDREN

The poet Hesiod believed that the oldest being in the universe was a shapeless mass, neither male nor female, called Chaos. The first child to emerge out of Chaos was Mother Earth, a mighty goddess. The Greeks called her Ge (1) or Gaia (2).* Other poets insisted that Gaia was only one of the many grandchildren of Chaos. In this version, Darkness was the oldest being and the mother of Chaos. When the mother and son mated, Darkness gave birth to four beings she named Nyx (Night), Day, Erebus (Underworld Darkness), and Air. Air and Day were the parents of Gaia and her brother, Pontus (Sea). Gaia's many first cousins were all children of her Aunt Nyx and her Uncle Erebus. Compared with Mother Earth, the children of Nyx (3) were small, and often winged. They had names like Old Age, the three Fates, Misery, Murder, Nemesis, Joy, Friendship, Pity, Hunger, Death,

---

* Throughout this and the following chapters, the single-digit numbers in parentheses refer to the correspondingly numbered character's or plant's name in the "Botany" portion of each section.

and Sleep. The last two children were twin boys. The Greeks called Sleep Hypnos, and the Romans called him Somnos (4).

Night's children took refuge on and inside their cousin, Mother Earth. The Roman poet Ovid wrote about the barren, frozen land of Hunger but preferred to describe the underground house of Somnos. The poet insisted that Sleep's cave could be found in a distant, misty land. It was easy to recognize, as the cave's mouth was fringed with poppies. Sleep usually drowsed as he held court. He was surrounded by a thousand dreams, as they were both his servants and his sons. Each dream took a different form when visiting a sleeping mortal. Icelos appeared to sleepers as various animals. Phantasos took the form of inanimate objects. Morpheus (5), as his name suggests, was the most cunning of shape-shifters. When we dream longingly of dead friends or family members it is only Morpheus tricking us with his many morphs.

Botany

(1) Ge. Plants that root in Mother Earth's soil are called geophytes. This growth habit is distinct from plants that colonize stones (lithophytes) or dwell in water (hydrophytes). If a plant bears such a short stem that its flowers bloom flush with the ground, or partially underground, it is said to be geoflorous. Because most plants grow in some sort of soil medium and many conceal their flower buds just under the soil's crust, their unexpected blooming appears to be a sudden and spontaneous caprice of the earth goddess. Botanists incorporated Ge into the prefix of up to twenty plant genera, but more than half were reduced to synonyms in the twentieth century. We continue to recognize *Geoblasta* (Ge's bud), *Geocarpon* (Ge's fruit), *Geocaryum* (Ge's nut), *Geocaulon* (Ge's stem), *Geocharis* (Ge's charms), *Geococcus* (Ge's mustard cress), *Geodorum* (Ge's gift), *Geogenanthus* (flower of Ge's people), *Geopanax* (Ge's cure-all), *Geophila* (Ge loving), *Geosiris* (Ge's iris) and *Geostachys* (Ge's spike).

Glue is the unexpected gift offered by the sixteen species of shepherd's crook orchids (Orchidaceae) in the genus *Geodorum*, distributed from India east to the Philippines and as far south as Australia. The flowering shoot pokes up out of the humus but then curves around, forming a hook or crook with dangling small, pinkish-white flowers. Shepherd's crook orchids usually conceal their squat storage stems (pseudobulbs) under the earth. These little barrel-shaped structures are natural glue pots that are gathered to make body paints that stick to the skin. The natural glue is also used as an adhesive in the construction of traditional musical instruments.

Botanists also invoke Ge when they describe the development of seedlings. Epigean (above Ge) germination occurs when seeds sprout underground and their young stems elongate carrying the thin, flat, embryonic leaves (cotyledons) up above the soil surface. Exposed to sun and air, the cotyledons usually expand and supply infant seedlings with their first photosynthetic foods, turning water and carbon dioxide into sugar. Note how the heart-shaped cotyledons are pushed upward by their baby stalk in edible mung bean and alfalfa sprouts.

When cotyledons remain underground and unexpanded, this is known as hypogean (below Ge) germination. The seed sprouts as usual, but the infant stems elongate without taking the thick, heavy cotyledons along for the ride up into the air. These big or lumpy cotyledons are already provisioned with stored sugars, and they are ready to nourish the seedling until it develops its first foliage leaves. Note the massive and paired cotyledons of an avocado seed, for example. The single cotyledon in each corn kernel and wheat seed also remains under the soil's surface within the remains of the seed's shell. Corn and wheat cotyledons act as stomachs, helping the young sprout digest stored food tissue (endosperm) and convert it into energy for growth and stem construction.

(2) GAIA. Although the name of the earth goddess enjoyed a revival during the back-to-nature movements of the 1960s, the scholarly Linnaeus employed her name far earlier, giving us the genus *Epigaea* (on top of Mother Earth). The genus consists of three species of miniature shrubs confined to temperate regions in Japan, eastern North America, and the Caucasus regions. The little bushes belong to the rhododendron family (Ericaceae) and rarely grow higher than four to eight inches. The creeping, branching stems appear to hug "Gaia's breast" as they grow through the humus of shady woodlands and forests.

Americans call *E. repens* the trailing arbutus. The tubular pink-white flowers produce a rich, spicy fragrance, and this led to the downfall of these shrublets through much of New England. Natural populations suffered decimation in the late nineteenth century, as there was an urban market for cute gift baskets filled with moss and uprooted, scented wildflowers fresh from the spring countryside. Cloying sentimentalism, rural industries, and delicate species are a disastrous combination. Now protected in many states, trailing arbutus will make a comeback if surviving plants are exposed to woodland ants. Their fruit is a dry capsule, but the seeds are connected to the inner fruit wall by stalks of sweet, pulpy placenta. Ants collect the seeds, eat the placenta, and then dispose of the seeds in their underground "garbage pits." The insects effectively plant the next generation of wildflowers.

(3) NYX. Like Gaia, the black-winged goddess of night has her share of devoted botanists who use her name as a prefix in eight genera. Members of the genera *Nyctaginia* (flowers open at night), *Nyctanthes* (Nyx's flowers), *Nyctialanthus* (Nyx's beautiful flower), *Nyctocalos* (beautiful at night), and *Nyctocereus* (Night's candle) share one thing in common. Either they delay flowering until later in the afternoon, remaining in bloom long after sunset, or they open their buds in the black of night.

For example, *Nyctaginia* consists only of *N. capitata*, native to Texas and northern Mexico. We call it scarlet musk flower, or devil's bouquet, as the flowers are satanically red. However, this tiny genus gives its name to the four-o'clock family (Nyctaginaceae), the source of many garden favorites, including *Bougainvillea*, sand verbena (*Abronia*), and the four-o'clocks (*Mirabilis*) still popular in summer gardens. Both four-o'clocks and scarlet musks typically open their flower buds late in the afternoon and keep them open through the night to wait for visiting moths.

In contrast, *Nyctanthes arbortristis* is the coral jasmine or tree of sorrow found from India east through the Indonesian island of Java. It belongs in the olive tree family (Oleaceae). Fresh, fragrant flowers open each evening and wilt and fall by morning. Their flowers are picked to yield a yellow-orange dye for silk. The blossoms of this large shrub figure in Hindu myths. In one version they represent the reincarnated soul of a princess loved and abandoned by the sun god. She continues to grieve in her woody form (*arbor* = tree, *tristis* = sad). By disposing of her flowers before the sun reappears she refuses to forgive him.

(4) SOMNOS. Clay tablets from the Sumerian civilization indicate that the opium poppy (*Papaver somniferum*) has been a pain reliever, sleep inducer, and "banisher of care" for more than 4,500 years. We can see why Linnaeus insisted on incorporating the Roman god of sleep into the species name of this commercially important herb. Just as night's children found refuge with Gaia, the great goddess whose body symbolizes the entire Mediterranean basin was undoubtedly the first protector of the opium poppy. The wild species probably came from Turkey or the Middle East, but its use spread quickly through Arab, Greek, Egyptian, and Roman civilizations. The Ebers Papyrus, a 3,600-year-old Egyptian compendium of medical recipes and magic spells, recommended a potion of poppy juice mixed with fly spots scraped off a wall to stop children from crying too much.

Every wealthy Roman reading Ovid would have smiled knowingly at verse referring to poppies fringing the cave of Somnos. By the second century C.E., Claudius Galen, surgeon to Rome's gladiatorial school, recommended opium for a number of ailments, including dizziness, colic, fevers, migraines, leprosy, melancholy, and most female complaints. Collecting opium has not changed much over the centuries. The green fruit begins to expand as soon as the short-lived petals drop to the ground. Workers slash the fruit's skin three to ten times during a period of several days to make it bleed a sticky, white, bitter "milk" (latex). Scrape off the dried milk, and you have harvested raw opium.

(5) MORPHEUS. Biochemical analyses of opium, starting in the early 1800s, identified more than twenty-six nitrogen-rich compounds known as alkaloids. Morphine, codeine, and papaverine are the most common, with the greatest commercial and

medical potential. Morphine remains the most addictive of these natural opiates. Until the second half of the twentieth century, it was one of the few dependable drugs one could give to patients recovering from surgery or war wounds. In the 1930s and 1940s, morphine was mixed with the nightshade molecule, scopolamine. This drug was given to women in labor so they could enjoy a "twilight sleep" during childbirth. Just as Morpheus is a favored son of Somnos, morphine is the preferred compound in *P. somniferum*. The derivation of heroin will be discussed in §6.1.

3.2 THE BIRTH OF THE TITANS

Gaia fell asleep and gave birth to a son without benefit of a male partner. She called the boy Uranus (1). He became the vaulted sky and the husband of Mother Earth. When Uranus fertilized his mate with rain, the land became clothed in mountains and forests. Uranus fathered seven beautiful goddesses and seven giant, handsome gods on Gaia. These divine children were known as the Titans (2). Uranus was pleased with his children and allowed them to remain on Mother Earth. Titan brothers married Titan sisters, making Mother Earth and Father Sky grandparents and great-grandparents.

Gaia had six more giant boys, but all were grotesque. Each of the three Cyclops (3) had only one large, wheel-shaped eye set in the middle of their heads. The remaining three sons were called the Hecatoncheires. Each of these giants had fifty heads and a hundred arms. Uranus could not stand to look at his ugly offspring and imprisoned them in Tartarus, a cold and dark underworld beneath Gaia.

Botany

(1) URANUS. Although Uranus is the sky father and Gaia's primary consort, his name is not widely applied in botanical nomenclature. In fact, the genus *Uranthoecium* (roof of Uranus) consists of only a single species, *U. truncatum* in the grass family (Poaceae). The genus name refers only to the small, single-seeded fruit (caryopsis), which is supposed to bear a vaulted roof like the sky. Known as flat-stem grass, it is found only in northern Australia, surviving in seasonally dry but tropical regions on dense soils. It sends up fresh growth after seasonal rains.

(2) TITANS. Poets throughout the centuries have imagined the male Titans as immense but handsome beings. When most botanists name a new species *titan*, they want the reader to know that they have found a mighty specimen, far larger than its closest relatives. *Amorphophallus titanium* is a member of the philodendron family

(Araceae) native to the Indonesian island of Sumatra. However, the full, scientific name means "titanic and irregularly shaped penis."

The name may sound unflattering to Gaia's handsome sons, but most botanical gardens prize this plant as a crowd-drawing curiosity. This species produces the largest unbranched flowering stalk (spadix) on earth. It may reach a height of greater than nine feet and weigh more than twenty pounds in full bloom. However, this massive reproductive organ rarely lives a full week. When receptive to sweat bees or dung beetles, the stalk emits an odor of carrion and overripe fruits and vegetables, explaining why some people call it the corpse flower. The plant makes only one giant parasol leaf each year, and the leaf withers when the plant has stored enough starch to flower. The flowering stem is so massive that it takes the bud at least four months to develop underground before it breaks through the soil's crust. Considerable horticultural skill is required to bring this species into bloom every two or three years. Some grow it in immense pots for decades and never see a spike. When one American garden brought its *A. titanium* into flower, it was considered larger and longer than other specimens blooming in a rival garden that year. The gift shop promptly sold a T-shirt featuring its garden's flowering stalk with the inscription, "Mine's bigger than yours."

There is one interesting exception to the rule that *titan* always means "big" in botany. *Titanopsis* (like a titan) is a genus of six species in the carpetweed or pig face family (Aizoaceae). Marketed as jewel plants or living stones, *Titanopsis* spp. live in deserts in southern Africa. The mature plants are rarely more than a few inches in height, as their grayish-green, thick, sculptured leaves mimic small, shiny pebbles. Naming this genus of petite succulent plants after the robust sons of Uranus reflects an obscure but old tradition upheld by the greatest English poets. The sun was characterized as a mighty, chariot-driving Titan named Hyperion (see §3.3). His equally titanic son, Helios, inherited the same shining chariot. Even Shakespeare referred to the sun as Titan in his long poem *Venus and Adonis*. When living stones bloom, they make disproportionately large, flat, yellow flowers, radiating many petals that remind some viewers of the sun's rays.

(3) CYCLOPS. The genus *Cyclopia* (like a Cyclops) consists of twenty shrubby species in the bean family (Fabaceae) distributed through southern Africa. Each pea or bean flower wears a broad, bonnet-shaped petal known as the standard. A dark, wheel-shaped blotch decorates the base of the yellowish standard petal on a *Cyclopia* flower. Here is the single eye of the Cyclops. Contrasting color patterns (nectar guides) on petals direct bees to the location of nectar in a blossom, so this odd blotch is probably adaptive.

South Africans of British descent call *Cyclopia* species "honey bushes." They pick, chop, and ferment heaps of leaves to make a sweet tea.

3.3 THE REIGN OF CRONUS

Gaia wanted her multilimbed giants and single-eyed Cyclopes freed from the underworld, so she encouraged her Titan sons to revolt. Cronus, the boldest and youngest, waited until his father fell asleep and then castrated Uranus with a flint sickle. Uranus's blood fell from heaven onto a grove of ash trees (*Fraxinus*) (1). The blood-spattered ash leaves grew into a new race of peaceful goddesses called the Meliae (2).

Unfortunately, the drops of blood that fell onto the ground spawned three terrible goddesses of divine vengeance. The Greeks were terrified of this winged trio. The brutal, winged Furies (Erinyes) were always looking for mortal sinners, especially those who harmed their parents. When these goddesses found their victim, they would beat him with clubs made of ash wood. Uranus cursed his son as he died: "Some day, one of your wife's children will overthrow you!"

Cronus now ruled all creation. He assigned the Titan men and women to the cyclical upkeep of nature and all natural bodies. His siblings did their work so well that it was regarded as a Golden Age. Hyperion and his wife Thia guided the sun while Coeus and his sister spouse, Phoebe (3), controlled the waning and waxing of the moon. Cronus held the respect of all but his own mother. Gaia hated her son because this king of the Titans forgot his sacred promise, and he never released his ugly brothers from Tartarus.

Botany

(1) ASH TREES. Historian and botanist Hellmut Baumann insists that Greek myths about ash trees refer, specifically, to the manna ash (*Fraxinus ornus*). The wood of the tree was revered because it made such fine, durable javelins and lances. The ancient use of ash wood in weaponry probably explains why it appears in such an early creation myth. After all, classical Greece was subdivided into warring city states. The Furies carry ash wood cudgels, and Nemesis (another goddess of divine vengeance) carries a rod of ash to show that her decisions are inflexible. King Peleus (the father of Achilles, see §7.3) was given a limb of ash, to make his own lance, when he married the nereid (§3.4) Thetis.

There are approximately sixty-five *Fraxinus* species native to the northern hemisphere. Historically, American white ash (*F. americana*) was the favored source of wood for tool handles, church pews, and baseball bats. European and American ashes are still cut to make hockey sticks, so their use as the wood of war is far from exhausted.

(2) MELIAE. Linnaeus named the genus of ash trees *Fraxinus* instead of *Melia* because he had to follow his own rules. *Fraxinus* is the oldest written name for the European ash in Latin. Even the Roman poet Virgil uses the same word to refer to the tree in one of his poems. Fortunately, Linnaeus did not let a good myth about goddesses arising from blood-soaked foliage to go to waste. His genus *Melia* refers to three species of Old World trees found from subtropical Asia to northern Australia. They are not close relatives of true ashes, but the branches of both *Melia* and *Fraxinus* bear pinnate (like a bird's feather), compound leaves. When Linnaeus named the genus *Melia*, he was saying, in essence, "Look, this genus of Asian trees has foliage just like a European ash." *Melia* gives its name to the family (Meliaceae) and is related to true mahogany (*Swietenia*) and *Toona* (Australian red cedar). The family name makes a fine memorial for goddesses generated by trees wearing the blood of the sky.

The wood of two *Melia* species is valuable, so they are often called white cedars or Ceylon mahoganies. *Melia azedarach* is so loved for its shade and blue-purple flowers that it is called the Indian lilac or pride of India. This species is grown as a street tree where winters are warm and mild. Is it my imagination, or does this inedible plum-size fruit release a pungent odor reminiscent of dog's urine?

(3) PHOEBE. *Phoebe* is a genus of seventy species of canopy trees native to South America and tropical Asia (especially the islands of Indonesia and Malaysia). They belong to the bay laurel family (Lauraceae) and are also related to the commercial avocado (*Persea americana*). Although *Phoebe* species usually grow taller than commercial avocado trees, they produce smaller, full moon–shaped fruits. The shape of the fruit alludes to the nocturnal sister of the big Titan boys.

3.4 THE ORIGIN OF NYMPHS

Mother Earth and her Titan daughter Tethys were so fertile that they produced a new race of female divinities known as nymphs (1). These little goddesses always appeared youthful and beautiful, occupying and protecting different realms on land or water. Gaia is mother of all the oreads (mountain nymphs) (2) and dryads (oak nymphs) (3). Each dryad lived in her own oak and died when the tree fell. Mother Earth also gave birth to the napaeae (4) and the limoniades. The napaeae inhabited dells and glens, while the limoniades guarded the flowery meadows. Tethys was the mother of three thousand sea nymphs known as oceanids. She was also the mother and grandmother of the naiads (5), a race of freshwater nymphs. Naiads protected springs, fountains, and ponds, and they herded the cattle of the river gods. Doris, a daughter of Tethys, married a sea god named Nereus. Together they had fifty more marine nymphs called nereids (6).

The ancient Greeks praised the beauty of the nymphs but feared meeting them. These minor divinities were easily displeased, often calling on more powerful gods to punish offending mortals. In contrast, wealthy aristocratic Romans erected shrines in their gardens to entice naiads to take up residence. As fountains and pools were status symbols during the hot Roman summers, freshwater nymphs had to be propitiated.

Botany

(1) NYMPHS. Although nymphs occupied every habitat in classical mythology, it is clear that Linnaeus was thinking only of naiads when he named the water lily genus *Nymphaea.* At least thirty-five *Nymphaea* species are found around the world, usually in slow-moving rivers or still ponds. Around the Mediterranean, the ancient Egyptians much admired water lilies. Tomb paintings and long, dried wreaths found in those tombs indicate that water lilies were used in funerary rites and for personal adornment by 2000 B.C.E. Two blue-flowered species (*N. caerulea* and *N. lotus*) were particularly favored in the headdresses of women at court. Egyptian doctors may have combined water lilies with more poisonous toad skin to make an early painkiller and anesthetic. In Egyptian art, water lilies are often confused with the Indian sacred lotus (*Nelumbo nucifera*), but Egyptians did not import and grow this Asian plant until after 500 B.C.E.

Fossil seeds, flowers, and leaves of extinct members of the water lily family (Nymphaeaceae) have been found in North America, Europe, and China. The oldest remains are probably more than ninety million years old (from the Cretaceous period), unintentionally justifying their status as daughters or granddaughters of old Mother Earth. Molecular studies using the DNA of live water lilies continually show that they are descendants of some of the most primitive flowering plants on this planet. The water lily family contains about sixty species, in six genera, including two giant and magnificent species in the genus *Victoria*. Knowing John Lindley's taste for the names of goddesses, you might assume that he named these huge South American plants after the Roman goddess Victoria (Greek, Nike; a daughter of the nymph of the river, Styx). In fact, the loyal Englishman honored Queen Victoria, in 1837, when it was still appropriate to name such a giant, flabby water plant after a young monarch who had not yet discovered the pleasures of royal banquets.

Taxonomists following Linnaeus also invoked the nymphs. The genus, *Nymphoides* (nymphlike) belongs to the bogbean family (Menyanthaceae). There are about twenty species distributed through the waterways of the world. The name *Nymphoides* acknowledges that floating leaves attached to the flowering stalk resemble miniature lily pads. However, *Nymphoides* and *Nymphaea* are distant relations, at best. Nurseries specializing in plants for garden ponds may sell *Nymphoides* as water fringes, owing to the frilly sculptures on the flower's petal tips blooming above the water's surface. Some species of *Nymphoides* offer edible tubers.

We should also take a brief look at *Petronymphe decora*, a solitary species from Mexico in the onion family (Alliaceae). *Petronymphe* means rock nymph. Unlike water-dependent *Nymphaea*, *P. decora* grows in harsh, rocky soil. Regarded as a rare and choice bulb by collectors, the plant dangles greenish-yellow blossoms from the tips of its umbrellalike flowering stalk.

(2) OREADS. When I first heard the name *Orestias*, I assumed it was derived from Prince Orestes, the avenging son of King Agamemnon (see §7.2). In fact, *Orestias* is an atypical spelling for the oreades (mountain nymphs). This rare genus of orchids (Orchidaceae) was not discovered until the second half of the nineteenth century. An expedition of botanists from Portugal visited the mountains on the western African island of St. Thomas. The new orchids were found clinging to tree branches in forests growing at elevations of more than 3,500 feet above sea level.

There are only three species in the genus *Orestias*. Their flowers are tiny, but when they are dissected, they show physical similarities with the more common Old World genus *Oberonia* (see §2.6). The taxonomist describing the new genus made an obvious attempt to compare classical nymphs with Shakespearean elves. Remember, much of the plot of *A Midsummer Night's Dream* takes place in a dark forest outside the city of Athens. Naming an orchid genus after the oreades is entirely appropriate for one simple reason. Orchids flourish in tropical mountain ranges. They rarely thrive under the dark, thick, sweaty canopies of lowland rain forests. Without appropriate drainage, air movement, and cool night temperatures, most tropical orchids lose their ability to flower and usually die of root rot. Many species of tropical orchids require a long cycle of low night temperatures before their stems will manufacture new flower buds. No one really knows exactly why these plants require shifting air currents to stay healthy. In either case, though, tropical mountains are ideal for cooler temperatures and breezes.

Most tropical orchid species spend their lives attached to bare rocks or tied to the branches of trees. Their fibrous, adhesive, and spongy roots are always exposed to the air and appear to benefit from daily mist baths provided by low, drifting cloudbanks. When you walk up a trail on a tropical mountain or a dead volcano orchids do not show much diversity until you hit the middle elevations of "good air exchange." At these altitudes, plants enjoy daily temperatures around 64 to 73 degrees Fahrenheit. So much for the Hollywood stereotype of orchids thriving in "steam bath" climates.

(3) DRYADS. The name of the race of goddesses who protected trees and lived in old oaks provided taxonomists with fodder for new plant genera. Six genera

survive that incorporate the word *dryad*: *Dryadanthe* (flowering dryad), *Dryadella* (little dryad), *Dryadodaphne* (dryad's laurel), *Dryadorchis* (dryad's orchid), *Dryas* (dryad), and *Drymaria* (forest and sea nymph). Ironically, none of them belong to the oak family (Fagaceae).

For example, *Dryadella* consists of more than forty species of miniature orchids (Orchidaceae) found in forests from southern Mexico to northern Argentina. They spend their lives perching on the limbs of trees producing small, mottled flowers. Naming yet another orchid genus after a tree nymph is only fair. It is estimated that 85 percent of all orchid species are epiphytes and must spend their lives clinging to limbs. Like the dryads of old, most arboreal orchids perish after storms or animals break their tree host's branches and they fall to the ground. Most epiphytic orchids rot and vanish if they end up on the forest floor.

The same story cannot be applied to the two species in the genus *Dryas*. They belong to the rose family (Rosaceae), and alpine and rock gardeners may know them as mountain avens or alpine dryads. They are found in the colder portions of the northern hemisphere in Arctic tundra and/or alpine zones in Europe, Asia, and North America. Mountain avens do not grow as trees or epiphytes. They are creeping shrubs, often forming thick mats. Why did Linnaeus name them after dryads? He said that the lobed leaves of *D. octopetala* reminded him of the lobed leaves of an oak.

(4) NAPAEAE. Two rather small genera honor the nymphs of glades and dells. *Napaea dioica* is a solitary species found from Pennsylvania south to Virginia, then west to Wisconsin and Iowa. Wildflower books call it the glade mallow and place it in the hibiscus family (Malvaceae). It is often recommended for shady gardens, as it prefers moist, cool, wooded dells and grows in stony soils left by past glaciers. In Greco-Roman mythology, all nymphs are females, but our glade mallow conceals a distinctly masculine side. The word, *dioica*, means dioecious (male and female flowers on separate plants). If you look into the white flowers on the same glade mallow plant, they are all either pollen makers (males) or seed makers (females).

In contrast, *Napeanthus* (flower of the dell nymphs) consists of more than fifteen species distributed from Central to South America. This genus belongs to the gloxinia family (Gesneriaceae). The plants are diminutive, and horticulturists who collect "dwarf gesneriads" recommend you grow them in a terrarium, or at least use a goldfish bowl with a lid, to keep their atmosphere moist. Shade tolerant, some species are found in tropical dells and glens. Once again, naming dinky plants after a race of nymphs makes sense if you believe the Napaeae, and their sisters, were cousins of those puny fairies.

(5) NAIADS. Linnaeus named the genus *Naias*, but the spelling was later changed to *Najas*. No one seems to know why, and the word is still pronounced NAY-as.

There are at least thirty-five species of these aquatic herbs found worldwide in bodies of fresh water. Known as naiads, water nymphs, or river nymphs, the plants spend their entire life cycle underwater. Even their tiny, unisexual flowers bloom below the surface. Their pollen grains are shed directly into the water to be carried by the currents.

Some species are sold as plants for goldfish ponds and are considered ideal "nurseries" for the fry of tropical fish. Prospective aquarists should take care, as discarded naiads can invade and clog waterways. Modern studies comparing flower development, pollen anatomy, and DNA strongly suggest that *Najas* may be the only genus in the family Najadaceae.

(6) NEREIDS. *Nerine* (nereid, or a nereid named Nerine) consists of about thirty species in the daffodil family (Amaryllidaceae). *Nerine sarniensis* is the famous Guernsey lily. However, all *Nerine* species are native to southern Africa, and not the Channel Islands between England and France where Guernsey (called Sarnia by Roman navigators) lies. What were taxonomists thinking? The story goes that a Dutch ship carrying choice bulbs ran aground on the island of Guernsey (Sarnia) in 1659. The sailors used the bulbs of *N. sarniensis* to barter with the locals, insisting the plants came from Japan, not the Cape of Good Hope! In another version of the story the holds of the ship burst and the bulbs washed up on the beaches taking root. In either case, the Reverend William Herbert (1778–1847) was aware of the stories explaining the arrival of these plants on the Channel Islands. He decided to treat them as gifts of a capricious sea goddesses, establishing the genus *Nerine* in 1820.

3.5 CHASTE OR CONSTANT NYMPHS

Powerful gods often took nymphs as lovers, giving the little goddesses unsavory reputations for promiscuity. But although Echo and Cyrene were interested in more than one male, the majority of nymphs were not nymphomaniacs. Some valued their chastity. Syrinx changed herself into a clump of giant reeds (*Arundo donax*) to avoid rape by Pan, the rural deity who guards flocks and herds. The goatish god was most disappointed when he lost the nymph, yet he was wise enough to cut the hollow stalks and fashioned them into the first musical panpipes.

Lotus (1) also became a beautiful plant, in this case to escape the fertility god Priapus. Queen Dryope saw the purple-flowered plant while walking in the woods and picked some of the pretty blossoms to please her infant boy. The queen was horrified when she saw the broken stems gushing blood instead of sap. The gods became vindictive when they saw how Lotus was violated. In revenge, they turned Dryope into an oak tree, and her

3. Plant genera named for the nymphs and the would-be lover of a nymph. Top left, leaves and flowers of a floating heart (*Nymphoides cordatum*) from *An Illustrated Flora of the Northeastern United States, Canada and the British Possessions* (1913). Top middle, an underwater stem of a naiad (*Najas major*) from Baillon's *Histoire Naturelle des Plantes* (1886–1903). Top right, a segment of a flowering branch of monkey grass (*Liriope graminifolia*), also from Baillon. Below is the odd couple of Smilax and Crocus. Bottom left, a flowering, prickly vine of sarsaparilla (*Smilax officinalis*). The name *officinalis* means it is the official species used in medicine. Bottom right, the saffron crocus (*Crocus sativus*). To the right of the plant is an enlarged pistil neck with its three arms (the source of commercial saffron). Both illustrations are taken from Baillon. All illustrations reproduced with the permission of the library of the Missouri Botanical Garden.

son grew up playing in her shade. Similarly, when the river god, Alpheus, pursued Arethusa (2), the nymph turned herself into a stream and trickled underground. Alpheus followed her and tried to mingle his waters with her, but Arethusa's stream flowed too fast for him. She reemerged on the island of Sicily and created a permanent spring.

The nymph Smilax (3), could never decide whether or not to accept the mortal boy, Crocus (4), as her lover. Her indecision irritated the gods, as well, so they turned the ill-sorted pair into plants with such different habits that they never shared each other's company again. Most say that Smilax became a woodland vine, but others insist she is the slow-growing, gloomy yew tree (*Taxus*).

Let us not forget nymphs constant in marriage. Numa Pompilius, one of the early kings of Rome, wed the nymph Egeria (5). When he died, as all mortals must, she would not be comforted and wept until she dissolved into a pool of water. The Romans also told the tale of Pomona (6), the apple tree dryad. She was courted by many rural deities but rejected all suitors. Vertumnus, a garden god, visited her in disguise and warned her of the cruel fate in store for cold-hearted maidens. She married him, joining orchards and vegetable gardens in mutual horticulture.

Botany

(1) Lotus. This unfortunate goddess protected her virginity only to fall prey to cows and sheep. Although the genus *Lotus* sounds like the name of the Asian water lotus (*Nelumbo*), Linnaeus gave the nymph's name to the genus of trefoils in the bean family (Fabaceae). Most are wildflowers of the northern hemisphere, but bird's foot trefoil (*Lotus corniculatus*) is now grown in temperate climates all over the world. It makes an excellent, nutritious hay or fodder for farm animals. In Sudan, this nymph takes revenge by storing up cyanide compounds in her leaves, poisoning beasts of burden.

(2) Arethusa. *Arethusa bulbosa* is a favorite orchid (Orchidaceae) of naturalists found through northeastern Canada and the United States. It prefers the protection of wet habitats, as did its chaste namesake. The largest populations of *A. bulbosa* grow in cool bogs on floating mats of sphagnum moss. Wildflower books often call it dragon's mouth, because the pink-purple flowers appear to have a "gaping maw and spiky ears" when viewed in profile.

(3) Smilax. Most Americans despise their native *Smilax* species, as the vines invade shady gardens and roadsides, covering trees and fences with their coiling stems armed with vicious hooks and prickles. I was brought up to call them catbriers because they scratch. However, some plants have pleasantly aromatic foliage, and

the dried underground stems of some South American species provide us with the commercial source of sarsaparilla for tonics and soft drinks. In fact, there are more than two hundred *Smilax* species distributed throughout the world in both temperate and tropical regions. The majority are long-lived vines that prefer the shade cast by forest canopies. Consequently, these plants rarely encounter the wild crocuses of sunny, exposed sites. Smilax now gives her name to the catbrier family, Smilacaceae.

However, until the end of the twentieth century, most taxonomists still treated *Smilax* and the genus *Smilacina* (little Smilax), as close relatives in the lily family (Liliaceae). Both genera prefer forests. Both have underground stems (rhizomes) and produce little white-greenish flowers. As noted above, though, *Smilax* now gets its own family, and gene studies put *Smilacina* in the lily-of-the-valley family (Convallariaceae). Superficial similarities are always deceiving, and the hardest part of plant classification is determining which characteristics are so dependable that they always point to close relationships and common origins. In this case, the genetic evidence suggests that an older generation of botanists should have placed greater emphases on major differences in leaf structure and the internal stem anatomy between *Smilax* and *Smilacina*. Hindsight is always twenty-twenty, but *Smilax* and *Smilacina* are proof that flower and fruit characteristics do not always offer a "royal road" to uncovering a plant's genealogy.

Smilacina, in turn, is a genus of thirty woodland herbs distributed from the Himalayas east through the temperate forests of North America. Wildflower books often call them false Solomon's seal, as they are easily confused with the true Solomon's seal (*Polygonatum*), yet another spring-flowering herb of temperate forests bearing small white flowers.

(4) CROCUS. *Crocus* is a genus of more than eighty bulbous species distributed throughout the Mediterranean basin, with a few reaching western China. The genus belongs to the iris family (Iridaceae). Descriptions of wild populations place them on open, often dry, rocky slopes and plains, quite unsuitable for *Smilax* vines. Most of us plant crocuses that flower in late winter or early spring. However, when this myth was first told, it was probably meant to explain the origin of the commercially important, autumn-flowering, saffron crocus, *Crocus sativus*. If you grow saffron crocus in the northern hemisphere, you know that its mauve flowers may not appear until dull, cold November.

Saffron was first domesticated somewhere within the Mediterranean basin, and it was a major export of the ancient Cretan Empire. In general, stories of supernatural origins of the most important domesticated plants occur in the nature religions of many cultures. They often involve a man or demigod changed into the preferred food, spice, or drug plant. He must die, and be reborn, for the good of all people.

The aromatic spice and yellow dye derive exclusively from the dried red arms of the tip of the female organ (pistil). Saffron crocus does not occur in the wild. Detective work, using the microscope, suggests that the saffron crocus was produced by a freak chromosome error in a clump of *C. cartwrightianus*, a common species still found wild in Greece and some Aegean islands.

Virtually all crocuses are cool- to cold-weather flowers, popping up when days are short. For example, winter-flowering *C. hyemalis* blooms in November and December in northern Israel and is so common that people call it Chanukah lights. The blossom has a golden yellow throat reminding viewers of candle flames on the menorahs displayed at the same time of year.

(5) EGERIA. We recognize only two South American species in the genus *Egeria*. Both are aquatic plants surviving well (perhaps, too well) in almost any freshwater pool. No nymph's tears are required to grow these plants. *Egeria* species belong to the pondweed family (Hydrocharitaceae), but some authorities feel that tropical American *Egeria* is best treated as a synonym of the Canadian pondweeds (*Elodea*).

Brazilian pondweed (*E. densa*) is the most popular species grown in bowls and ornamental pools for pet goldfish and tadpoles since the late nineteenth century. The curly leaves were believed to add lots of oxygen to still water. Unfortunately, it escaped from aquaculture and now clogs once clear lakes, irrigation ditches, and dams in much of the United States and New Zealand. The lawmaking and practical-minded Egeria would continue to cry if she knew her name was now associated with a noxious pest.

(6) POMONA. Pomology is the scientific study of all fruit, a fittingly academic tribute to the nymph Romans believed protected their apple orchards. The name *Pomona* and the botanical term *pome* have common origins in Latin. A pome is a fleshy fruit in which the core consists of five hard-papery, seed-filled chambers. These are the five original ovaries produced by the flower. The skin and edible flesh of the fruit are both derived from a short sleeve of tissue made by fusing together the bases of the other floral organs (sepals, petals, and stamens). Following fertilization, the inedible ovaries that make up the fruit's core are surrounded and engulfed by the fleshy sleeve. This produces a typical apple (*Malus*), pear (*Pyrus*), or quince (*Cydonia*). If you do not believe me, flip an apple upside down and look at the dimple with a hand lens. Those reduced, triangular flaps outside the entrance to the core are just withered sepals.

3.6 NYMPHS AND THEIR CHILDREN

Miracles may happen if a child has a nymph for a mother. King Icarius rejected his newborn daughter by the naiad Periboea (1). He had the baby tossed into the sea, but the infant was rescued and nurtured by a flock of ducks (probably Eurasian widgeons, *Anas penelope*). Icarius decided that this phenomenon was divine proof he must reclaim his discarded child.

Feronia (2), another woodland nymph of orchards, and patroness of Roman freedmen, was most devoted to her son, Erulus, an early king of Italy. At his birth, she gave him three lives and six arms to defend himself. King Erulus was invulnerable to all, except the child of another nymph. Evander, son of Carmenta (a fountain naiad), defeated Erulus by killing the king three times on the same day.

Acis was the handsome son of the river nymph, Simethis (3). The poet Ovid insisted that Acis became the lover of the sea nymph Galatea when he was only sixteen years old. The nymph tried to hide and protect him, but Polyphemus, the jealous Cyclops, crushed Acis to death with a rock. His blood turned into rushing water, and Acis was reborn as a river god.

Of course, the most famous child of a nymph was the son of Liriope (4), a blue-haired naiad. From an early age, Liriope's boy attracted suitors of both sexes. The perplexed nymph took him to the famous seer, Teiresias. "Your son, Narcissus (5), will live to a ripe old age provided he never knows himself," said the prophet. Narcissus grew up to be a beautiful youth of awesome vanity who rejected the love of numerous nymphs and mortals. One man committed suicide after Narcissus ignored him. Before he died, this lovesick victim cursed Narcissus, condemning him to experience the same passion for an unobtainable object: "So may he love—and never win his love!" One day, Narcissus discovered a clear, silvery pool and promptly fell in love with his own perfect reflection. Unable to possess the beautiful boy in the water, he pined away. All that remained of him was the flower that bears his name.

Botany

(1) PERIBOEA. We are not certain which Periboea the German botanist Karl Sigismund Kunth (1788–1850) had in mind when he named the genus. At least four queens of Greece share the same name, and Homer nicknames the love goddess Periboea in at least one lyric within his *Iliad*. Kunth insisted he named the genus after a nymph, so it is quite likely that it is the supernatural wife of Icarius who gives the genus its name.

There are only two species in the genus *Periboea*, and both are found in southwestern Africa, near the Cape of Good Hope. These lilylike herbs are now classified within the hyacinth family (Hyacinthaceae), another flower with an important mythological connection (see §6.2). The derivation of the name remains obscure but appears to follows a long, continuous tradition of naming herbs with pretty flowers after nymphs or queens of Greece. *Periboea* may be found along the coast to Cape Town within plain sight of the ocean. Is she still waiting for sea ducks to return her child? Unfortunately, some taxonomists prefer to treat this genus as a synonym and submerge it within the much larger genus of Cape cowslips (*Lachenalia*), sold as tender bulbs.

(2) FERONIA. Some gardeners and horticulturists continue to refer to the solitary species of wood apple, or elephant apple, as *Feronia limonia*. This is an old and persistent error surviving on Web sites and standard books on Asian fruit trees. Its real scientific name is *Limonia acidissima*. Linnaeus gave it its official name, but *Feronia* is still preferred by many. Wood apples are members of the citrus fruit family (Rutaceae), and this tree is native to southeastern Asia. The fruit's rind is so hard it is often cracked open with a hammer to reach the soft pulp, an appropriate feature for an overly protective orchard nymph. Wood apple pulp is eaten raw or mixed with sugar and water to serve as a refreshing drink, but the flesh is also used as a soap substitute. The tree's wood is a source of useful timbers and a natural gum used in glues and watercolor paints.

The name *Feroniella* (little Feronia) still survives as a genus, named properly by Walter Tennyson Swingle (1871–1952). It consists of three species that also come from southeastern Asia, are also members of the Rutaceae, and share growth habits and flower characteristics in common with wood apple.

The tree *F. lucida* is grown from Cambodia south to Java and has many common names, including kabista batu, krassand, and ma sang. The fruit rind is used in traditional medicines, and the pulp is usually eaten raw. As Linnaeus was the first to place all internationally commercial oranges, lemons, tangerines, and grapefruit in the genus *Citrus*, only minor botanists (like Swingle) named minor fruit crops (like kabista) after minor nymphs (like Feronia).

(3) SIMETHIS. *Simethis* is a genus of one or three species of wildflowers native to western Europe. Classification of this tiny genus keeps changing, and recent DNA work insists it belongs to the daylily family (Hermerocallidaceae). *Simethis planifolia* is the white-flowered Kerry lily whose stamens bear fuzzy stalks. There is no explanation for the genus name, and it appears to be another of Kunth's attempts (see above) to give a pretty plant a pretty name. Greco-Roman goddesses are known for their white limbs and complexions.

(4) LIRIOPE. The poet Ovid often color-codes minor divinities in his epic, *Metamorphoses*. Water nymphs have blue hair, whereas minor marine gods have sea green scalps. Look at a stalk of monkey grass or lily-turf (*Liriope spicata*) before it is in full bloom, and you will see it is covered with blue buds, like a naiad's tresses. We know monkey grass as a common, often invasive, groundcover, forming tight tufts in shade or poor soils where real grasses refuse to thrive. For centuries, though, Chinese folk

medicine has recommended using the underground portions of these plants to treat asthma and flagging male virility. Chinese pharmacologists continue to identify and analyze glycoside molecules in the plants' extracts.

Placed within the lily-of-the-valley family (Convallariaceae), four *Liriope* species grow wild from China to Vietnam and Japan. The Portuguese Jesuit, João de Loureiro (1717–1791), was responsible for the genus name. He lived in Cochin, China, for more than thirty years, searching for medicinal plants. Although the name suggests he felt homesick for Mediterranean landscapes and Latin poetry, he was probably thinking of obvious similarities between monkey grass and daffodil flowers. Like most botanists of the eighteenth century, João de Loureiro would have seen a close alliance between *Liriope* and *Narcissus* based on flower structure. Both blossoms contain a solitary pistil surrounded by six stamens. By the nineteenth century, though, the two genera were placed in separate families. Late-twentieth-century studies on the molecules in plant genes confirm that monkey grass and daffodils (see below) require different classifications.

(5) NARCISSUS. Because the propagation and merchandising of daffodils, jonquils, paperwhites, and angel's tears is part of the centuries-old Dutch trade in bulbs, it is easy to forget that *Narcissus* is a genus native to the Mediterranean basin, not Holland. There are more than twenty-five wild species distributed from western Spain and Morocco east through Israel and other Middle Eastern countries. They are placed in the amaryllis family (Amaryllidaceae) and are no longer viewed as particularly close relations of *Liriope* by modern taxonomists (see above).

The word *narcissus* embellishes Greco-Roman poetry. In a hymn attributed to Homer, Hades abducts his niece, Persephone, after she picks a poet's narcissus (*N. poeticus*, see §5.2). Sophocles refers to a coronet of narcissus flowers worn by the great mother goddesses. Theocritus describes Princess Europa carrying the same blossoms just before Zeus, in the form of a white bull, carries her off. All Linnaeus had to do was formalize a common name. The words *narcissus* and *narcotic* appear to have a common Greek origin. The Furies, the three spirits of divine vengeance (see §3.3), twine narcissi in their snaky hair before flying off to confront and stupefy mortal criminals. Because most garden daffodils reflect the human preference for large flowers and vivid colors, many homeowners have never smelled the numbingly sweet odors of the little blossoms of *N. tazetta* or its intensely scented relatives.

Narcissus bulbs travel so well that they have escaped from cultivation all over the world. The flower buds of most *Narcissus* species develop inside bulbs stimulated by weeks of summer baking in harsh soils. That explains why one encounters forgotten clumps of "daffs" by abandoned houses from Texas to southern France to Australia. The Chinese sacred lily is really a narcissus hybrid, *N. ×incomparabilis,* forced into bloom in ceramic planters in time for the Chinese New Year festival. It is easy to hybridize wild narcissi with heirloom garden bulbs. In the 1890s, there were only thirty cultivated breeds of narcissus. By 1987, more than ten thousand varieties were registered. Japanese horticulturists are known for their breeding of promising new hybrids.

3.7 THE FIRST CENTAUR

Cronus married his sister, Rhea, but was unfaithful to her. The Titan king seduced his niece, the nymph Philyra (1). Rhea looked down from heaven and saw them making love. Exposed, Cronus turned himself into a stallion, ejaculated in haste, and then galloped away. He never looked at Philyra again. Fleeing the scene was a prudent measure, as Rhea was vindictive by nature. When her acolyte, a boy named Cyparrisus (2), accidentally killed her sacred stag, she turned the youth into a cypress tree.

Philyra gave birth to a boy that appeared human only from his head to his waist. The baby had four hoofed legs and the tail of a horse thanks to his father's cowardice. Mother of the first centaur (3), the horrified nymph abandoned her offspring and turned herself into the first linden tree (*Tilia*). Philyra's shame was premature, as her infant, Chiron (4), grew into one of the most respected beings on Mother Earth. He was famed as a prophet, educator, and herbalist. That explains why the root collectors of Greece (the rhizotomi) referred to several wildflowers with medicinal properties as "centaury herbs." Chiron probably knew the virtues of gentians (*Gentiana*) long before King Gentius (5) of Ilyria popularized their use in medicine.

Chiron married the nymph Chariclo and they had a daughter, Ocyrrhoe (6), but his lineage stops here. Ocyrrhoe inherited her father's powers of divination, but her visions were so awful that she resigned from soothsaying and turned herself into a mare.

Botany

(1) PHILYRA. Linnaeus was forced to name the linden tree *Tilia,* as this is the oldest name for the plant in Latin texts. However, he was not about to waste the perfectly good name of a Titan's child who became a tree. The genus *Phillyrea* refers to two to four tree species with bluish-green leaves sold as mock privets. Their fruit reminds people of an olive. That is not surprising, as the genus belongs to the Oleaceae family, which contains both the species of garden privets (*Ligustrum* species) and the edible olives (*Olea europea*) of commerce. Mock privets grow wild on many Mediterranean coasts and islands, so why not impose the name of a Mediterranean nymph?

(2) CYPARRISUS. The genus *Cupressus* contains thirteen to twenty-five species of magnificent trees distributed through the warmer, drier temperate zones of the

northern hemisphere (only one species grows up in the cold Himalayas). They produce cones instead of flowers. Since ancient times, the Italian cypress, *C. sempervirens*, has enjoyed immense popularity as either a garden or cemetery tree within the Mediterranean basin. Perhaps the tale of the boy who killed the tame stag promoted this early and widespread use of cypress in graveyards.

Wind-sculpted, contorted specimens of the Monterey cypress (*C. macrocarpa*) are native to coastal California and may enjoy a lifespan of two centuries. The cypress family (Cupressaceae) is cosmopolitan, with 113 species in 17 genera. The closest relatives of *Cupressus* include junipers (*Juniperus*) and white cedars (*Thuja*). The Cupressaceae is allied to the pine family (Pinaceae). Pines (*Pinus*) are Rhea's sacred trees. No wonder the Greeks associated the evergreen, needle-leafed, cone-bearing cypress with the ill-tempered wife of Cronus.

Egyptians used cypress wood for sarcophagi, whereas Greeks craved it into statues of their gods. An essential oil is still distilled from the young shoots to scent soaps or refresh smelly feet. So-called cedarwood oil from China is distilled primarily from weeping or mourning cypress, *C. funebris*. Greek housewives must have cherished their cypress chests, as clothes moths hate the aromatic compounds in the wood, protecting homespun woolens.

4. A small limb of a weeping cypress (*Cupressus funebris*) from China. Note the scales (modified needles) on the smaller branches and the two round and spiny cones. The illustration was taken from *Paxton's Flower Garden* (1882), a magazine produced by John Lindley, Sir Joseph Paxton, and Thomas Baines. Reproduced with the permission of the library at the Missouri Botanical Garden.

(3) Centaur. There are two old taxonomic traditions naming genera after centaurs to honor Chiron, the harmonious monster of herbal remedies. The genera *Centaurea*, *Centaurodendron* (centaur's tree), *Centauropsis* (centaur-eyed), and *Centaurothamnus* (centaur's bush) all belong to the daisy family (Asteraceae). *Centaurium*, though, belongs to the gentian family (Gentianaceae).

Centaurea and *Centaurium*, although placed in very different families (and only distantly related), share one thing in common that kept these wildflowers in apothecary shops for thousands of years. Both plants bear underground stems and/or roots extremely bitter to human taste buds. Biochemists now insist that these harsh flavors derive from a broad spectrum of plant molecules known as glycosides. Tinctures made of several unrelated herbs, all called century plants, were added to tonics in the belief that they stimulated the flow of both saliva and stomach acids, returning appetites to invalids and other sickly folk.

The first genus, *Centaurea*, consists of more than 450 species of herbs and bushy plants distributed through Eurasia, with a few species native to North America and one in Australia. Blue and bluish-purple flowering heads are common. When sold as beloved garden flowers, they are known as bluebottles, bachelor's buttons, and cornflowers. When these same species escape from cultivation and devour farmland or natural grasslands, we call them knapweeds. Those remaining three genera in the daisy family (*Centaurodendron*, *Centauropsis*, and *Centaurothamnus*) make flowering heads that resemble ornamental cornflowers and knapweeds.

Centaurium, on the other hand, contains far fewer species (about thirty), and most are distributed through the northern hemisphere. They are still called centaury plants, but odder common names include bitter clover, Christ's Ladder, and wild succory. Easier to grow than their cousins, the true gentians (*Gentiana*, see below), centauries offer showy, rosy-purple flowers. Many species found in North America are Eurasian in origin, descendents of garden escapees.

(4) Chiron. *Chironia* is another taxonomic word game of Linnaeus to show close similarities between different genera. The father of plant taxonomy wanted us to know that *Chironia* must be a close relative of *Centaurium*. As expected, *Chironia* is placed in the gentian family (Gentianaceae). There are fifteen, bushy, *Chironia* species, all plants of Africa and Madagascar. Christmas berry (*C. baccifera*) is now grown as a low shrub in dry gardens, but traditional African medicine has many uses for it.

Hesperochiron means Chiron of the West. Two small wildflower species are found only in the far west of the United States. I cannot say *Hesperochiron* without producing a mental image of the venerable centaur wearing a cowboy hat. This genus name was coined in 1871 by the American botanist Sereno Watson (1826–1892). He disagreed with British botanist George Bentham (1800–1884), who first described the new plant as another mountain foxglove (*Ourisia*), in the snapdragon family (Scrophulariaceae). After dissecting some specimens, Watson came to the conclusion that this wildflower really belonged to a new genus in the gentian family. Of course, he followed the usual tradition of naming members of that family after the myth of Chiron, the first herbalist.

Hesperochiron californicus produces a ring of fuzzy, ground-hugging leaves, and a small bouquet of dainty, bluish-white flowers sprouts from its center. Some wildflower books call it the monkey-fiddle flower. This adds an ironic twist. Watson's classification was all wrong. We now understand that this innocent-looking plant made monkeys out of both Bentham *and* Watson. Monkey-fiddles are not snapdragons *or* gentians. They belong to the waterleaf family (Hydrophyllaceae). Their squat, compact growth forms and their five-pointed petal cups made them look enough like a tiny gentian to confuse Watson. Consequently, monkey-fiddle flowers enjoy the dubious distinction of belonging to the only plant genus honoring the centaur Chiron that is not a member of either the daisy or gentian families.

(5) GENTIUS. We can find references to gentians in the work of the herbalist Theophrastus by the fourth and third centuries B.C.E. Once again, a plant's name follows the Greek root collectors' ancient tradition of naming an herb with medicinal properties after a powerful monarch or deity. It is disturbing to realize that, for thousands of years, people have destroyed millions of these beautiful wildflowers to extract false hopes. Some gentians are still known as agueweeds, suggesting they were once doomed to an ineffective career fighting fevers.

The genus *Gentiana* consists of more than three hundred species that prefer the mountains of Europe, Asia, and North America. In more tropical latitudes of South America or northwestern Africa, these herbs are found at higher, perpetually cooler altitudes. Flower colors vary, but most collectors prize species bearing deep indigo blue petals. Emily Dickinson's famous poem "Fringed Gentian" refers to the North American native, *G. crinita*. The gentian family (Gentianaceae) contains more than twelve hundred species in seventy-four genera. The majority grow as herbs, rarely taking the forms of shrubs or small trees. Other genera in this family are also favored as ornamental plants and are grown under such names as rose pinks (*Sabatia*) or Arabian violets (*Exacum*).

(6) OCYRRHOE. The genus *Ocyroe* was renamed *Nardophyllum*. Only seven species are found on the dry, southern slopes of the Andes. They are low-growing cushion shrubs of poor, sandy soils, but when their flowering heads burst into bloom, it is easy to see they are members of the daisy family (Asteraceae) and closely related to *Centaurea*. I have included this synonym to give you another example of how a later taxonomist comprehended and then extended the classification and wordplay of Linnaeus, transforming dry terminology into an inside joke and mnemonic.

5. Zeus and his sacred eagle survey plants growing in his cloudy realm (with apologies to Ingres). A spray of *Pandorea jasminoides* hangs over the god's head while a *Typhonium venosum* blooms at his feet. The eagle sits in the shade of a Brazilian cabbage palm (*Euterpe edulis*). Trading Elysium for Olympus, a specimen of *Asphodeline lutea* flowers in the right-hand corner. Illustration by John Myers.

CHAPTER 4

⋙⋘

The Triumph of Zeus

Let us begin our singing
from the Helikonian Muses
who possess the great and holy mountain
of Helikon
and dance there on soft feet
by the dark blue water
of the spring, and by the altar
of the powerful son of Kronos. . . .

—HESIOD, *Theogony*
(translation by Richard Lattimore)

4.1 THE BIRTH OF ZEUS

Cronus now ruled the universe, but he ruled in fear of his father's curse: "Someday one of your wife's children will overthrow you!" Unfortunately, his wife, Rhea, was a fertile mother goddess who gave birth to five babies. Each time, Cronus snatched the infant from its mother's arms and swallowed the newborn whole. The king of the Titans thus disposed of three daughters and his first two sons. Rhea was determined that her sixth child would escape. She gave birth in the dead of night on a mountain in Arcadia where her husband could not see her. Unattended, Rhea's only physical relief from the throes of childbirth was to plunge her two hands into the soil. Ten finger gods, or dactyls (1), popped out of the ten holes in the dirt, ready to serve her and her baby boy. Mother Earth transferred her newest grandchild and the dactyls to a cave on the island of Crete. The following day Rhea presented Cronus with a stone wrapped in swaddling clothes. The Titan king gulped it down as usual.

Rhea named the baby Zeus, but his future worshipers also called him Dyaus (2), Jupiter (3), or Jove. It would be Zeus's destiny to father a new race of gods, so the Romans honored him as Diu-pater (2). Tall, ancient oaks (*Quercus*) became his sacred trees.

Botany

(1) Dactyls. Botanists have found "fingers in flowers" and other plant organs for hundreds of years. The species name *dactylifera* means "having fingers," whereas *dactyloides* means "fingerlike." Finger-shaped structures are so obvious that at least fifteen genera continue to incorporate the finger gods as *Dactyladenia*, *Dactylaea*, *Dactylaena*, *Dactylanthus*, *Dactyliandra*, *Dactyliophora*, *Dactylocladus*, *Dacyltopsis*, *Dactylorhiza*, *Dactylorhynchus*, *Dactylostalix*, *Dactylostegium*, *Dactylostigma*, and *Dactylostelma*. Let's look at two of my personal favorites.

Dactyliandra (male finger/stamen finger) is an Old World (Africa and southwestern India) genus in the pumpkin family (Cucurbitaceae), consisting of only two species. The name indicates that each pollen-making stamen (*andra*) found inside a male flower resembles a finger. *Dactylorhiza* (fingered orchid root), in contrast, refers to thirty-five species of orchids (Orchidaceae) native to North America and Eurasia. Dig up the plant and you will see that its lumpy storage organ, known as a root-stem tuberoid, subdivides into longer, fleshy clusters resembling elongated fingers. A much earlier generation of English peasants often called these orchids "dead man's fingers" and even entertained a superstition that they grew out of the hands of a corpse of a convict who had died on the gallows. In contrast, the vast majority of soil-dwelling orchids with tuberoids produce organs that are more likely to remind the collector of a pair of testicles. Tuberoids resembling testicles are the subject of a completely different Greek myth (see §5.7).

Curiously, Linnaeus did not have fingers in mind at all when he named the familiar but solitary species of Eurasian orchard grass *Dactylis glomerata* (now a common, naturalized plant in American meadows). *Dactylis* refers to something that resembles a cluster of grapes. Orchard grass masses its tiny flowers into spikelets that hang together on the flowering stalk like bunches of inedible, flat, greenish grapes.

(2) Diu or Dyaus. The carnation (*Dianthus caryophyllus*) you buy in a florist's shop has pagan significance. *Diosanthos* has meant the "flower of Zeus" since antiquity. Hellmut Baumann, author of *The Greek Plant World*, emphasizes that the blossoms were worn in floral crowns during religious rituals. Archeologists unearthed remains of decorative murals depicting flowers of the shrubby Cretan pink (*D. arboreus*) at the famous palace of Knossos site on Crete. The genus *Dianthus* contains at least three hundred species found throughout Europe, Asia, and down into South Africa. They all belong to the pink and chickweed family (Caryophyllaceae). Many more species and hybrids are popular garden flowers, including the sweet william (*Dianthus barbatus*).

Translations of Greco-Roman poetry insist that all gods smell good. It is, therefore, easy to understand why carnations and pinks were used to honor mighty deities, as some species have sweet-spicy aromatic flowers. In Britain, the flowers

6. Plant genera that include one of the names of Zeus. Top left, a flowering stem of *Dianthus cruentus,* a wayside field pink of Eastern Europe and Turkey. Top right, a fruiting twig of a Mauritian persimmon (*Diospyros amplexicaulis*). Although most flowers shed all their floral organs as their ovaries ripen, the calyx cap continues to cling to most persimmons and date plums. Bottom, a branch of Persian or common walnut (*Juglans regia*) with a close-up of the short-lived stalks bearing male flowers (catkins). All illustrations were derived from *Paxton's Flower Garden* (1882) with the permission of the library of the Missouri Botanical Garden.

with the spiciest scents flavored alcoholic drinks from the days of Chaucer through Shakespeare's time, giving the plants such quaint names as "sops-in-wine" or clove pinks. British cooks also pickled carnation petals in vinegar or chopped them up to make a sauce for mutton. Whole open flowers were dipped in egg white and sugar to make candied ornaments for puddings. We now understand that the appetizing fragrance of the flower is fully functional, because it attracts pollinating butterflies by day and/or noctuid moths (loopers, foresters, and owlets) through the evening.

Diospyros (Diu's fruit or pear) refers to the genus that gives us persimmons, date plums, and velvet apples. There are more than 475 species found wild on every major continent except Antarctica. Tropical regions are always richest in these small trees and shrubs of the ebony family (Ebenaceae). At least a hundred species are found only on the island of Madagascar. The name *diospyros* is probably as old as *diosanthos*, and Linnaeus would have found it either in the third-century B.C.E. works of Theophrastus and/or the *Materia Medica* of Dioscorides, from the first century C.E.

However, Linnaeus did not understand that when ancient authors used the word *diospyros*, they usually referred to the fruit of European hackberry (*Celtis australis*) not the native Mediterranean date plum. He named the hackberry *Celtis*, reserving *Diospyros* for the new genus of date plums, and this scientific name still sticks. Hellmut Baumann notes that modern Greeks prefer the larger fruit of the commercial Japanese persimmon (*D. kaki*) to their own native date plum (*D. lotus*). As the scientific name suggests, the Greek species of date plum is also a candidate for the delectable lotus fruit eaten by Odysseus's crew during their attempt to return to Ithaca (see §7.5).

(3) JUPITER. Gastronomic Romans held walnuts in such high esteem that Pliny the Elder called them the acorns of Jove (*glans Jovis*). Linnaeus translated this into botanical Latin as the genus *Juglans*. There are twenty-one *Juglans* species distributed through North America and Eurasia. *Juglans*, in turn, gives its name to the family, Juglandaceae, with sixty-five species of trees and bushes found mostly in cooler regions of the northern hemisphere, although members grow as far south as tropical Malaysia. This family also contains the genus of commercial pecans (*Carya*) that will figure prominently in a later myth (see §5.7).

Have you wondered why so few shade-tolerant plants grow well under the black walnut (*Juglans nigra*) in your garden? As leaves, twigs, and fruits of this tree drop to the ground, they release red crystals containing the molecule juglone (literally, Jupiter's nut's ketone). Such crystals can remain in the soil for decades, killing or suppressing the roots of both seedlings and mature plants of other species. Chemical warfare between plants to reduce competition is known as allelopathy.

Once again, the king of the gods exerts ultimate power over his smaller and younger subjects.

4.2 THE CHILDHOOD OF ZEUS

Rhea hung Zeus's Cretan cradle from an oak tree so that Cronus would not find him in heaven, sea, or earth. Like all babies, Zeus wailed and cried, and Rhea feared the noise would attract her husband's attention. The mother of Zeus created the Corybantes (1), a race of helmet-wearing warrior priests, out of rain. They drowned out the infant's cries by shouting, dancing, and clashing their spears against their shields. When Cronus complained of the commotion, Rhea told him that her devotees were engaged in solemn worship.

Rhea could not nurse her own son, so she gave her baby the she-goat, Amaltheia, a beast who never ran dry. As the young god grew, he enjoyed wrestling with the giant goat until, one day, he broke off one of her horns by accident. It became the cornucopia (2), the miraculous horn of plenty, spontaneously filling up with food and drink for its owners, a sign of divine abundance.

Little Zeus also had a trio of divine nursemaids. Some say they were the original ash nymphs (Meliae, see §3.3) born from the castration of Uranus. Others say they were children of the sea Titan Oceanus (3) and his sister-wife, Tethys. Adrasteia (4) and Melia gave the baby goat's milk. Their sister, Melissa (5), collected honey that dripped from the trees in that plentiful Golden Age. Melissa was transformed into the first honeybee (*Apis mellifera*) for her services.

The child god had two special playmates. One was the young nature god, Pan. The second was Celmis (6), a son of the nymph Alciope (7). One day, Celmis rejected the godhead of Zeus. Vindictive Rhea punished Celmis for his blasphemy by transforming him into an iron bar or magnetic lodestone.

Botany

(1) CORYBANTES. The genus name *Corybas* means "dancing priest" and represents a hundred species of shade-loving, helmet orchids (Orchidaceae). Most grow in forest floors on the islands of Indonesia and Malaysia south to Australia and New Zealand. The flower resembles a miniature helmet because the broad, dorsal sepal forms a hollow dome over the lower, broader, sculptured lip petal. Some tropical Asian helmet orchids are beautifully exaggerated. The floral surfaces have striped, fluted, feathery, or scalloped surfaces that remind me of highly ornamented helmets

in illustrated books about the Trojan War. Some flowers have curving, narrow lateral petals, reminiscent of decorative plumes or crests.

In eastern coastal Australia, helmet orchids usually bloom on mossy forest floors, popping up during late winter rains paralleling the myth of Rhea's priests. These flowers probably mimic the fruiting bodies of mushrooms that also grow during this pleasantly cool and damp season. The orchids are pollinated by pregnant fungus-gnats, and fine sculpturing inside the flower mimics a mushroom's gills. Some Australian helmet flowers produce an uncanny smell like buttery, cooked mushrooms.

(2) CORNUCOPIA. There are only two Eurasian species in the genus *Cornucopiae*. They are placed in the grass family (Poaceae), but neither is a source of edible grains. However, *Cornucopiae* species are most abundant producers of dry, single-seeded fruits (caryopses), distributed generously on the branching flowering stalks.

7. Plant genera named after some of the caretakers of the infant Zeus. All three are still found in eastern Australia. Top, *Adrastaea salicifolia*, a shrub of swamps. Bottom left, a mountain snow daisy (*Celmisia*) showing the typical parachute on the dry, single-seeded fruit. Bottom right, a fringed helmet orchid (*Corybas fimbriatus*) with the typical dorsal sepal forming an inflated cap (the helmet) over the top of the flower. All drawings are from *Flora of New South Wales* (edited by Gwen J. Harden, Kensington, New South Wales, 1993) under the copyright of the Royal Botanic Gardens (Sydney) and Domain Trust.

I have looked at pressed, dried specimens in the herbarium of the Missouri Botanical Garden. The fruits do not resemble little horns, in my opinion. There are references to these fruits becoming entangled, en masse, in clothing and in the hair of farm animals, including goats. Obviously, they remain "much attached" to the kids of Almatheia.

(3) OCEANUS. How do you indicate plant geography in cabinets holding international collections? The largest plant museums (herbaria) subdivide the world into a minimum of five broad regions. Plants found on islands of the eastern half of the southern Pacific basin (Australia, Fiji, New Zealand, Samoa, Tahiti etc.) belong to a region botanists call Oceania. The Swiss botanist Augustin Pyrame de Candolle (1778–1841) may have remembered Adrasteia, a daughter of Oceanus, when he named an Australian wetland shrub *Adrastaea*.

(4) ADRASTEIA. *Adrastaea salicifolia* is the only species in the genus. This waist-high shrub belongs to the elephant apple family (Dilleniaceae) and is restricted to swamps and lakesides of eastern Australia. It produces tubular yellow flowers in late winter to early spring (August–September). Like so many of the aquatic daughters of Oceanus, *Adrastaea* stands in shallow water or reposes on wet banks. When Candolle named this genus, he was probably considering its wetland distribution in the botanical realm of Oceania.

Beware of the natural protectors of *Adrastaea*. I collected twigs in yellow bud the August day I found the shrub in a drying swamp in Royal National Park in New South Wales. This meant getting wet. Upon returning to the herbarium of the Royal Botanic Gardens in Sydney, I found blood on one of my socks. A huge horseleech had come back to town with me.

(5) MELISSA. The importance of flowers to the ancient, rural, honey industry is commemorated in their scientific names. Blossoms smelling like honey may be given the species name *melliodorous*. If hand lenses detect the presence of nectar droplets (see §4.7) inside a fresh flower, it may be named *melittus*. However, the bee nymph, *Melissa*, gives her *full* name to only three species of fragrant herbs found naturally from Europe to Iran. *Melissa* belongs to the mint family (Lamiaceae). Britons and Americans call *M. officinalis*, bee balm. When Linnaeus named these herbs after the industrious nymph, he probably knew the ancient legend that bee balm leaves attract swarms of honeybees. In fact, the foliage of *M. officinalis* has a nice, lemony fragrance and is used traditionally to flavor medicinal teas and liqueurs.

Melittis is also in the mint family. It is similar to *Melissa* but consists of only one European species (*Melittis melissophyllum*), known as bastard balm. Linnaeus obviously derived the word *Melittis* from *Melissa* to show it was a close relative of the preferred *Melissa officinalis*, but like most bastards, not quite good enough.

(6) CELMIS. *Celmisia* is the genus of mountain and alpine snow daisies (daisy-sunflower family, Asteraceae). Sixty-one species are restricted to the southern hemisphere, but fifty-eight are found *only* on the islands of New Zealand. Most grow as tufted herbs, but some are twiggy bushes. Originally, Candolle placed most daisy bushes of the southern hemisphere in a genus he named *Alciope* (see below). This did not suit his contemporary, Alexandre Henri Gabriel Cassini (1781–1832). Taxonomists regard Cassini as the "Parisian father" of the modern classification of the daisy family. Cassini was unsatisfied with Candolle's lumping so many daisy-like plants together just because they grew in temperate regions so far south of the equator. By 1836, Cassini finished revising the New Zealand and Australian snow daisies. He took them out of genus *Alciope* and placed them in his new genus, *Celmisia*. He was trying to show other taxonomists that his new genus was closely related to the old *Alciope*. He wanted botanists to discriminate between the South African "mother genus" (*Alciope*) and her larger, Australasian "son" (*Celmis*).

From the nineteenth through the early twentieth century, some botanists believed they could help geologists and prospectors by identifying "indicator plant species" which *always* grew on soils that formed over lucrative ores, minerals, and gem deposits. Yes, *Celmisia* was once associated with rocks rich in iron, but with so many species of wild snow daisies they were *never* precise indicators of hidden metals.

(7) ALCIOPE. The dust has long settled on Cassini's major revision of the daisy family. Two bushy species of *Alciope* are all we have left in the original genus once erected by Candolle. As we mature we often surpass our mothers in size, but *Celmisia*, with greater than sixty species, is now more than thirty times larger than *Alciope*. The two remaining *Alciope* species are confined to the west side of the Cape of Good Hope. They grow in dry valleys or on rocky mountain slopes and offer yellow flowering heads.

4.3 ZEUS AND THE TITANS' DAUGHTERS

Gods mature quickly. Zeus, or Jove (1), grew a beard the silvery white color of the clouds he would one day rule. His Titan aunts and nymph cousins found him attractive. They hid him from Cronus, offered excellent counsel, and became his lovers. He had many children by Titan woman and most were dutiful daughters who would, one day, help him control the elements, the virtues, and all arts and sciences. By the Titan Themis (Justice), he fathered the Horae (the seasons). By Eurynome, he had the three Graces or Charites (2).

Mnemosyne (Memory) was much favored by Zeus, and she gave birth to nine daughters by the fountain of Pieria on Mount Olympus. The gods called them the Pierides (3), but we know them better as the Muses or

Musae (4). All nine sisters lived together on mountaintops and inspired the lives of many later generations of talented mortals.

Botany

(1) BEARDED JOVE. *Anthyllis barba-jovis* is a shrubby, Mediterranean member of the pea family (Fabaceae), commonly known as silver bush or kidney vetch. The dense, large, evergreen, compound, silvery white leaves resemble a giant beard. The plant had a respectable history as an ornamental bush in the gardens of Roman aristocrats. Linda Farrar, author of *Ancient Roman Gardens*, suspects the shrub was grown in imperial gardens as early as the first century C.E., but it was clipped into a rounded form following the Roman love of topiary. Shrubs with silvery gray foliage were much favored in landscapes of the wealthy and powerful.

Please do not confuse *A. barba-jovis*, the kidney vetch, with a European herb sold commonly as Jupiter's beard (*Centranthus ruber*). *Centranthus* belongs to the valerian family (Valerianaceae), and is not a close relative of true peas and vetches. *Centranthus ruber* has pretty, tubular, pink-reddish or purple flowers and remains a popular groundcover in California gardens dominated by dry soils. Unfortunately, it soon takes over and will smother stone walls, pushing its way into old fields.

Jovibarba (beard of Jove) consists of five European species of houseleeks, or hen and chicks, within the stonecrop family, Crassulaceae. David Gledhill, author of *The Names of Plants*, states that *Jovibarba* refers to the delicate, beardlike fringes on the flower petals. However, many taxonomists no longer think it is a distinctive genus and sink all five species into the much larger genus, *Sempervivum* (forty-two species), distributed through Europe, Morocco, and western Asia. Many horticulturists and collectors are displeased with this reclassification and continue to refer to *Jovibarba* species in nursery catalogs and on Web sites. The much cultivated *J. heuffelii* escaped from cultivation in the United States and is now a naturalized weed in Ashland County, northern Wisconsin. In either case both jovibarbas and sempervivums (as they are known popularly by astute collectors) are hardy plants, often grown in crannies of ornamental stones or walls. Some species produce dense white, wooly beards from the centers of each rosette of succulent leaves.

The name *Jovibarba* also reflects a strange superstition about houseleeks in general, at least as old as the Roman Empire. If these plants were grown on the roof of a house, they would protect the building from lightning (Jove's weapon of choice). The late Joseph Reis, an American nurseryman from Merrick, New York (and a jovibarba fancier himself), told me, when I was a boy, that some ethnic Germans also grew them on their roofs as proof against lightning. This probably went back to pagan days when German-speaking people lived in fear of the thunder god, Thor or Donner.

(2) CHARITES. Botanists used the word *Charis* without ever consulting with classical scholars. We should note that, in Homer's *Iliad*, Charis is the name of the wife of the lame god of smiths (Hephaestus or Vulcan). Some authorities insisted that Charis was another of the many names for Aphrodite, goddess of love. Others said that Charis was the married name of one of the Charites, Aglaia (§5.9), the second wife of Hephaestus, after he divorced unfaithful Aphrodite. If this is correct, then all references to Charis in plant taxonomy refer to at least one of the three Graces (the Charites).

Ironically, the genus *Anticharis* is an unflattering piece of word play, as it means without any grace or charm. The genus belongs to the snapdragon family (Scrophulariaceae), with fourteen species distributed through Africa and southern Asia. Most are weedy, annual plants of arid zones and seasonal riverbeds, known as wadis. They are hardy survivors with few resources to invest in elegant growth habits or large, attractive flowers. In fact, earlier generations of botanists often honored the three Charites, or the minor goddess Charis, whenever these taxonomists described a new genus and were enchanted by beautiful flowers or graceful growth forms. Unfortunately, five genera in five different families (*Charesia, Charia, Charidia, Chariesis,* and *Chariessa*) are now reduced to synonyms.

We still have the genus *Charianthus* (flower of the Charites). It contains about ten species in the glory bush family (Melastomataceae). *Charianthus* species grow as shrubs and small trees preferring the cooler, mossy mountains of the islands of the West Indies and Antilles. The flowers are charming, wearing silky pink, red, or purple petals that form nodding bells or urns. They are so attractive that some people call them "mountain fuchsias," although they are not related to the genus *Fuchsia* in the evening primrose family (Onagraceae).

(3) PIERIDES. *Pieris* (of the Muses) consists of seven species of evergreen bushes in the rhododendron-heath family (Ericaceae) found in temperate, eastern Asia and parts of North America. David Don (1799–1841), a British botanist, named this genus. We will see that he plainly favored classical names for other members of the heath family, trying to emulate Linnaeus. In the eighteenth century, Linnaeus named a little heath he found in Lapland after Princess Andromeda (see §6.6). Don continued the pretty tradition with three new genera: *Leucothoe* (§5.11), *Pieris,* and *Cassiope* (§6.6). By giving these new genera the names of mythological characters he was pointing out that his newly described shrubs were closely related to the *Andromeda* of Linnaeus.

Unfortunately, these look-alike genera, all named after mythical Greek females, continue to provoke confusion among gardeners and commercial horticulturists. Even today your local nursery sells bushes labeled as andromeda, when most are usually cultivated forms of the Asian *Pieris japonica*. The confusion is best explained in the botanical explanation in §6.6. *Pieris japonica* is particularly favored in temperate gardens with moist, acid soil. Owners trying to create a "Japanese landscape" employ these shrubs because they offer nodding tassels of white-pinkish, bell-shaped flowers in spring and their young, emerging leaves are so shiny and scarlet. *Pieris floribunda* is the American fetterbush found from Virginia through Georgia. It is not as popular in gardens as its Asian cousin.

The Roman poet Ovid describes the Pierides as nine silly girls who were the daughters of a wealthy man named Pierus. These Pierides challenged the real Muses to a song contest, and when they lost, the goddesses changed their mortal rivals into magpies that can only cackle scornfully and mimic their superiors. All botanical lexicons, though, continue to insist that *Pieris* refers to the nine daughters of Zeus and Mnemosyne.

(4) MUSAE. Because the Muses prefer mountains, some scientists gave the name *musarum* (of the Muses) to montane plants of southern Europe. In 1854, Theodoros Orphanides, a father of Greek plant taxonomy, discovered a yellow-flowered knapweed on the limestone cliffs on Mount Parnassus, in Greece. He named it *Centaurium musarum* (see the myth of the first centaur in §3.7). It was not collected again until 2004, when botanists finally revisited the same, bizarre, vertical cliffs. Are muses most helpful to mortals willing to undergo extreme exertion and personal sacrifice?

In fact, physical discomfort and long journeys do not await everyone seeking these daughters of Zeus. You ate the muses this morning if you sliced a banana onto your breakfast cereal. *Musa* is the genus of all thirty-five banana species, whether they are grown for fruit (*M. acuminata*) or fibers (*M. textiles*). Linnaeus named this genus, and his publication, *Critica Botanica,* insisted he wanted one new word to do the work of three.

Musa represents an amazing piece of etymological acrobatics. First, European botanists wrote the old Arabic word for banana as *muz* or *muez.* The ancestors of all edible bananas came originally from wild plants that grew in the forests of Thailand and the islands of Indonesia and Malaysia. Their popularity spread west slowly, over more than two thousand years ago, and is attributed to Arab traders passing fruits and cuttings on to enthusiastic farmers in India and Africa. By naming the genus *Musa*, Linnaeus acknowledges the popularization of bananas by Muslim cultures. Muslims called banana plants "trees of paradise," and that is why Linnaeus named the most common commercial, edible breed *Musa paradisiaca*. During the twentieth century, chromosome studies exposed this favorite, yellow-skinned fruit as a cultivated hybrid, not a true species at all, and we now write the scientific name *Musa ✕paradisiaca.*

Second, Linnaeus insisted that he wanted to honor Antonio Musa (63–14 B.C.E.), doctor to the first Roman emperor, Augustus (but he never tells us why). Third,

Antonio's family name, Musa, is merely a Latinized version of the Greek *Musae*. By honoring the Roman physician Linnaeus claimed he also honored the nine daughters of Zeus.

4.4 THE MUSES

As daughters of Mnemosyne (Memory), each muse became a goddess of an art or science requiring a great act of memorization in those days when paper and books were rare. Men would call on them for divine recall and inspiration. Each muse was easy to recognize because she always carried the tools of her trade. For example, the Muse Euterpe (1) played the flute and encouraged men to set lyric poetry to music. Polymnia (2) wore a veil, sang sacred songs, and taught oratory and rhetoric. Her sister, Erato (3) carried a lyre because she supported love poetry and marriage songs. Thalia (4) was the most lighthearted of the sisters. She inspired comic theater by donning the comic's mask, carrying a shepherd's staff, and keeping thin-soled shoes (favored by Greco-Roman comedians) on her beautiful feet. The Muses preferred lofty mountains, and they were particularly fond of Mount Helicon (5). They had a temple there where they performed their graceful dances.

Botany

(1) EUTERPE. There are twenty species of palms with feathery (pinnate) fronds in the genus *Euterpe*, and most are native to South American rain forests. A palm specialist, C. Martius (1794–1868), working in Brazil, compared the slender and graceful trunks of these palms bending in the wind to one of the dancing muses. The stem shoots of the Brazilian cabbage or acai palm (*E. edulis*) provide us with that exotic and expensive delicacy, hearts of palm salad. Harvesting the tender core in the shoot of the stem tip kills the young tree. Another species, *E. oleracea*, is favored more as a small, ornamental tree, which dances in warm humid breezes.

(2) POLYMNIA. *Polymnia* refers to twenty species in the sunflower family (Asteraceae) found through the western hemisphere. In particular, the South American yacón (*P. sonchifolia*), is cultivated in the Andes Mountains for its sweet, crunchy tubers. Once again, Linnaeus named a mountain plant after a mountain goddess. The taste of yacón reminds some people of water chestnuts (others say apples). The sugar in the tuber is fermented to make a source of alcohol.

(3) ERATO. *Erato* once referred to four species in the sunflower family (Asteraceae) found in the tropical Americas. Candolle was originally trying to show that *Erato* was in the same family as *Polymnia* (see above) and some species of *Erato* and *Polymnia* prefer mountain habitats, as did the nine muses. Recently, the genus *Erato*

became a synonym and was submerged within the larger genus *Liabum*, with thirty-seven species distributed from Central America through the Andes.

(4) THALIA. Unfortunately, Thalia is another all-too-common common name in Greco-Roman mythology. Zimmerman warns that one Thalia is the muse of comedy. The second is one of the *Charites*, and a third is an obscure water nymph. Historians of botany agree that Linnaeus erected the genus *Thalia* to do double-duty. It honors one of the Charites (Graces) and the memory of Johannes Thal (1542–1583), an herbalist who collected plants in the Harz Mountains. To read a full explanation of the genus *Thalia*, see §5.9.

(5) HELICON. European expeditions to Central and South America brought back specimens of large herbs from wet warm forests. Linnaeus compared the flowers of these tropical American plants to those of the Asian banana, *Musa*. The Swedish taxonomist noted that the flowers of edible bananas and the little blossoms of the new plants were very similar. Both contained the same numbers of sexual organs, although they came from very different parts of the world. Linnaeus decided he would erect a new genus for the tropical American plants. The new name would indicate the close alliance between the nine muses and their favorite home, Mount Helicon.

Heliconia is now a genus of about a hundred species distributed through the New World. These large, often bulky, herbs grow in deep shade, or they invade gaps after large canopy trees fall over following storms or earthquakes. Some are true epiphytes, colonizing and growing on the limbs of larger, supportive trees. Most *Heliconia* species protect their small, tubular blossoms in large, boat-shaped, enfolding leaves known as bracts. *Heliconia* flowers are pale and ephemeral, but their bracts are often long-lived and gaudy, wearing contrasting hues of yellow and scarlet. No wonder they are often sold as lobster claw plants. The relationship between ornamental heliconias and commercial bananas continues to change. Nineteenth-century botanists thought Linnaeus was on the right track and placed heliconias in the family Scitamineae with bananas (*Musa*) and the bird-of-paradise plant (*Strelitzia*). In 1941, Japanese taxonomist T. Nakai gave them their own family, the Heliconiaceae.

4.5 ZEUS DEFEATS ATLAS

Zeus conspired with his mother, Rhea, and his current love, the ocean nymph, Metis. Rhea presented Zeus to her husband as a new cupbearer. Cronus did not recognize his own offspring. Meanwhile, Metis mixed a powerful emetic with water and honey on the first night that Zeus served his father. When Cronus took his bedtime drink, he vomited up the stone in swaddling clothes and all of Zeus's siblings. The two gods and three goddesses emerged alive and fully grown. They immediately swore a thankful oath of loyalty to their liberator, Zeus.

With such powerful siblings, Zeus declared war on the Titans. The male Titans appointed the gigantic and wealthy Atlas as their warlord. Atlas's wealth came from the many countries he owned. More important, he had many virginal daughters by each of his three wives: the evening star, Hesperis (1); Pleione (2); and Aethra. Atlas knew very well that he stood to lose the most if his army was conquered by this new, seductive son of Rhea. The war lasted a decade, but Zeus and his two brothers ultimately crushed the Titan army because these sons of Rhea kept their promise to their grandmother, Gaia. They freed the Cyclops and Hecatoncheires from Tartarus. The multilimbed Hecatoncheires were irresistible in battle. The peaceful Cyclops proved to be inspired smiths, and they provided Zeus with wonderful weapons, including the first thunderbolts.

Zeus showed his gratitude to all female Titans and nymphs, absolving them from any punishment. Instead, all male Titans who supported Cronus were exiled to Tartarus, where the hundred-handed giants prevented any future escape. Atlas was separated from his troops and condemned to carry heaven on his shoulders for eternity. As anticipated, his daughters became the servants, nursemaids, and concubines of a new race of gods.

Botany

(1) HESPERIS. Anyone who grows dame's rocket (*Hesperis matronalis*) knows that the sweet spicy odor of its blossoms is always strongest by late afternoon, persisting into the twilight as the evening star begins to glimmer. Although its fragrance is far fainter when the purple, pink, or whitish flowers stand in full sun they continue to attract many nectar-drinking insects. In particular, dame's rocket is loved by the butterflylike skippers of the insect family Hesperiidae. Obviously, both the Latin name of this genus of wildflowers and the family name in the Lepidoptera share a common origin, because both organisms remain "active" in the evening.

The genus *Hesperis* consists of about thirty species in the wallflower or cabbage family (Brassicaceae), and Linnaeus derived the name from scented plants mentioned by Theophrastus. Whereas *Hesperis* species are distributed naturally from the Mediterranean east into Central Asia and western China, dame's rocket is such an old garden favorite in Canada and the United States that it has escaped and become naturalized in all but ten U.S. states.

Remains of first-century manuscripts by Dioscorides indicate that the Romans favored certain members of the wallflower family for their ability to scent gardens.

Hesperis matronalis and its close relatives, wallflower (*Cheiranthus cheri*) and scented stocks (*Matthiola incana*), were all lumped together as *aeukolov* herbs.

(2) PLEIONE. *Pleione* is a genus of orchids (Orchidaceae) with fifteen species distributed from the Himalayas east into southern China, Thailand, and Taiwan. Some plants attach themselves to tree branches and others grow on mossy rocks. Dried and live specimens began arriving in England during the early nineteenth century, booty of the famous East India Company. David Don (see §4.3) was the author of this genus. He must have taken the advice of John Lindley, that a taxonomic name should be harmonious and nondescriptive. Don left no obvious clue to explain why these plants honor an obscure, female Titan who gave birth to the stars we call the Pleiades.

Consulting Ovid's *Metamorphoses,* we note that Atlas is turned into Mount Atlas when he gazes on the decapitated head of Medusa. Some *Pleione* species are mountain-loving and are found at altitudes between eighteen hundred feet to more than three thousand feet above sea level. Singchi Chen et al.'s astonishingly beautiful yet educational *Native Orchids of China in Colour* (Beijing: Science Press, 1999), offers one startling photo of dozens of flowers of *P. hookeriana* blooming on a mountain slope, forming pinkish-white constellations against the rock face. Was Don suggesting that Pleione still clings to her mountainous husband, Atlas?

8. *Pleione humilis* shows two developmental features typical of most of the species in this genus of orchids. First, the plants usually bloom after they've shed their seasonal leaves. Second, the fringed lip petal of the flower is often longer and broader than the succulent storage stems (pseudobulbs). The plate was taken from *Paxton's Flower Garden* with the permission of the library of the Missouri Botanical Garden.

4.6 Zeus and His Brothers Divide the Universe

Who ruled the universe following the defeat of the army of Atlas? Zeus and his two brothers drew lots. Zeus reigned in heaven. Poseidon (1) (Roman, Neptune) (2) received the sea. Hades drew the underworld, but all three gods reserved dry land as their freehold, sharing the territories once owned by Atlas. To subdue the Titans, the three Cyclops had presented Hades with a helmet of invisibility. He continued to use it after the Titan army was defeated. The Greeks claimed that is why we never know the moment when the King of the Dead claims us.

The Cyclops gave Poseidon a trident that would cause earthquakes when its points were plunged into the ground. As he continued to use it after the Titans were exiled to Tartarus, Zeus called his brother "Earth-Shaker." The easily angered god of the sea became used to taking whatever he wanted by force. However, Oceanus, the original, sea-ruling Titan, took no part in the Titan war. Poseidon decided it was politic to marry into his new kingdom. The Earth-Shaker knew that, as king of the sea, he would receive the "tribute" of the river gods, all sons of Oceanus, if he ruled by legitimate right of succession.

In a rare moment of civility, Poseidon proposed to Amphitrite, a granddaughter of Oceanus. Amphitrite rejected the offer. She knew of her suitor's thuggish reputation, and the nymph fled to the headwaters of a river in the Atlas Mountains. Poseidon sent Delphinus (3), the first dolphin, after her to propose until Amphitrite agreed to the wedding. The god was so delighted with the gentle results achieved by the matchmaking mammal that he placed Delphinus in heaven as a new constellation.

Botany

(1) Poseidon. Technically, the genus *Posidonia* (city of Poseidon) is named not for the sea god but for a now-vanished seaport founded by Greek colonists in Italy. Ancient adherents of Greco-Roman religions often named cities in honor of a patron deity; for example, Athens is named after Athena (see §5.12).

Posidonia consists of about three species of sea grasses that are often given their own family, the Posidoniaceae. *Posidonia oceanica* lives in the Mediterranean, while the other two species are found in shallow bays and coastal shelves off the coast of Australia. The Mediterranean species is often called tape grass owing to its long, ribbonlike foliage. Before we had modern insulation technology, the stalks of tape grass were collected and dried to serve as packing material for fine Italian glassware. Poseidon is also the god of horses, and Roman art often depicted him on a chariot pulled through the water by aquatic steeds. Did the German-born and London-based botanist Carl Dietrich Koenig (1774–1851) imagine giant seahorses grazing in salty, tape grass meadows when he named the genus in 1805?

Posidonia species are so well adapted to marine life that their little male flowers open underwater, releasing flexible, microscopic, eel-shaped pollen grains that drift toward female flowers on gentle currents. The threadlike pollen wraps itself around the pistil tips. After flowering and setting seeds, the reproductive tips of tape grass and many other sea grasses snap off. The action of gentle waves and a shallow sandy bottom may roll the fibrous fragments into relatively large, buoyant globes or egg-shaped bodies. Divers, beachcombers, and marine botanists refer to such flotsam as "Neptune's balls."

(2) NEPTUNE. Speaking of Neptune, the genus *Neptunia* contains a dozen species of shrubs or herbs in the bean family (Fabaceae) found primarily through the wet tropics of southeastern Asia and coastal, northern Australia. Some species grow in seasonally wet, monsoon soils, and *Neptunia prostrata* gives the genus its name because it is a naturally floating shrub. Each bush resembles a waterlogged mass of flabby stems, remaining afloat on ponds and sluggish rivers, as its shoots are filled with the buoyant air-containing tissue, known as aerenchyma. Preferring fresh water, *Neptunia prostrata* bobs over the domains of the tributary river gods.

In addition, *Neptunia* species have "sensitive" compound leaves that close up when touched or stroked, just like their close relatives in the genus, *Mimosa* (sensitive plants). Classical poets complained that quarrelsome Neptune was easily provoked and quick to respond. The sensitive leaves on *Neptunia* contribute to his irritable reputation.

(3) DELPHINUS. Generations of Mediterranean kings and peasants have seen the dolphin in the fat flower bud of a *Delphinium*. The head and snout of the dolphin are the unopened petal tips. The dolphin's "tail" is a special, modified sepal known as the spur, which contains nectar (see §4.8) after the petals open. The genus *Delphinium* consists of more than two hundred species of wildflowers in the buttercup family (Ranunculaceae). Most seed catalogs these days sell them as delphiniums to discriminate between true *Delphinium* species and their look-alike siblings, the larkspurs (*Consolida*; §7.3). Classic herbalists, including Dioscorides in the first century c.e., used the word *delphinium* long before Linnaeus formalized the genus in 1754.

Delphiniums are *not* restricted to the Mediterranean basin. Different species are distributed through temperate Europe and Asia and are common through North America. The greatest number of American species are found in the Pacific coast states eastward into the drier regions of the U.S. southwest. We should not assume all delphinium flowers wear shades of blue, either. Some have yellow flowers. Red-flowered, odorless species are found from southern California through Arizona.

These scarlet blossoms are usually visited by hummingbirds. In the nineteenth century, biochemists began to extract and identify the pigment molecules in flowers. Pigment chemicals were often named after the flowers from which they were first extracted. Some blue delphiniums gave chemists the compound delphinidin.

The delphinidin molecule belongs to a class of common and vivid pigments known as anthocyanins. Research confirms that anthocyanins produce most of the reds, blues, and purples we see in flower petals. Floral beauty is literally skin deep when it is based on anthocyanins, as these pigments are dissolved within water bags (vacuoles) inside the cells that comprise the surface of petal skin. We now understand that the blue color expressed by delphinidin changes with the chemistry of the water bags in petal and sepal cells. Alkaline water in a cell gives us blue delphinidin, but lower the pH to acid, and delphinidin loses two atoms of oxygen and two atoms of hydrogen. The molecule is transformed into pelargonidin, which now appears red to the human eye. Pelargonidin is a molecule once associated with the scarlet petals of the common, potted, African geraniums (*Pelargonium*).

4.7 THE KINGDOM OF HADES

Hades inherited cavernous gloom, but he became the wealthiest deity, owning all the seams of precious metal and caches of gems. Four subterranean rivers flowed through Tartarus, but the mightiest was the dripping malodorous Styx (1). We still speak of foul or underground conditions as stygian. Hades's earliest subjects included only the imprisoned Titans, their hundred-handed guards, and various demons like the three Empusae (female vampires with the legs and hooves of asses) (2), and the Mormolyca (a sort of hobgoblin) (3).

However, the underworld became the most populous place in the universe once the gods created short-lived humans. After death, the shade or phantom (*mormos*) (4) of each man and woman spent eternity wandering through the Elysian meadows of ever-blooming asphodels (5) in the underworld of Tartarus. The Etruscans, a people from northern Italy, insisted there were many gods in hell. Some were divine children or grandchildren of Jove like the boy god, Tages (6). If you plowed the earth, Tages would rise up out of the furrow and teach you divination by reading the livers of sacrificed animals.

Botany

(1) STYX. Poets and storytellers depicted the Styx as a thoroughly unpleasant body of water weaving its sluggish way through the infernal darkness bordering the land of the dead. When botanists thus name a species, they are describing a plant that

grows in unpleasant habitats. Specifically, those habitats are less than pleasant for the botanist attempting to collect a new specimen. Many plant species thrive under conditions that a refined taxonomist would describe as stygian. Fascinating species have earned the name *stygia* for no better reason than that they were found floating in stagnant, smelly water. For example, both the Nordic bladderwort (*Utricularia stygia*), an interesting carnivorous plant, and one of the Australian floating hearts (*Nymphoides stygia*) are comfortable in muddy pools, ditches, or bogs.

A plant could also earn the name *stygia* if its roots or its underground stem (rhizome) penetrated dense, infertile, and rocky soil. Going to some inhospitable site where it grew was no picnic for a botanist, and there was little pleasure to be gained trying to dig a specimen out of its hard substrate. Consider the attractive, blue-flowered *Globularia stygia*. It is found through Greece and countries of southeastern Europe growing as a small, matted shrub colonizing the driest crevices and stony slopes. This little bush anchors itself by pushing its underground stems through the holes in porous limestone. Collectors were rewarded for past discomfort and sweaty work. *Globularia stygia* has become a favorite in European rock gardens.

(2) EMPUSAE. Botanists have wondered why John Lindley attempted to "curse" a few small, species of orchids (Orchidaceae) with the name of the filthiest she-demons in Greek mythology. It is worth trying to guess Lindley's riddle even though his genus, *Empusa*, was reduced to a synonym of the orchid genus *Liparis*. Here is my answer. Lindley, unlike many plant taxonomists of his day, examined living plants as well as flat, dried herbarium specimens. The flowers of many *Liparis* (or *Empusa*) species have small, dull, brownish-greenish flowers that produce a persistent smell reminiscent of stale urine (usually a sign of fly pollination). I think someone sent Lindley one of these stinkers in bloom, and he responded professionally with the foulest name in the classical arsenal. I have never cared for the acrid odor of an American orchid species known as the large twayblade (*Liparis lilifolia*), either. Back in the late 1970s, I met an amateur Australian orchid grower who had a pot of native *Liparis reflexa* and referred to the flowers as dog's widdle. One sniff and I had to agree.

The genus *Liparis* was named in 1818 by the French botanist L. C. Richard, and it means fatty or greasy (referring to the shiny slickness on the leaves and stems). Most are tropical plants, but a few grow in the humus of forest floors in temperate North America and Europe. There are at least three hundred *Liparis* species, so smelling bad is obviously a successful ploy. Orchids blooming in deep shade are unlikely to attract bee or butterfly pollinators, as these insects are sun worshipers. The debris on the forest floor is a natural nursery for many fly species. As winged adults, many are attracted to the stench of animal waste products. *Liparis* fertility is obviously dependent, in part, on pollinator gullibility.

(3) MORMOLYCA. Some orchids have ugly flowers. If you think *Liparis* (*Empusa*) orchids sound homely, have a look at the genus *Mormolyca*. The Austrian plant taxonomist Eduard Fenzl (1808–1879) offered it as his own take on the Greek underworld back in 1850. Fenzl decided he would reexamine, revise, and compliment John Lindley's creepy sense of humor. Fenzl studied a Central American orchid that Lindley had first named, *Trigonidium ringens*, back in 1840. Fenzl decided to rename the genus *Mormolyca*. This new genus name stuck, but to date it contains only one species, *M. ringens*, found from Mexico to Costa Rica. Like the genus *Mormodes* (see below), *Mormolyca* colonizes tree branches and also prefers warm, inland valleys. Although its flower has yellow-pink sepals and lateral petals, it spoils any overall cheerful effect with muddy purple blotches on its lip petal. The solitary flower that tips each stalk is so small it must be classified as a grotesque goblin instead of a big, flapping phantom.

(4) MORMOS. *Mormodes* (phantomlike) is yet another genus in the orchid family (Orchidaceae) that John Lindley slapped with a classically macabre name. About twenty species are distributed from southern Mexico through South America, usually attached to trees and often growing in relatively warm central valleys. The flowers are decorated with dense brownish-red streaks and dark purple spots. The somber presentation is exaggerated in flowers of *M. aromatica*, in which the sepals and lateral petals form an overlapping hood shading the lip petal. It reminds me of theatrical depictions of Charles Dickens's Ghost of Christmases-Yet-to-Come. In *M. lineata* the lip petal is so deeply lobed that it resembles a ghastly, hairy, three-fingered claw or dark glove.

(5) ASPHODEL. The flowers of the dead grow in the Greek sunlight. There are eighteen species in the genus *Asphodelus* distributed through the Mediterranean and five species that grow east into the Himalayas. There are also nineteen species in the related genus, *Asphodeline*, and they have a similar distribution. Both *Asphodelus* and *Asphodeline* species are lilylike wildflowers commonly called asphodels. Botanists place both genera in the family Asphodelaceae, and they are distant cousins of edible asparagus.

Many modern Europeans find asphodel species attractive and grow yellow *Asphodeline lutea* in their gardens. Why did ancient Greeks and Romans regard them as death flowers? Robert Graves insisted that the earliest people to settle the Mediterranean ate the edible bulbs and starchy roots of *Asphodelus* and *Asphodeline*. These plants were gathered as emergency or famine foods; indeed, some Bedouin tribes still gather and eat *Asphodelus fistulosus*. Graves reasoned that once an old, wild food is abandoned by a culture in favor of more nutritious and easily prepared crops, it becomes food for ghosts. Ancestral spirits are always traditional and conservative, continuing to eat the same foods they foraged for in life.

Hellmut Baumann put a different spin on the presence of asphodels in hell. Like Graves, he acknowledged that their roots were mashed and mixed with figs only when ancient communities were on the brink of starvation. In pre-Christian Greece, asphodels were regarded as "a frugal meal to the dead." Baumann departed from Graves's explanation after he observed goats and sheep avoiding asphodels in meadows. When stony Greek fields are overgrazed, asphodels are the only plants that thrive and flourish. As phantoms can no longer plow, herd, or farm, they inherit weed-choked, fallow pastures for all of eternity.

(6) TAGES. Mexican marigolds (*Tagetes erecta*) are such cheerful annuals of summer window boxes and autumn borders it is astonishing that Linnaeus named the genus after an Etruscan underworld god. Domesticated by inhabitants of Mexico and Guatemala, long before conquistadors brought the seeds to Europe, marigolds were death flowers. The Aztecs used them in rituals of human sacrifice. In modern Mexico some graves are strewn with marigolds on the Day of the Dead. Mayan descendants, living in the mountains of Guatemala, left trails of marigold petals from the graveyard to their houses when I visited Chichicastenango back in 1976. A marigold trail allowed the spirit of a loved one to find its way back to the nether-world after enjoying the hospitality of the living.

Although the flowers are attractive, the leaf glands give marigold plants a dis-agreeable, (perhaps charnel-like) smell. Seeds sprout quickly and easily in sunny, plowed beds. Obviously, Linnaeus did not want to attempt to Latinize the tongue-twisting names of Mexican deities like Xochiquetzal, the goddess of flowers (represented by the marigold). The obscure Etruscan Tages would do. There are at least fifty wild species in the genus *Tagetes*, native to the subtropical–tropical Americas and Africa. They belong to the daisy family (Asteraceae). Traditional cultures use various species as sources of yellow dyes, medicines, and pesticides. Growing marigolds between rows of potatoes may protect root vegetables from attacks by eelworms (nematodes). Tages still aids humanity on agricultural soil.

4.8 THE PALACE OF OLYMPUS

Zeus continued to celebrate his victory by constructing a heavenly palace suspended above Mount Olympus (1) in Greece. The banquet hall held space sufficient to seat twelve deities. The members of this dodekatheon (2) were all siblings and/or children of Zeus, and only they were permitted to vote in affairs determining the rule of nature and mankind. The dode-katheon spent most of their time at a perpetual feast. The food of the gods (3) was called ambrosia (4), and they drank nectar (5), which kept them youthful, strong, and beautiful.

Botany

(1) OLYMPUS. *Olymposciadium caspitosum* is a species in the celery family (Apiaceae) native to Turkey and Greece (the country of Mount Olympus). *Olymposciadium* means the parasol of Olympus. Most members of the celery family produce a flowering stalk in which the smaller branches resemble the spokes of an umbrella. Do the gods sit under parasols when they admire the view from their heavenly terraces? *Olymposciadium caspitosum* is still used to make traditional herbal teas, and there is some discussion of farming it as a novel source of aromatic oils.

(2) DODEKATHEON. The genus *Dodecatheon* consists of fourteen species of perennial wildflowers that Americans know as shooting stars. British horticulturists often call them American cowslips. One species is found in Siberia, but all the rest are unique to North America. They are members of the primrose family (Primulaceae) and flower in early spring. Selective breeding produced some forms hardy in shady gardens. The tinted flowers nod on their stalks, and the petals curve backward, giving them the appearance of comets or falling stars. Like all members of the primrose family, *Dodecatheon* species produce floral organs in whorls of five, not six or twelve. Linnaeus's name for this genus looks inappropriate until we consider what true primroses meant to Greek culture.

The ancient Greeks believed that their native oxlip (*Primula elatior*) was a cure-all. Because it conquered every ailment, the plant must have enjoyed the approval of each of the twelve Olympians. Consequently, root collectors (the rhizotomi) called the oxlip the dodekatheon. The oldest herbals and treatises on medicinal plants always referred to oxlips, primroses, and cowslips as primulas (the first ones of spring). Linnaeus had to follow his own rules, and he named the primrose genus *Primula*. He then transferred the name *Dodecatheon* to the shooting stars to establish that these North American flowers were close relatives of Grecian oxlips, sharing similar flower, stem, and leaf characteristics.

(3) FOOD OF THE GODS. *Theobroma* (food of the gods) is a tropical American genus of twenty species of large bushes and small trees placed in the cola nut family (Sterculiaceae). It contains the cocoa bush of commerce, *Theobroma cacao*. Surely the genus that gives us commercial chocolate could not have a more appropriate name. Although Christopher Columbus recorded the natives of Nicaragua drinking cocoa, it was the Spanish conquistador, Hernán Cortés, who brought the drink from Aztec Mexico back to Europe. The Aztecs, in particular, regarded it as a gift from their deity, the plumed serpent Quetzalcoatl. Therefore, Linnaeus may not have been referring to the Greco-Roman pantheon when he named it food of the gods.

The woody pod of a cacao bush yields twenty to sixty seeds packed in a fragrant pulp. The familiar smells and flavors of chocolate develop only after the seeds are fermented, cleaned of pulp, and roasted for up to seventy minutes at 212 to 248 degrees Fahrenheit. Cocoa butter and chocolate liquor are extracted from the processed embryo inside each seed. Both the embryo and the shell of the cacao seed produce minute quantities of caffeine and its sister molecule, theobromine (literally, food of the gods' alkaloid). Theobromine stimulates the human body much like caffeine. It relaxes smooth muscles in the bronchial system, making it easier to take deep breaths, inducing a sense of alertness and twitchy or restless activity. One thing is certain. Although Linnaeus drank chocolate and probably enjoyed chocolate-flavored cakes or sauces, he never ate a chocolate bar or molded bon-bon in his life. Recipes for solid chocolate candies were not marketed until 1847. Chocolate liquor, even when sweetened with sugar, refuses to hold its shape unless it is thickened with extra cocoa butter and/or condensed milk.

(4) AMBROSIA. Naming the genus of inedible ragweeds, hogbrakes, and bursage bushes after the food of the gods sounds like a cruel joke. Linnaeus was probably acknowledging those ancient herbals that recommended using the Mediterranean species, *A. maritima*, in medicinal liqueurs to treat upset stomachs (dyspepsia). Indeed, some modern Egyptians still believe that *Ambrosia* preparations soothe kidney ailments. Unfortunately, recent tests show that the old claims that *Ambrosia* tinctures in water kill eggs of liver flukes and larvae of malaria-carrying mosquitoes are largely ineffective.

There are approximately twenty-four species in the genus *Ambrosia* distributed in North and South America, but only one species, *A. maritima*, grows wild from the Mediterranean through Eurasia. They belong to the daisy family (Asteraceae). The herbaceous, annual species are the much-despised ragweeds, a primary source of pollen-based allergies. Unlike most members of the daisy family, *Ambrosia* species are wind-pollinated, and the pollen grains swell up and rupture when they become immersed in the fluids of our tear ducts, nostrils, sinuses, and lungs. This causes symptoms from mild hay fever to life-threatening asthmatic attacks, depending on the sensitivity of the individual. You cannot escape ragweed by avoiding the dry countryside, as European *A. maritima* is now an invasive weed in North America. It grows happily in cracked pavement or waste places in almost all cities and suburbs, spewing pollen during warm months.

(5) NECTAR. The Roman poet Virgil was the first to refer to sweet plant secretions as nectar. Until the invention and use of magnifying lenses by the early seventeenth century, most Europeans believed that heavenly droplets fell into waiting flowers where they ripened and sweetened until harvested by honeybees. That is why Pliny the Elder called honey "the saliva of the stars."

We now understand that watery liquids containing dilute amounts of sugar, amino acids, and vitamins are secreted by specialized glands located inside many flowers and/or on the surfaces of some leaves and stems. These glands are called nectaries. One or more "veins" of sugar-transporting tissue, known as phloem, are usually located directly below each nectary gland, supplying the nutrients consumed by visiting animal pollinators. Nectar secretions are usually restricted to narrow niches on the floor of the flower, at the base of a long floral throat, or inside a hollow petal sac or spur. How do day-flying bees, butterflies, flies, and certain birds find the fluid hidden in the blossom? Animals with color vision follow the contrasting patterns of speckles, streaks, or bulls-eyes advertising the location of the liquid reward. Botanists call these colorful patterns nectar guides. Some petals wear ultraviolet reflecting pigments, invisible to the human eye. Humans cannot see into the UV range, and we miss a lot of natural designs on white or yellow petals.

Botanists are often impressed by the sheer amount of nectar found in some flowers, as well as where the nectar glands are located in the flower. In the case of the genus *Nectaroscodum* (garlic nectar plant), examine the nodding, brownish flowers and note the disproportionately large, clear droplets inside the bell-shaped cups. There are only two species of *Nectaroscodum* distributed from southeastern Europe to western Asia. They are members of the onion family (Alliaceae) and are available in many bulb catalogs. The genus *Nectandra* means nectar-man. As in so many members of the bay laurel family (Lauraceae), the male pollen-making organs (stamens) in *Nectandra* flowers secrete the divine drink for bees and flies. There are more than a hundred species of *Nectandra* scattered through the forests of the tropical Americas. They are often called silverball trees, carunjes, canelas dura (hardwood cinnamons), and purchury bean trees.

4.9 BATTLES ON OLYMPUS

Now it was Zeus's turn to be hated by Gaia. She loathed him because the new king of the gods sent her Titan sons and grandsons into the underworld for eternity. Gaia gave birth to the twenty-four huge gigantes (1) who were human to the waist but had the legs and tails of dragons. They stormed Olympus when they were full grown. Fortunately, Zeus was forewarned of this plot, thanks to a prophecy by his sister, Hera. She also predicted that the monsters would be defeated with the aid of a magical herb. Zeus commanded that the sun and moon stop shining. He descended to earth and procured the plant in darkness so Mother Earth never saw him. When the gigantes attacked, the gods were prepared, and they destroyed the invaders.

Gaia's second and final attempt to depose the Olympians came with the birth of her last son, the winged monster Typhon (2). His body was made of entwined snakes, and he had the giant head of a fire-breathing ass. The gods were so terrified that they fled Olympus and hid in Egypt, transforming themselves into various animals so their enemy would never find them. Zeus finally defeated Typhon by crushing him under Mount Aetna in Sicily. The smoke issuing from its volcanic cone is all that remains of the monster's foul breath. Now unopposed, Zeus spared or ignored Typhon's mate, Echidna (3). Half giant nymph and half serpent, she slithered off to give birth to a new generation of destructive beasts (see §6.6 and §6.8). Some deities employed these monsters as servants or exploited these vicious creatures as challenging adversaries for their half-mortal sons.

Botany

(1) GIGANTES. Botanists give the names *gigantes* and *giganteum* to species that are unusually taller than their closest relatives. *Allium giganteum* is the giant, ornamental onion of spring bulb gardens. *Carnegia gigantes* is the much-admired giant saguaro cactus. Sometimes the word is modified to apply to an oversized part of the plant, so *giganthes* (giant flowers) refers to species with atypically large blooms.

Gigantochloa (giant grass) is a genus of approximately thirteen species distributed through the islands of Indonesia and Malaysia. They are all giant bamboos in the grass family (Poaceae). In early stages of growth some species provide us with edible bamboo shoots. In contrast, mature stems may reach more than sixty feet in length and be greater than a foot in diameter. In Indonesia, these giant stems provide people with traditional building materials and water pipes.

(2) TYPHON. The Austrian botanist Heinrich Wilhelm Schott (1794–1865) was the reigning expert on the classification of new members of the jack-in-the-pulpit family (Araceae), inventing names for thirty-seven new genera (a record for taxonomists working on this family). Schott is the author of the genera *Typhonium*, *Typhonodorum*, and *Echidnium* (now a synonym for *Dracontium*, see §6.8). It is obvious he enjoyed his classical education and that he retained a healthy sense of humor when adding new genera to the Araceae.

Most species in this family have small, bumpy flowers arranged along a fleshy stalk called the spadix. Sterile buds confined to the tip of the spadix are odor makers, and this portion of the blooming stalk often resembles an undeveloped ear of corn, a porcupine's quill, or a scaly snake's tail. The spadix is usually enfolded in or hooded by a larger, inflated leaf known as a spathe. Spathe leaves comes in different colors, from white-greenish and yellow to lurid shades of maroon and rusty red. Spathe shapes and colors have been compared to the hoods of cobras, donkey ears, dog's heads, warrior's shields, and nun's habits. The flowers are often pollinated by dung beetles, carrion flies, or fungus gnats and may emit nauseating stinks in full bloom, as their odor molecules are often based on ammonia and methane "building blocks."

Schott obviously felt that such monstrous flowering stalks should be named after monsters. He gave us the genus *Typhonium* (the lesser Typhon). It contains thirty species of shade-loving plants found from southern China to northern, coastal Australia. In bloom, the spathe and spadix of *Typhonium* species resemble the lower jaw of an ugly creature sticking out its narrow tongue. A new *Typhonium* was found recently in northeastern Australia, but it still lacks a species name. The new plants are known from only four threatened locations. Local naturalists call them "stinky lilies."

Typhonodorum means "smelling horribly like Typhon." We are left to wonder whether Schott was honoring or insulting the great John Lindley when he named the solitary species *Typhonodorum lindeleyanum*. The huge plant is found only in Madagascar and nearby islands. Known as the mangibo, it is an aquatic tree, monstrously large (like its namesake) compared to most other members of the jack-in-the-pulpit family. An important component of Madagascar mangrove forests and river vegetation (rheophytes), the mangibo produces a gross, column-shaped trunk like a banana or palm.

(3) ECHIDNA. In contrast, *Echidnopsis* (Echidna's branch) belongs to the milkweed family (Asclepiadaceae), and an estimated thirty species are distributed from east Africa through the Arabian Peninsula. Many members of the milkweed family are tough, succulent plants in dry regions of Africa. *Echidnopsis* species have long, often leafless, but turgid stems frequently armed with little prickles. They grow by trailing along the ground like the tail of mythology's snake woman. Such plants are prized by the sort of people who enjoy collecting and growing other Old World succulents in the milkweed family such as the closely related starfish flowers (*Stapelia*).

4.10 ZEUS AND THE FIRST WOMAN

Zeus was uninterested in the mortals made by his mother and grandmother. He wanted his own human race to worship him and his family. The king of the gods commissioned two remaining Titans, Prometheus (1) and Epimetheus, to make living men out of clay. Prometheus soon preferred his creations to his patron. To benefit humankind, Prometheus played two devastating tricks on Zeus. He fooled the Olympian monarch into selecting the fat, bones, and offal of every animal sacrificed to the gods, so humans always kept the best cuts of meat. Zeus was so angry he tried to spite Prometheus by issuing a divine imperative that "man must eat his meat raw." What did Prometheus do in response? To give humans physical comfort and warm food, the Titan stole fire from the sun chariot. Prometheus hid the coals in the hollow stalk of a giant fennel (*Ferula communis*) (2) and carried it down from Olympus.

As punishment, Zeus's servants chained Prometheus to a rock or pillar high in the Caucasian Mountains, and a giant vulture came every day to rip out the Titan's liver. The king of the gods took revenge on his all-male race of men for accepting stolen fire from heaven. Zeus fashioned a female image in clay, and the four winds breathed life into her. She became the first mortal woman. The other gods delighted in giving her beauty, grace, fine clothes, cunning, and other talents. When she acquired all their divine gifts (*pan* = all; *dora* = accomplishments) the gods named this first mortal woman Pandora (3).

Pandora was given to Epimetheus, and he married her, despite the prophetic warnings of his brother, Prometheus. To show his generosity, Zeus gave Pandora a pretty box as a wedding gift. "Don't ever open it," said the king of the gods. Of course, one of the goddesses gave Pandora curiosity. In due course, this first woman lifted the lid, and all the spirits of plagues and woes escaped. The spirit of Hope remained in the box, but some say she only stayed with humankind to prevent future generations from committing suicide and ending the divine punishment on our race much too soon.

Botany

(1) PROMETHEUS. *Prometheum* is a genus of two to six species of small, colonial herbs. Like most members of the stonecrop family (Crassulaceae), *Prometheum* species survive drought by storing water within succulent clasping leaves. They are relatives of the jovibarba plants discussed in §4.3. *Prometheum* plants prefer to grow between the chinks of old garden walls. Their roots and creeping stems invade stony crevices until they are well attached to a boulder, just as poor Prometheus was chained to his rocky mountaintop.

(2) GIANT FENNEL. It surprises people to learn that giant fennel exists. Baumann insisted that dead, naturally hollow, flowering stalks of *Ferula communis* have an ancient and honorable history of transporting coals to start new fires. In fact, there are more than 172 *Ferula* species distributed from the Mediterranean basin east through Afghanistan. These herbs belong to the celery family (Apiaceae), and their stems and roots yield both edible resins and true gums. Sold as asafetida and galbanum, they continue to flavor Worcestershire sauce. The gum is also a traditional remedy for flatulence and cramps. When herbalists called it silphion or silphium, it was used as a contraceptive and aphrodisiac. The orgiastic wine god (see §5.6 and §5.7) was often depicted holding a flowering stalk of *Ferula* in his hand.

(3) PANDORA. The flowers of bower vine (*Pandorea jasminoides*) are unusually beautiful, like the first mortal woman. Tropical gardens often display their large pink-magenta trumpets. However, if the flower is pollinated, a large pod develops,

crammed with many seeds. Each seed wears glider wings. When the ripe pod splits open, spontaneously the seeds flutter away. One botanist compared this simple act of seed dispersal to Pandora's opening the lid of her box and freeing myriads of malevolent spirits.

Pandorea is a genus of six species of woody vines distributed from the Indo-Malaysian archipelago south through New Caledonia and Australia. It is one of the few genera in the catalpa tree family (Bignoniaceae) native to the Old World tropics. Most other members of this family are restricted to the New World tropics. Some native Australians (kooris) call *Pandorea* species wonga vines. The vines provide them with lengths of narrow, flexible wood that can be tempered in a fire to make spears for warfare or hunting.

CHAPTER 5

☙ § ❧

The Gods of Olympus

So weeps the wounded balsam: so
The holy frankincense doth flow.
The brotherless Heliades
Melt in such amber tears as these.
I in a golden vial will
Keep these two crystal tears, and fill
It till it do o'erflow with mine;
Then place it in Diana's shrine.

—ANDREW MARVELL,
  "The Nymph Complaining for the
  Death of Her Fawn"

5.1 DIVINE MESSENGERS

With mortals confined to earth, and many gods living in the sea or the under-world, Zeus needed dependable messengers to carry his proclamations. His first herald was Iris (1), winged daughter of a Titan and a sea nymph. She used the rainbow to run from heaven to earth. His second messenger was his own son Hermes (2) (Roman, Mercury) (3). The boy's mother was Maia (4), one of the many daughters of Atlas. The month of May is named in her honor. Hermes was an unusually precocious baby. Within twenty-four hours of his birth he made a lyre out of a tortoise shell, stole his half-brother's cattle, invented winged sandals, and learned to make fire by rub-bing two sticks together. If he was this fast and clever, thought Zeus, he would make a superior messenger. Athletes, heralds, travelers, merchants, orators, and thieves all thought of Hermes as their patron.

Botany

(1) IRIS. The genus *Iris* is aptly named for the obedient and glittering messenger goddess of Greek and Roman poetry. Consisting of nearly three hundred species, taxonomists attempt to make it easier to identify *Iris* species by subdividing the genus into "sections" according to consistent differences in roots, underground stems, leaf, and floral characteristics. Distributed through much of the northern

9. With apologies to Botticelli, we see Aphrodite rising out of the venus's flytrap (*Dionaea muscipula*). She carries flowers of the butterfly mariposa (*Calochortus venustus*). In the upper right-hand corner a cupid glides down to offer her blossoms of *Paphiopedilum* orchids. Illustration by John Myers.

hemisphere, *Iris* species show so much color variation that the genus duplicates all the hues in a rainbow. In fact, some iris flowers produce colors that you cannot find in white light refracted by raindrop prisms.

For example, we have all seen wild and domesticated iris flowers with silvery white petals. In contrast, fewer gardeners are familiar with the forty, or more, *Iris* species placed in the section Oncocylus. They are all wildflowers of seasonally dry regions or true deserts from Turkey south through the Middle East. It is typical for "Onc" flowers to display veins and blotches so dark they appear black or brown to the human eye. They are difficult to grow, and the few, lucky horticulturists who succeed compare the flowers to mourning silks. Curiously, red and orange are rare colors in this genus. Only the copper iris (*I. fulva*) of U.S. southern swamps displays these hues. This is also the only *Iris* species pollinated by hummingbirds, which learn to follow red-orange signals to obtain the richest nectar rewards. The copper iris is easily hybridized, and most commercial breeds of Louisiana irises with reddish petals derive from *I. fulva*.

Iris, in turn, gives its name to the family Iridaceae, with more than eighteen hundred species worldwide. Although we think of irises as plants of boggy soils in northern zones, the center of diversity for the whole family is in southern Africa. Iridaceae provides us with many garden bulbs, including *Crocus, Freesia, Gladiolus,* and *Tigridia*. Once again, wildflowers in the family offer all colors of the rainbow, but if you find iris flowers too deficient in scarlet pigments, consider growing *Crocosmia* or *Tritonia*, as red-orange flowers are the rule, not the exception.

Historical records and archaeological evidence suggest an ancient association between native *Iris* plants and the most complex civilizations of the Mediterranean basin. The arching blossoms of purple and bluish irises were associated with the early art and religious beliefs of Greece, Egyptian dynasties, and Minoan Crete. For example, irises were planted on the graves of Greek women. Stylized motifs of iris flowers are found in some frescoes and on other artifacts excavated at the Knossos sites on Crete. Pieces of wall decorations resembling iris flowers survive from the reign of the Pharaoh Thutmosis III (1479–1425 B.C.E.). Moving from the sublime to the ridiculous, a Viennese museum in 2003 released a translation of a prescription written on a smudged piece of Egyptian papyrus. The artifact was dated back to the fourth century C.E. Written in Greek (once the preferred language of Egyptian physicians), it called for a pounded mixture of dried iris flowers, rock salt, mint, and black pepper to clean and whiten teeth.

(2) HERMES. *Hermodactylus* (fingers of Hermes) consists of only one European species, *H. tuberosa,* and it also belongs to the iris family (Iridaceae). The genus name refers to the modified, jointed bulbs (corms) that reminded the British horticulturist Philip Miller (1691–1771) of fingers. Hermes, after all, is the light-fingered

god of pickpockets and merchants (who deal with dubious weights and measures). Undoubtedly, the taxonomist wanted to show that *Hermodactylus* was closely related to the genus *Iris*, so he coined a name that would remind us that Olympus had two divine messengers. As Philip Miller was both a commercial florist and gardener at the Chelsea Physic Garden, it is likely he planted some of the first corms of *H. tuberosa* to bloom in England.

Bulb catalogs sell this species as widow's iris, because the flower color contrasts green bands with tips so dark they appear black, like a woman in mourning. They bloom in spring, even on chilly days, and have a nice, sweet fragrance best appreciated by cutting their stalks for vases in warm rooms. Enjoy this charming genus name while you can, as it is headed for synonymy. Molecular studies confirm older analyses of plant anatomy insisting that *Hermodactylus* is just another small, bulbous *Iris* species from rocky Mediterranean soils.

(3) MERCURY. Two explanations account for the derivation of the genus *Mercurialis*. the first is that Linnaeus found a Latin reference to a plant named after the god Mercury in the writings of Cato. A second version is that *Mercurialis* honors the Italian doctor Hieronymus Mercurialis (1530–1606), who recommended various herbal treatments for athletes. As we now know, Linnaeus was quite capable of naming the same plant after two different sources, and the god Mercury is a patron of athletes.

In either case, the eight or so *Mercurialis* species grow from Mediterranean Europe to Thailand and are placed in the spurge family (Euphorbiaceae). They have a dubious history in herbals for treating a number of unrelated illnesses. Dog's mercury (*M. perennis*) was once cultivated as a source of dyes. Several species of Mercury plants escaped from cultivation long ago and are now regarded as annoying garden weeds in Europe and the United States.

(4) MAIA. *Maianthemum* (flowering in Maia's month) is a small genus of three wildflower species associated with cool woodlands in the northern hemisphere. They bloom by May, and American wildflower books still call them mayflower or wild lily-of-the-valley. One legend says that after their first, terrible winter at Plymouth Rock, surviving pilgrims found forest floors filled with *M. canadense* in spring. Here was a divine sign that the Puritans were meant to stay. Mayflowers plants are now placed in the lily-of-the-valley family (Convallariaceae).

5.2 ZEUS AND HIS SISTERS

Zeus married his fellow conspirator Metis (the nymph who concocted the potion that made Cronus vomit). She became pregnant with a new goddess, but Gaia prophesied spitefully that if Metis ever conceived a god, that boy would depose his father. Zeus pretended he wanted to play. He suggested a

contest of shape-changing with Metis. When she turned into a fly, he swallowed her and no one saw her again. After Metis "vanished," Zeus considered consorting with his three sisters. Because Hestia (Roman, Vesta) (1) tended the sacred hearth on Olympus, he allowed her to remain a virgin in perpetuity. Demeter (Roman, Ceres) (2) attended to the cycle of crops, so he fertilized her and they had a girl, Persephone.

Although Zeus always considered Persephone his most beautiful daughter, he betrothed her to dour Hades without Demeter's knowledge. One day, as Persephone and her friends picked flowers in a Sicilian meadow, her uncle claimed her. Some say he created the first poet's narcissus (*Narcissus poeticus*) to lure her to the exact spot where his chariot burst from the earth. When Demeter learned of the abduction, earth's vegetation withered and starvation came to the new race of men. The Olympian deities were in danger of losing all their worshipers. Persephone starved herself during her stay in Hades's palace. She ate only a few seeds from a single pomegranate (*Punica granatum*).

Rhea, who you will remember was the mother of Demeter, Zeus, and Hades, agreed to act as a mediator in the dispute. Thanks to her forceful persuasion, the gods agreed that Persephone would return to Demeter annually but she must also reign in Hades's palace for one month each year for each seed eaten. When Persephone returned to hell, Demeter imposed winter on the earth, but this time she taught humans how to preserve crops against lean times. Demeter also instituted religious mysteries at Eleusis (3) near Athens, where Greeks were initiated into the service of mother and daughter. Hades's concubine Menthe (4) refused to welcome Persephone as her rightful queen. Persephone, now resigned to the marriage, disposed of Menthe by trampling her underfoot until the nymph turned into mint, the herb of hospitality.

Botany

(1) VESTA. Vesta's virtue is never in doubt. Like the color white, this goddess is an old symbol of purity in European culture. Species named *vestae* or *vestalis* almost always bear white flowers. For example, *Calochortus vestae* (*Calochortus* means "beautiful grass") is a coastal mariposa lily found only in California. The three broad petals have pure white tips, graduating into red and yellow patterns at their bases.

Vesta's virtue carries over to her historical priestesses. Laelia is the name of one of ancient Rome's vestal virgins. John Lindley erected the orchid genus *Laelia* as an honorific. Taxonomists currently recognize about fifty *Laelia* species distributed through the tropical Americas. These plants colonize tree branches or rocks.

Undoubtedly, John Lindley was most familiar with a common, lowland species (*L. rubescens*) from Mexico to Guatemala. It is a hardy epiphyte of seasonally dry forests. The tough plants survived long voyages to Europe, surprising their new owners with sprays of many flowers with delicate white petal tips.

(2) CERES. When a species is named *cerealis*, it honors Ceres as goddess of agriculture. She persuaded humans to grow edible grains. Because the grass family (Poaceae) gives us most of our edible grains, and forage for livestock as well, a finger millet has been named *Eleusine cerealis* (see the next entry). Tef is a traditional grain of Ethiopian cuisine derived from a domesticated species of bluegrass (*Poa cerealis*). The seeds are harvested, made into a sourdough, and cooked into a unique bubble-filled breadstuff with a texture between that of a pancake and a thick tortilla. Some taxonomists prefer to give this grass the scientific name of *Egragrostis tef*.

(3) ELEUSIS. Barley, wheat, and spelt have such old names in Latin and Greek that taxonomists could not justify naming them after the center of worship of the two grain goddesses. The traditional millets of African cultures, however, were largely unknown to Greco-Roman civilizations and could be named after the famous site of religious mysteries. The genus *Eleusine* consists of nine species of tropical grasses (Poaceae) found wild in Africa and South America. I have mentioned *E. cerealis* just above, but *Eleusine coracana* has been in domestication for more than three thousand years. Africans call it ragi or kurakkan. Goose grass (*E. indica*) escaped from cultivation and is now a common weed of lawns and gardens in much of the northern hemisphere.

(4) MENTHE. *Mentha* is the genus name of the plants that Greeks and Romans used extensively to flavor their food and drink and to scent their perfumes. Spearmint (*M. ×spicata*) is a hybrid between *M. longifolia* (horse mint) and *M. suaveolens* (apple mint). Peppermint (*M. ×piperita*) is a double hybrid between spearmint and water mint (*M. aquatica*). Most of the gourmet mints, including Scotch, black, and pineapple are also of hybrid origin. Pennyroyal (*M. pulgeium*) is an important exception. It grows as a good, wild species from Mediterranean Europe through Asia Minor. Although this herb has a long, respectable history of scenting soaps and cosmetics, its use as a tea taken to effect miscarriages may be far older. All mints belong to the mint or dead nettle family (Lamiaceae). About twenty-five species are found naturally in Eurasia and northern Africa, but most are so popular they now are grown around the world.

Marcel Detienne, the author of *The Gardens of Adonis*, interprets the myth of Mentha as the accepted career of a concubine in classical Greek culture. Mistresses were luxury items of powerful men but these women could not bear fruit (legitimate children). Persephone, the legal wife, symbolizes seeds in the soil that yield the next life-sustaining generation. Mentha cannot stand up to her and is turned

into a perfume plant devoid of edible fruits. I think Detienne misses the irony in the story. Myths, poems, and plays suggest Greeks and Romans regarded mint as a spice of hospitality. Fresh leaves might be rubbed on furniture to scent a room or used to flavor various dishes including wedding cake. In one version of the myth, Demeter searches for her daughter, grows thirsty, and is welcomed by a king's servants who refresh the goddess with a drink of barley water flavored with mint. In contrast, Mentha refuses hospitality to Persephone. The nymph's punishment is to become the herb of hospitality.

5.3 THE WEDDING OF ZEUS AND HERA

Zeus decided that his third sister, Hera (Roman, Juno) (1), would marry him and become the queen of Olympus. Of all the goddesses, she had the most beautiful figure. Hera augmented her beauty by selecting the peacock as her sacred bird. There was no courtship. Hera was the proudest of Zeus's sisters, and she rejected his proposal with obvious disdain. Zeus made it rain outside Hera's door and then transformed himself into a cuckoo. His pathetic chirps brought Hera to his aid. She picked up the cold, wet bird and warmed it between her breasts. Zeus regained his godly shape and violated his sister. Hera could no longer decline her brother's proposal without losing her reputation.

The king of Olympus decreed that all of Creation must attend their wedding and bring gifts. The nymph Chelone (2) refused to attend. She even had the audacity to mock the bride and groom. The nymph was destined to suffer a fate so humiliating it would be recorded in one of Aesop's fables. The immortal wedding guests brought splendid presents. Hera was particularly delighted with the tree she received from her grandmother, Gaia. It bore golden apples. Hera planted it in her private garden, on some distant mountain, far to the west. She sent the three daughters of Atlas and Hesperis, the Hesperides (3), to guard the fruit and maintain the garden. These Hesperides—Aegle (4), Hespere, and Erytheis—were attractive but untrustworthy, and they started stealing the golden fruit. Hera sent the multiheaded snake, Ladon (a son of Echidna), to coil around the tree, providing the ultimate protection.

Following the wedding, Zeus and Hera retired to the island of Samos for a three-hundred-year honeymoon. They had several children, including Ares (god of war), Eris (a personification of strife or discord), Eileithyia (goddess of childbirth), Hephaestus (god of smiths), and the goddess of youth, Hebe (5). Some say that Zeus was not Hebe's father. Hera became pregnant after eating a lettuce (*Lactuca sativa*).

Zeus summoned Chelone to Olympus the day after he and his queen returned from Samos. "Why did you miss my wedding?" he thundered. Chelone resorted to a sentimental excuse. "Home is dear. Home is best," she replied in the tone one uses to silence an impatient child. Zeus turned her into a turtle. Chelone lost her voice and was forced to carry her home on her back.

Botany

(1) JUNO. We know of two attempts to name a genus in the iris family (Iridaceae) after the wife of Roman Jupiter. In Ovid's *Metamorphoses,* Juno always prefers Iris (see §5.1), as her messenger, so the association between the goddess Juno and the iris family is entirely appropriate. Two taxonomists named two genera *Juno* and *Junopsis,* but the names did not endure. Studies showed that they were nothing more than species best placed in the old genus *Iris.* However, plant breeders and catalogs continue to refer to fifty-five species of Juno irises. Each "Juno" has a bulb that wears a papery wrapper (tunic) and produces several, fleshy roots. The leaves on each stem are channeled and stacked on each other, like narrow trays, in two opposite rows. Look for the crest on each of the three, dangling petals (the falls) on each flower. Do they remind you of the feathered crest on the head of Juno's favorite fowl, the peacock?

(2) CHELONE. *Chelone* is a genus of half a dozen species of perennial plants native to North America. These wildflowers belong to the snapdragon family (Scrophulariaceae). They are known as turtleheads, as they reminded Linnaeus of a smooth reptile's head with open jaws. It is as if Zeus froze the nymph in the act of uttering her last word. *Chelone glabra* is the most commonly grown and sold species in this genus. It is often recommended for shady backyards with wet soils. Because the white and pink flowers do not appear until late summer, it adds a most welcome touch of color, as most woodland herbs and bushes bloom in spring.

It is interesting to note that botanists kept the nymph's full name, whereas zoologists classifying reptiles modified the word. *Chelodina* is the genus of freshwater, snake-necked terrapins from Australia and New Guinea. *Chelonia* is the genus of green sea turtles.

(3) HESPERIDES. As mentioned earlier (see §2.9), poets and ancient geographers never agreed on the precise location of the garden of the Hesperides. Was it in Spain, northwestern Africa, or some mysterious island(s) out in the Atlantic Ocean? David Gledhill, of the Bristol University Botanic Garden, wrote that taxonomists used the word *hesperides* to describe some species native to western Spain. I have since examined five books on the regional floras of Spain, though, and failed to find a single species named *hesperides.*

We do know, though, that a much older generation of botanists believed that classical tales of golden apples were evidence of an ancient trade in large citrons (*Citrus medica*) with yellow rinds. Mediterranean civilizations first imported the fruit from India. The use of the citron (*etrog*) in the Jewish festival of Sukkoth is often dated to the period in which the empire of Alexander the Great extended from the Middle East through northern India. Fruits are named and classified according to the construction of ripe tissue layers once the seeds in the ovary reach maturity. Berries are multiseeded, fleshy fruits. Some modified berries also have a thick, aromatic peel (exocarp) and a segmented pulp (mesocarp) composed of little juice sacs. The sacks are "pumped" up by a central core of hollow, fleshy hairs (endocarp). This type of fruit is classified as a hesperidium, and it is unique to a select number of species in the citrus tree family (Rutaceae). The best known, of course, are all the commercial *Citrus* species and hybrids, including citrons, limes, lemons, oranges, grapefruits, and tangerines.

(4) AEGLE. The genus *Aegle* consists of only three species of tropical trees found from western Africa to Malaysia. The genus belongs to the citrus tree family (Rutaceae). Therefore, the berries of *Aegle* species share some important anatomical features in common with commercial oranges, lemons, and other citrus fruits (see above). Both *Aegle* and *Citrus* bear the "golden" apples of the Hesperides. *Aegle marmelos* is the Bengal quince or bael fruit, popular in India. It is associated with the Hindu god, Shiva. Like true citrus fruits, bael pulp flavors cold drinks, fruit ices, and marmalades. Unlike an orange or lemon, a hammer may be needed to break through the hard rind of a bael. Of course, we must expect that golden apples resist cracking.

(5) HEBE. Despite the rather odd myth of Hera's salad-induced pregnancy, the genus *Hebe* is not related to wild or commercial lettuces (*Lactuca*) in the daisy family (Asteraceae). *Hebe* is placed traditionally with snapdragons and turtleheads (*Chelone*) in the Scrophulariaceae (see above). The genus contains nearly seventy-five species of shrubs distributed through the temperate mountains of the southern Pacific (especially New Zealand), with a few in South America. The flowers of *Hebe* species come in many colors—blue, pink, red, and purple—but a large proportion of New Zealand species offer plain white blossoms. This is probably another example of a genus with pale, fragrant flowers named after a beautiful goddess or princess. Hebes are popular as ground covers and alpine shrubs in colder countries of the British Commonwealth. They are not well known in the United States.

Hebe has another meaning in the language of botany. Young creatures, like newly hatched chicks and kittens, as well as the limbs of adolescent boys and girls, are rather downy, so the word *hebe* is added to some genera to indicate that the plant has fuzzy "bits." For example, the genus *Hebecladus* means "downy branch."

5.4 Leto's Children

Following his marriage to Hera, Zeus resumed his conquest of goddesses and nymphs, but he now attempted various disguises to hide his affairs from his official wife. He temporarily transformed himself, along with the Titan woman Leto, into quails and mated in the bushes. The result was a splendid pair of twins, brother and sister. Artemis (1) (Roman, Diana) (2) remained a virgin, like her Aunt Hestia, but she rarely stayed on Olympus. This goddess preferred hunting in forests, and she did not confine her sport to animals. When she dipped her arrowheads in the juice of yew foliage (*Taxus*) (3), she executed impious mortals and nymphs. The Romans believed her father appointed her to drive the moon chariot (see §5.11). Apollo (4) was the most beautiful of Zeus's sons. When not engaged in such pursuits as public debate, medicine, and music, he cultivated an interest in mortals, muses, and nymphs. The Romans believed his father appointed him to drive the sun chariot (§5.11).

The chaste naiad Daphne (5) was most famous for fleeing from Apollo. By the time he caught her, Daphne's father, a river god, transformed her into the first bay laurel (*Laurus nobilis*), but Apollo would not abandon her. The laurel became his sacred tree, and he wore a wreath of bay leaves in times of victory. Few nymphs or princesses, however, could resist Apollo. He had sons by Acacallis (6), Calliope, Cyrene, and Dryope (6), just to name a few, and they all grew up to become talented demigods or cultured rulers. The Romans also insisted that Apollo fathered Janus (7) on an unknown mortal woman. Janus ruled the Kingdom of Latium in Italy. When he died, he was deified as the double-faced god of beginnings and endings. Janus guarded gates, roadways, and doors. That is why the Romans began their year with the month of January.

Botany

(1) Artemis. *Artemisia* is another name Linnaeus plucked from Pliny, the Roman natural historian. The genus consists of more than three hundred species distributed through much of the warmer, drier regions of the northern hemisphere south into parts of South America and Africa. Placed in the daisy family (Asteraceae), the wormwoods, dusty millers, mugworts, commercial tarragon, and American sagebrushes are all *Artemisia* species. As the Mediterranean species have such a long history in folk medicine and witchcraft, it is no surprise that ancient herb collectors (the rhizotomi) put them under the protection of a powerful, often predatory, goddess who ruled the magical moon. However, there is a second explanation for the name. Queen Artemisia of Helicarnassus fought on the side of King Xerxes of

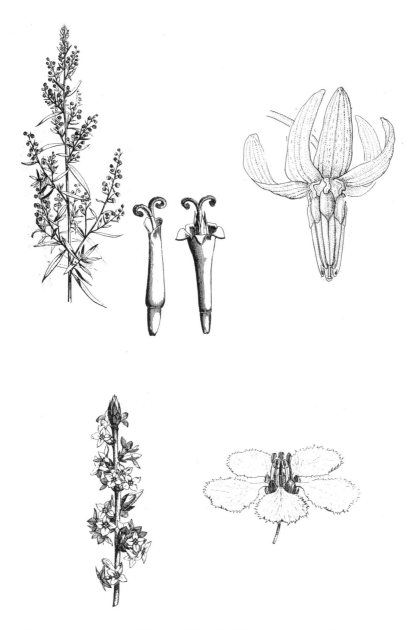

10. Plant genera associated with Leto's children. Top left, a flowering stem of tarragon (*Artemisia dracunculus*) and two much magnified florets of wormwood (*A. absinthium*). Top right, a magnified and dart-shaped flower of an Australian flax lily (*Dianella caerulea*) drawn by John Myers. Bottom left, a flowering twig belonging to the shrub mezereon (*Daphne mezereum*). Bottom right, a normal, bisexual flower produced by a vine in the genus *Janusia*. With the exception of the flax lily, all illustrations came from Baillon's *Histoire Naturelle des Plantes* (1886–1903). Reproduced with the permission of the library at the Missouri Botanical Garden.

Persia in the fifth century B.C.E. The original name of the plant may be associated with this real and powerful female warrior.

The power of these plants cannot be doubted. The Chinese have used *Artemisia annua* since 340 C.E. to combat malaria; it is a source of a parasite-killing molecule known as artemisinin. Europeans put *Artemisia* to another use. When fresh stems of some wormwood species are bruised and soaked in a solution of 85 percent alcohol, they release thujone molecules. Distilled, diluted with more water, and sweetened, the thujone solution becomes the greenish liqueur sold as absinthe. The nineteenth-century French elite believed absinthe sharpened the mind and other appetites. That is why its consumption is associated with Paul Verlaine, Henri de Toulouse-Lautrec, Vincent van Gogh, Charles Baudelaire, and Oscar Wilde (in his Parisian exile). Jurists, criminologists, and politicians believed it produced illusions and severe addictions that fostered frenzied crimes and early deaths. France banned absinthe in 1915, but many other herbal liqueurs remain legal provided they lack *Artemisia*. A glass of Pernod is supposed to replicate the flavor of absinthe.

(2) DIANA. By the second half of the eighteenth century, the French were conducting large-scale scientific expeditions to the southern hemisphere that promoted a "bring-them-back-alive" policy for unusual animals and plants. The first *Dianella* species grown in the Jardin de Roi were mistaken for a new kind of *Gladiolus,* but the two plant groups are not considered close relatives anymore. French gardeners called the exotic wildflower *dianelle de bois* (little Diana of the woods), as they thrived in woodland shade on the Isles de France and Bourbon. All that the French botanist Adrien-Henri Laurent de Jussieu (1797–1853) had to do was formalize this common name as *Dianella* (little Diana). The genus *Dianella* is now placed in the daylily family (Hemerocallidaceae). Why did the plants remind horticulturists of a pagan goddess? Jussieu says nothing on the subject, but let's consider three facts. First, *Dianella* likes the woods, and the goddess Diana hunts in the woods. Second, the nodding flower looks like a tiny arrow or dart. Third, if a flower is pollinated, it produces an unusually shiny, moon-shaped berry (white, blue, or purple), which is easily associated with Diana and her moon chariot.

The genus *Dianella* contains twenty-five lilylike perennial herbs. Their scattered distribution through the southern hemisphere suggests they evolved as "island-hoppers." Different species grow from east Africa to Madagascar and on the islands of the Indian Ocean. Then these wildflowers reappear again through much of the southern Pacific basin (Hawaii, Australia, New Zealand). Because they produce such bright, colorful, and juicy berries, it is reasonable to assume their seeds were transported from island to island in the bellies of hungry, migratory birds.

(3) YEW. Although the link between Artemis and the herbal drink absinthe is comparatively recent and eccentric, the relationship between the goddess and the

yew tree (*Taxus*) is ancient and macabre. For thousands of years, European archers favored yew wood for their bows. In this light, the association between the tree and the goddess of the hunt follows a natural progression. However, both Greeks and Romans knew that the flat, green needles of their Mediterranean yews (*Taxus baccata*) yielded poisons fatal to human beings. Artemis is a vindictive goddess, and Theophrastus insisted that her Grecian temple stood in a yew forest. Baumann notes that the Furies favored yew, as well as ash (see §3.3). Like Artemis, these goddesses also drew poison from yews to punish sinners.

Taxonomists recognize only seven yew species, all native to the northern hemisphere. Modern biochemists confirm that yew leaves, bark, and the interior of their hard seeds contain toxins known as taxanes. Some animals appear immune to taxanes. American hunters insist that deer can graze on yew foliage without ill effect. If you live in the suburbs, you can watch birds gorging on the reddish seeds (they are not true berries) without ever seeing feathered corpses under the shrubs. Perhaps they strip off the red flesh (arils) without ever cracking open the seeds. And there is another side to the story. Yes, Artemis was a ruthless deity, but she also protected women in childbirth and prepubescent girls, and her twin brother, Apollo, was a patron of medicine (see §5.5). Medical research suggests that some taxanes may be useful in combating some human cancers. Taxol, derived from Pacific yew (*T. brevifolia*) is the best studied of these molecules.

(4) APOLLO. *Apollonias barbujana* is the Canary Island laurel tree. It belongs to the bay laurel family (Lauraceae) and is unique to the Canary Islands. Specimens are particularly common on the island of Madeira, where they survive in the humid, lowland, laurel forests with other species in the Lauraceae. Although it is a handsome, strapping tree, suitable for such a god as Apollo, its genus name is an obvious reference to the myth of Daphne transformed into a bay laurel (see next).

(5) DAPHNE. Here we have yet another nymph turned into a plant whose name was beloved by taxonomists. Linnaeus followed the old Latin references and named the genus of commercial bay trees *Laurus*. The name *Daphne* would later serve many other botanists in the world of plant classification. Linnaeus himself used the nymph's name for the genus *Daphne*. It consists of about fifty species of bushes distributed from southern Europe east through China. Like their namesake, they are considered choice possessions, but they resist captivity. Daphnes die quickly if they do not receive precise soil and temperature requirements.

Most daphnes are small shrubs producing thick clusters of pink or white flowers, offering what may be the sweetest scents of any garden plant. Winter daphne (*D. odora*) was particularly favored by the Chinese, as early as the tenth century C.E. It blooms by February in milder climates, filling drab winter gardens with scent. *Daphne* is placed in the gauze tree family (Thymelaeaceae), which also contains a related genus, *Daphnimorpha*, meaning "shaped like Daphne," found only in Japan. The genus *Actinodaphne* (Daphne's wooden beam) returns the nymph to her proper place in the laurel family (Lauraceae). It is a large genus (sixty to seventy species) of tropical Asia and the Indo-Malaysian archipelago. *Adendodaphne, Afrodaphne,* and *Nesodaphne* are now synonyms placed in other genera of the Lauraceae.

Can you guess the identity of *Antidaphne* (Daphne's enemy)? They are two mistletoe species (family Loranthaceae) from South America. Of course they are her enemy. Flowering shrubs, identified as mistletoes, grow as parasites on living branches of host trees and large bushes. Mistletoes weaken trees by penetrating their host's branches and stealing the water conducted up from the roots via the cells in the host tree's sapwood.

(6) ACACALLIS AND DRYOPE. Because Apollo claimed the most beautiful women, some botanists of the nineteenth century named orchids (Orchidaceae) with the most beautiful (or complex) flowers after two of his mistresses. Both have been reduced to synonyms. John Lindley gave us *Acacallis*, but these South American epiphytes are now placed in the genus *Aganisia*. *Dryopeia* was a genus from southern Africa and Madagascar associated with grassy hills and moss beds. All of its species are now placed in the genus *Dispersis*.

(7) JANUS. Adrien-Henri Laurent de Jussieu was also interested in the pitanga or Barbados cherry family (Malphigiaceae). His treatment of this largely New World group of woody plants was published in 1840. Jussieu noted that the flowering stalks of many pitangas terminated in only two, paired flowers. The god Janus had two faces. The genus *Janusia* is characterized by two flowers at the tip of each stalk. There are about a dozen species in the genus, and they prefer to grow on the west coast of the western hemisphere. Their vines are found from the U.S. southwest through Argentina.

Slender janusia (*J. gracilis*) is an attractive vine native to Arizona, but it blooms from April to October, not in January. It produces two kinds of flowers. The normal flowers have glands on their sepals, five yellow petals, and three ovaries in each pistil. The abnormal flowers lack glands, cannot make petals, and have only two ovaries. I have seen some photos in which a normal flower and an abnormal flower pair off on the same stalk. The Romans often depicted Janus with an old bearded face and a young smooth face on the same head. I would bet that Jussieu was aware of this odd iconography when he named the genus.

5.5 APOLLO AND THE GODS OF MEDICINE

Apollo's interest in medicine was replicated in his favorite son, Asclepius (1), son of the princess Coronis. Educated by his father and Chiron, this demigod became the greatest doctor in Greece. When Asclepius started bringing the dead back to life, Hades accused him of robbing his kingdom. Zeus solved the matter by killing Asclepius with a thunderbolt, but Apollo, as god of eloquence, convinced his father to resurrect Asclepius as god of medicine. At the time of his death, Asclepius had a family of his own. His sons became surgeons to the Greek fleet during the Trojan War (see §7.3). The daughters were deified as Hygeia (public health) (2) and the cure-all Panacea (3).

The quarrel between Hades and Asclepius never ended. When Hades suffered an arrow wound, he was healed by the dactyl (see §4.1) Paeonius (4). Intolerant of rivals, Asclepius threatened to kill Paeonius. Hades "protected" his healer by turning him into the first peony (*Paeonia*). Greek and Roman herbalists would not gather peony roots or seeds by day. They believed that if Hades saw them, the underworld god would send a woodpecker to pick out their eyes!

Botany

(1) ASCLEPIUS. When a species is named *asclepiadea, asclepiadum,* or *asclepiadus,* it usually means that herbalists believe some part of the plant has medicinal virtues. Considering the overuse of gentians (see §3.7) in folk remedies, it is no surprise that the European willow gentian is named *Gentiana asclepiadea.* Furthermore, the genus *Asclepias* contains more than 120 species found throughout much of the western hemisphere with the majority distributed from the United States through Mexico. These are the milkweeds of prairies, woodlands, and roadsides.

American tribes found extensive internal and external uses for milkweed medicines. For example, Chippewa healers steeped the root of swamp milkweed (*A. incarnata*) in water and used the solution as a foot soak for weary adults or as a bath for sickly children. They also washed, stewed, and ate the flower buds of common milkweed (*A. syriaca*) to whet weak appetites. European colonists picked up a number of milkweed remedies favored by American tribes long before Linnaeus formalized the genus name in the second half of the eighteenth century. Pleurisy root (*A. tuberosa*) was the preferred name pioneers gave to what we now call orange butterfly weed, so popular in native plant gardens. It was believed to cure various lung ailments (pleurisy), including pneumonia. Viewed as a cure-all in folk medicine it is no wonder Linnaeus named the plants after the divine physician. The chemistry of the white milk (latex) is so complex that it can be made into a rubber substitute. Modern clinical trials continue to test whether some milkweed molecules can be used to treat certain types of cancer.

The genus *Asclepias* gives its name to the family Asclepiadaceae, with almost 3,000 species arranged in 350 genera. Although *Asclepias* is primarily a North American genus, the family is especially diverse in dry, southern Africa where it evolved into a number of succulent forms popular with collectors. Members of this family also grow as vines in wetter regions of Africa and Madagascar or Indonesia and Malaysia. The Madagascar jasmine (*Stephanotis floribunda*) produces such large scented flowers that it is favored in corsages and wedding bouquets. Many gardeners feel their greenhouse is incomplete without a climbing *Hoya*, as their leaves are so shiny and the flowers look as if they have been carved out of wax or ivory.

(2) HYGEIA. Given that the gloxinia family (Gesneriaceae) produces brilliantly colored, tubular and lobed flowers, a few nineteenth-century botanists named some New World genera after minor goddesses (*Napeanthus*, see §3.4) and beautiful princesses (Hippodamia, §6.5). That is the only explanation I can offer for German botanist Johannes von Hanstein's (1822–1880) naming a Chilean wildflower *Hygea barbigera*, back in 1853. Hanstein never explained why he named a new genus after a daughter of Asclepias, god of medicine. *Hygea barbigera* (*barbigera* means there is a beard inside the flower's tube) has no medicinal virtues. It does not even have a common name. The gloxinia family is not closely related to the biochemically sophisticated milkweeds (Aslecpiadaceae), either.

(3) PANACEA. Hanstein's naming of the genus *Hygea* remains inexplicable. In contrast, Linnaeus's earlier decision to give the Greek goddess of all remedies to the ginseng genus (*Panax*) seems obvious. Traditional Chinese medicine regarded ginseng roots as cures for almost everything for millennia (and still does). The half a dozen ginseng species are herbs of deeply shaded forests in temperate North America and eastern Asia. They are camouflaged amid the low, mixed greenery, and a hunter of wild plants has to look for the herb's parasols tipped with little red fruits rising above the woodland floor. Traditionally, ginsengs belong to the ivy family (Araliaceae), but DNA evidence suggests that they are better placed with celery and its relatives (Apiaceae).

(4) PAEONIUS. Hybrids based on Eurasian species of peonies remain garden favorites, but Asclepius's greatest rival "retired from medicine" only recently. For thousands of years, herbalists pounded peony roots or seeds to extract oil used to treat nervous afflictions and violent spasms (including epilepsy). In the first century C.E., Pliny the Elder recommended this extract against nightmares induced by goatish spirits known as fauns. Later, biochemists found a glycoside in the oil and named the molecule paenol. As late as the eighteenth century, English housewives draped peony roots around the necks of infants, believing they prevented convulsions caused by the emergence of first teeth or attacks of whooping cough and rickets. At least one Native American tribe used the leaves of the Californian peony (*P. califonicum*) in a vain attempt to cure tuberculosis contracted from white settlers.

The tree peony (*P. suffruticosa*) is an old symbol of prosperity in Chinese culture and is a pervasive subject for paintings and poetry; its domestication probably predates the Qin Empire (before 200 B.C.E.).

Earlier attempts to place peonies in the buttercup family (Ranunculaceae) were incorrect, and the family, Paeoniaceae, remains distinct. There are about thirty species in the genus *Paeonia*, distributed through temperate Eurasia. Two species with brownish flowers are restricted to the Pacific northwest of the United States (California, Oregon, Idaho). They probably offer evidence of an earlier geological history when western North America was still joined to eastern Asia as part of the northern supercontinent of Laurasia.

5.6 HERA AND HER MORTAL RIVALS

Zeus enjoyed many mortal princesses with, and without, their consent. Hera often ignored the females he visited once and abandoned, but as goddess of marriage, she refused to suffer Pandora's descendants if her husband retained them as mistresses. The Queen of Heaven killed the children that Lamia (1) of Libya had with Zeus. Then she turned this princess into an evil spirit with a monstrous gullet and a serpent's body. Greeks and Romans believed Lamia adopted a beautiful, seductive form before she devoured children or sucked the blood of handsome youths.

In contrast, Hera's destruction of the princess Semele (2) was subtle. When the goddess appeared in the palace as an old friend of the royal family, Semele took her into her confidence. The silly princess bragged that her lover ruled the universe. Cunning Hera replied, "All men are deceivers and will say anything to get what they want, dear. You need proof. Have him visit you as he appears to his wife on Olympus." The next time Zeus appeared in Semele's chamber the princess made an impossible demand. He must show himself to her as he did to Hera. Zeus consented, but mortal Semele could not withstand the heat of heavenly glory. She burst into flames, and Zeus had only time enough to rescue the fetus in her womb, incubating it in his own thigh. Thus, the father of the Olympians gave birth to his own son Dionysus (3).

Zeus gave Dionysus to Princess Ino, Semele's sister. Hera responded by driving Ino's lover mad (see §6.9), and the royal line of the kingdom of Ochromenus collapsed. Only immortal nursemaids would do. Five more daughters of Atlas were pressed into the rearing of Dionysus. These mountain nymphs attempted to hide Dionysus from Hera by dressing him as a girl. Consequently, the god grew up with a taste for flamboyant clothes.

Nevertheless, Zeus was so pleased with the nymphs' selfless devotion to his son that one day he transferred Nyssa (4) and her four sisters to the sky. They became the constellation of the Hyades, controlling when it rained.

Although only a demigod, Dionysus was a prodigy and invented vine culture and wine while still a child. This most pleased his inseparable tutor, the fat, horse-eared Silenus (5). The woodland god remained drunk and drooling because he always carried a brimming cup of wine.

Botany

(1) LAMIA. Linnaeus found an herb named *lamium* in a work of Pliny the Elder. Old Pliny probably had the myth of the child-eating wraith on his mind when he described a flower with pouched petals that resembled a gullet (lamium). Now observe the pale flowers in any of the forty species of the genus *Lamium*. They do look like gaping, hungry maws, but so do so many other flowers in the mint family (Lamiaceae).

Lamium species are Old World herbs distributed from northern Africa into Europe and Asia. They are usually easy to procure, as they are often sold as ground covers for shady gardens. Most wildflower books still call them dead nettles, but don't worry. A true dead nettle lacks stinging hairs (its power to harm is dead). All it can do to frighten you is grow stalks of ghostly flowers.

(2) SEMELE. Like the doomed princess in the myth, many plant and animal species use up all of their adult resources in the act of reproduction. They mate once, often produce many offspring, and then die. Like Semele, they will not survive to see the birth (or germination) of their own children. In the second half of the twentieth century, ecologists and evolutionary biologists coined the term *semelparous* to refer to once-in-a-lifetime breeders. The majority of bedding plants sold as annuals (zinnias, marigolds, and pansies, to mention only a few) are semelparous. Once the plant converts all its growing shoots into flowers, it cannot change back and dies because it cannot make new stems or leaves. However, relatively large plants may be semelparous, as well. This includes the Hawaiian silver sword plants (*Agryroxiphium*) as well as Mexican magueys (*Agave*). The maguey's myth appears below (see §5.7).

In contrast, *Semele androgyna* is the climbing butcher's broom native only to the lowland forests of the Canary Islands. It is classified as a member of the butcher's broom family (Ruscaceae), second cousins to edible asparagus. Kunth obviously enjoyed naming white-flowered, lilylike plants after Greek princesses favored by lusty gods. It is useful to note that *Semele* grows in the same forest as the *Apollonias* tree (see §5.4), so Zeus's mistress shares her island home with her son's half-brother.

The vine has unusually shiny foliage and produces lots of tiny, white, unisexual flowers. Some flowers are males and make only pollen, while the rest are female blossoms and make only seeds. That is why this species was named *androgyna* (males and females live together). The female flowers of *S. androgyna* turn into bright red berries and look splendid next to their shiny, evergreen foliage. Europeans, living in balmier climates, grow climbing butcher's broom to hide blank or crumbling walls. Ironically, *Semele androgyna* is not semelparous, because the same vine makes fresh fruit year after year. This vine's fecundity fails to influence its mortality.

(3) DIONYSUS. The genus *Dionysia* refers to forty-two species of cushion shrubs colonizing rocky crevices on the mountains of Iraq, Iran, and Afghanistan. They belong to the primrose family (Primulaceae). Eduard Fenzl (1808–1879) established the genus in 1843, but it is unclear why he named it after the wine god. Considering the geography of these plants, we note that Dionysus spread his wine cult through Central Asia before returning to Greece (see §5.7). However, the primrose family is, at best, a very distant relation of the grape family (Vitidaceae). One thing is certain: *Dionysia* species are as flamboyant in bloom as their namesake is when he wears women's gowns. The buds of yellow, pink, or purple flowers crowd the tufted twigs of *Dionysia* bushes and bloom en masse. The shrubs look like brilliant floral pillows.

(4) NYSSA. Because the Hyades send rainstorms from heaven, scholars and scientists often confused them with water nymphs (naiads). Consequently, the genus *Nyssa* represents five species of tupelo trees that prefer "wet feet." In North America and China, tupelos are almost always associated with riverbanks and freshwater swamps. Furthermore, tupelo timbers resist rot, and traditional uses for the wood include construction of barrels, wharves, and hollowed-out water pipes. *Nyssa* was once placed in the dogwood family (Cornaceae) but now gives its name to its own family, Nyssaceae.

(5) SILENUS. There are two standard interpretations as to why Linnaeus named the large catchfly genus *Silene* after the drunken tutor of the wine god. First, if you look into the cup of a fresh catchfly flower, you will see large beads of nectar. This is the wine goblet of Silenus. Second, many catchflies wear glistening, glandular hairs on their flowering stalks and they release natural glues. These adaptive secretions slow and reduce attacks by munching pests. Small insects often land on the little glands and become stuck for good. That is why we call these wildflowers catchflies. For once, the drool of an alcoholic is adaptive.

There are more than five hundred species in the genus *Silene* distributed through much of the northern hemisphere, and dozens are native to Greece. We also call them campions and place them in the carnation family (Caryophyllaceae).

5.7 THE DEIFICATION OF DIONYSUS

Hera struck Dionysus with madness when he matured. Always restless, he wandered across the world introducing vineyard culture and the orgiastic cult of wine. His nursemaids and tutor followed him eastward, as did a growing entourage of mortals and lesser divinities. Some kingdoms welcomed the wine cult, whereas others warred with the god's retinue. Lycaste (1), a daughter of Atlas, was wounded during one skirmish, and Dionysus cured her by rubbing her face with white chalk. Recalcitrant monarchs met terrible fates. King Pentheus of Thebes rejected the worship of his cousin Dionysus. When he went out to spy on an orgy, he met with wine-frenzied women. His own crazed mother, Agave (2), mistook him for a wild beast and cut off his head.

Dionysus fell in love with Carya (3), princess of Laconia, but she died before they could marry, and the gods changed her into a walnut tree (*Juglans*). He later found princess Ariadne (4) on the island of Naxos, abandoned by her first love, Theseus. Dionysus married her instead, and the wine god gave the princess an undying crown of flowers at their wedding. When Ariadne died, he threw the crown into the night sky, and it became the corona borealis (5).

With wine established as the sacred drink throughout Greece and Central Asia, Dionysus could enter Olympus. He was the last son of Zeus to join the dodekatheon (see §4.8). He finally met his great-grandmother, Aphrodite, and they had a baby, Priapus. Hera was disgusted and cursed the new god to an eternity of grotesque features and exaggerated genitals. Priapus became a god of garden fertility and always carried pruning tools. His own son, Orchis (6), attempted to rape a priestess of Dionysus, but the women tore him to pieces. Priapus appealed to heaven to resurrect his son, but the Olympians despised Orchis's antics and decreed that only his testicles would live on as a wildflower. It is said that men who eat the plant's root are provoked to shamefully lustful behavior, little better than satyrs (7), the horned, shaggy-legged race of goat men loyal only to Dionysus.

Botany

(1) Lycaste. The next four entries take us to tropical and temperate regions in the western hemisphere. We will begin at higher, tropical elevations before hiking down the slopes of extinct volcanoes and traveling northeast. *Lycaste*, for example, refers to about twenty-five species of orchids (Orchidaceae) found from Mexico to South America. Most prefer higher altitudes, growing on the limbs of mountain trees or on porous volcanic boulders where incoming clouds bathe roots with mist. Their comparatively large flowers remind collectors of waxy tulips. These blossoms dress up in pure white, pastel pinks, and yellows, or they wear mysterious dark blotches. Their sweet and spicy fragrances remind some people of oil of cloves.

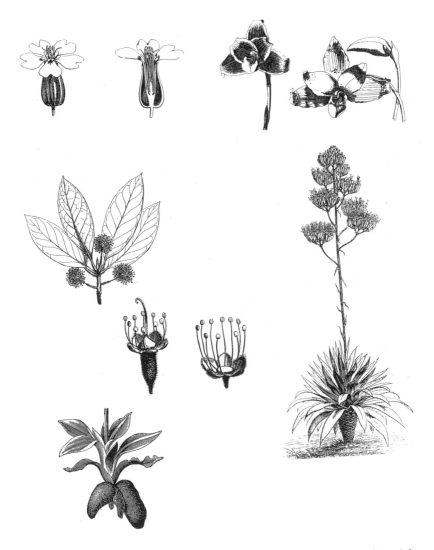

11. Plant genera and a plant organ named after servants and relatives of the wine god. Top left shows a typical ladder campion (*Silene*) flower and how the sepals fuse together to form a bladder (from Baillon's *Histoire naturelle des Plantes*, 1886–1903). Top right, the flowers of *Lycaste leucanthe* from *Paxton's Flower Garden* (1882). Middle left, a flowering twig and magnified flowers of swamp tupelo (*Nyssa biflora*). The congested, ball-shaped flowering stalk of a tupelo is made of many bisexual and male flowers (from Baillon). Bottom right, a century plant (*Agave americana*) in bloom (from Baillon). All preceding illustrations are reproduced with the permission of the library of the Missouri Botanical Garden. Lower left, this arrangement of underground orchis tuberoids is typical of many soil-dwelling orchids. Note that short, fleshy roots may grow in between the paired "testicles." The drawing comes from the 1882 edition of M. C. Cooke's *Freaks and Marvels of Plant Life; or, Curiosities of Vegetation* (London, The Society for Promoting Christian Knowledge) (from the author's library).

John Lindley, applying his standard rule that a new genus should have a pretty, lyrical, easy-to-remember name, selected one of the most obscure nymphs in mythology. Orchid taxonomists still debate her identity. Indeed, only recently has Lycaste been identified as a nursemaid and follower of Dionysus. Earlier lexicons of orchid names insisted that Lycaste was a daughter of King Priam of Troy (see §7.1), who kept nymphs as concubines and fathered half-nymph daughters. Priam's Lycaste married a cousin who fought for Troy, according to Zimmerman's *Dictionary of Classical Mythology*. We also know that Lindley's model species for the new genus was the famous white nun orchid (*la monja blanca*) of Central America (*Lycaste skinneri*). Although the face of this flower is often tinged with purple or pink, the most prized form is as white as the chalk that healed the wounded nymph. This orchid remains the national flower of Guatemala, and commercial products like mayonnaise are often named *la monja blanca*, testifying to their quality and purity.

(2) *AGAVE*. Next we encounter much larger plants occupying far hotter and drier lands. *Agave* means "noble" or "splendid," but is that all Linnaeus had in mind when he named the genus of magueys and century plants? I doubt it. The stiff, spirally arranged, narrow-tipped foliage gives the plant the appearance of a giant crown. The toothed, sharp-pointed leaves look like huge serrated knives used to decapitate large animals (or kings). More important, when the thick stems of *Agave mexicana* reach sexual maturity, Mexicans process them to become the source of alcoholic drinks like pulque, mescal, and tequila. Surely, the image of the homicidal (and highly intoxicated) queen occurred to Linnaeus when he named this genus.

As Linnaeus was Swedish, he may have been less familiar with that popular French saying, *noblesse oblige* (roughly, "special responsibilities come with aristocratic birth and status"). The genus *Agave* also denotes a generous monarch providing benefits far beyond cocktails with funny names and lurid stories. The Aztec and Mayan civilizations also cultivated some species as sources of durable leaf fibers. We continue to derive sisal from *A. sisalana* and henequen from *A. fourcroydes*. By the second half of the twentieth century, chemists discovered the second gift inside the sisal maguey. It produced a molecule that could be turned into the drug cortisone to help reduce the discomfort of inflammation. Today, natural sweeteners sold as agave are made from another Mexican species (*A. vera-cruz*) and consist primarily of the simple sugar fructose.

There are one hundred species of magueys growing in the warmer, and usually drier zones, of the western hemisphere. We find wild plants from the southwestern United States down through South America. Queen Agave also gives her name to the family Agavaceae, and many of the more than four hundred species share the same life cycle. Individual plants take up to a decade to reach sexual maturity. Then they transfer all their stored carbohydrates into a massive flowering stalk and bloom once. As the parent plant dies, it offers its last resources to its seeds still developing inside its many fruits. This is ironic when we realize that, in Greek mythology, Queen Agave is Princess Semele's sister. Most members of the *Agave* family are semelparous (see §5.6).

(3) CARYA. We are likely to see more trees in the genus *Carya* if we move further northward and stay away from true deserts. There are seventeen species in this genus distributed from eastern Canada to Central America. American hickories, pignuts, and the commercial pecan (*C. illinoinensis*) belong to this genus. *Carya* is placed in the walnut family (Juglandaceae). Linnaeus, as we know, erected the walnut genus, *Juglans,* based on classical writings (see §4.1). Much later, Thomas Nuttall (1786–1859), an adventurous naturalist who left England to live in the United States, returned to the original story of the dead princess who became a tree. He resurrected Carya to show plant taxonomists that true walnuts and American pecans were closely related.

Many Native American tribes favored wild hickories and pecans and protected them from animal attacks, weeded out competitive vegetation in wild nut groves, and offered them water. Thomas Jefferson popularized pecan domestication and convinced former president George Washington to grow them at his home at Mount Vernon, Virginia. It is my impression that residents of east Texas still consider their courthouses unfinished unless the front lawn is landscaped with a couple of pecans.

(4) ARIADNE. Botanists were unusually sensitive to the myths of beautiful women isolated on islands. Theseus abandoned the Princess Ariadne on Naxos. Her genus, *Ariadne,* is restricted to the island of Cuba. The two species of bushes belong to the coffee family (Rubiaceae). They are considered close relatives of the Cuban bush *Eosanthe* (see §5.10), but recent treatments suggest that *Ariadne* is best treated as a synonym of the genus *Mazaea.* Another classical allusion is lost to botanical accuracy.

(5) CORONA BOREALIS. The ring of petals is usually the showiest part of a flower, but some petals make themselves look even gaudier by developing an extra rim, tube, or halo known as a corona. Look at a daffodil (*Narcissus*). The three inner petals unite and push up an interconnected corona that resembles a pleated sleeve or funnel. Other examples of coronas include the dainty, white cup made by the petals of mahogany (*Swietenia*) flowers and the intricate, multirayed, haloes produced by the petals in each passionflower (*Passiflora*).

(6) ORCHIS. For thousands of years, herbalists dug up the underground storage organs of soil-dwelling orchids, like those of *Orchis* species, because they looked like testicles. These paired tuberoids (the orchis system) are filled with storage starch. The older, crumpled "testicle" is last year's bag of starch releasing its nutrients to

fuel the growth of springtime foliage and flower stalks. The newer, smoother, and whiter testicle saves sugars made by this year's leaves to store during the cold months of winter dormancy. The harvested "testicles" were pounded to make porridges or drinks, sold as salep. It was believed that such gruels acted like invigorating tonics, good for many complaints, and could make a man as randy as a satyr. Roman men, so obsessed with their own virility, believed they were consuming the *herba priapis-cus* (herb of Priapus). A market for salep survives today in rural Turkey. Modern preparations also whip in sugar and milk to produce a chilled, nougatlike dessert. The orchis tuberoid system is found in many different soil-dwelling orchids. That explains why country folk in Elizabethan England gave wild orchids such vulgar names as male fool herb, bull's bags, or dog's stones. One superstition insisted that orchids were generated spontaneously by semen spilled by thrushes and robins when these birds copulated on the ground.

The actual genus *Orchis* retains thirty-five species of long purples and monkey orchids most common in temperate Europe and Asia. The small but attractive flow-ers have lip petals painted with purple spots, streaks, or blushes. Charles Darwin studied the British species growing near his country home to better understand how the flowers were cross-pollinated by nectar-drinking insects. His investigations involved poking the flowers to see how the sexual organs released their pollen lumps (pollinia) that glued themselves to needles and pencil points. Ironically, *Orchis* is the genus that gives its name to the huge, primarily tropical, family of orchids (Orchidaceae). Only a few thousand species of orchids live exclusively in cool, tem-perate zones. In contrast, an additional fifteen thousand species are restricted to the equatorial belt.

(7) SATYRS. European herbals depicting paired tuberoids often referred to wild orchids as satyrions (satyr plants) in the belief that their consumption ensured a man's return to a level of potency comparable to a nymph-chasing rustic god. *Satyrium* is a more common genus of Africa and the Middle East, containing 130 species. The plants native to Arab countries were also gathered to make saleps, suffering the same, sad fate as *Orchis* species (see above). A cottage industry in saleps thrives in rural Turkey, taking one thousand to four thousand wild orchids every year. A number of native Turkish species appear to be threatened.

5.8 THE MANY NAMES OF THE LOVE GODDESS

The goddess of love and beauty had a convoluted and contradictory history to match her capricious personality and many names. Some said she was the daughter of Zeus and the sea nymph, Dione, so they called her Dionaea (1). Others said she appeared full-grown when the bloody genitals of Uranus splashed into the sea, and thus they called her the "foam-born one," or

Aphrodite. She rose up to the water's surface on a giant scallop shell and sailed it to Cyprus, so she is also called "the Cyprian one" (2). The port of Paphos on Cyprus was her favorite earthly residence. Cypriots called her "the Paphian one" (3). When she entered Olympus, Zeus married her to Hera's ugly son, Hephaestus. The love goddess continued to dispense her sexual favors with great generosity and slept with Ares, Poseidon, Apollo, and Dionysus. This may explain why her fellow deities called her Doritis (4), "the bountiful one."

Greek girls prayed to her as Verticordia (5), the turner of hearts, in the hope she would not allow them to fall in love with untrustworthy men. When her cult spread to Asia and the Middle East, she was identified with the goddess Astarte (6). The Romans called her Venus (7), "the charming one," and said she improved the fertility of garden plants. Whatever her name, she was a goddess of cosmetics, especially perfumes. The good smelling parts of plants were sacred to her. This included the fruit of the edible quince (*Cydonia oblonga*), the flowers of sweet violets (*Viola odorata*), and the leaves of wild myrtle (*Myrtus comunis*). Flocks of sparrows and doves followed her wherever she went.

Botany

(1) DIONAEA. We all are familiar with this form of the goddess's name as the solitary species of Venus's flytrap, *Dionaea muscipula*, native only to nutrient-poor bogs in the southeastern part of the United States. Dried and living plants were exported to Europe after 1760 to the delighted astonishment of anyone owning a "nature cabinet." American colonists and British horticulturists looked at the hinged, self-shutting leaves with their reddish interiors and comblike margins, and thought they resembled a woman's vagina. Some called the plant tipitiwitchet, in the slang of the day. Rural Americans continued to refer to a bordello-crowded avenue as tiwitchet or twitchet street well into the twentieth century. The smutty name did not suit plant importer John Ellis (1710–1776) or botanist Daniel Solander (1733–1782). Ellis provided the first scientific description of the new species. He took Solander's advice to honor the garden goddess who represents the beauty of all women, leaving us with *Dionaea* (Dione's daughter). Ellis also helped popularize the "more refined" common name of Venus's flytrap. Ever since, astute collectors of carnivorous plants have kept their heads out of the gutter.

Dionaea muscipula belongs to the family of insect-eating sundews (Droseraceae). Sundews have leaves that secrete an insect-trapping glue. Venus's flytrap, in contrast, lures its victims to its reddish pads by secreting droplets of nectar (the divine drink) before closing its hooked hinges and releasing digestive enzymes. There is a worldwide correlation between the evolution of meat-eating plants and soil chemistry. Roots growing in pure sand or, more commonly, in the drowned peat of bogs have trouble acquiring the building blocks of nitrogen and phosphorous. By evolving leaves that catch and digest bugs, sundews, Venus's flytraps, pitcher plants, and rainbow plants have been able to supplement their diets (see §6.2 and §7.4).

(2) "THE CYPRIAN ONE." Aphrodite's devotion to her adopted isle of Cyprus is reflected in two genera, *Cypripedium* and *Cyprinia*. In particular, *Cypripedium* offers more solid evidence that Linnaeus was a closet pagan. For centuries almost all European authors of herbals called lady's slipper orchids *calaceolus mariae* (Mary's shoe). They wanted to honor the Virgin Mary. Linnaeus, whose native country of Sweden was among the last of the European nations to adopt Christianity, named the genus *Cypripedium* (Aphrodite's slipper or sandal).

We now recognize thirty-three to thirty-five *Cypripedium* species in the orchid family (Orchidaceae), all confined to the northern hemisphere. Although thirteen are found from Alaska south to Mexico, the majority are native to China. The flower resembles a shoe or sandal in three ways. The two longer, narrower, lateral petals look like untied straps or laces. The sexual organs (column) have a central, flattened, triangular segment (staminode) that resembles a shoe's tongue or buckle. The third petal (labellum) is always inflated and hollow like a wooden clog or sabot, and then it curves back on itself forming a narrow "heel" with the base of the column.

Prettily painted, polished, and perfumed, the flowers always lack nectar. Bees, small wasps, or fruit flies are lured into the open fissure on the "open sole" of the shoe and are trapped inside the chamber. The only way to escape is to crawl under the tip of the female organ (stigma) and out through a tortuous canal, forcing the insect to contact a sticky anther that swabs its head or thorax with greasy pollen grains. If the same insect is stupid enough to visit a second lady's slipper (and some are), it will leave some grains on the next stigma, effecting cross-pollination. Once again the devious goddess ensnares overenthusiastic innocents.

Far fewer people have ever seen living specimens of *Cyprinia gracilis*. This member of the milkweed family (Asclepiadaceae) is unique to Cyprus and southeastern Turkey. It is a slender, woody vine scrambling through blackberry, rose, and oak thickets on mountain slopes that are two thousand to four thousand feet above sea level. Greek poets made much of the white limbs of Aphrodite (see §6.7). Some botanists describe the petals of *C. gracilis* (it has no common name) as "white as snow," but blossoms vary, and some are a disappointing greenish-yellow.

(3) "THE PAPHIAN ONE." The flowers of tropical Asian orchids in the genus *Paphiopedilum* (slipper of the Paphian one) also resemble shoes and are closely related to *Cypripedium*. The year 1886 is infamous to an older generation of orchid fanatics. That is when German taxonomist E. Pfitzer (1846–1906) published a treatment

subdividing the slipper orchids into the cold-weather genus, *Cypripedium,* and three additional tropical genera. Many British orchidophiles continued to sneer at the treatment for another seventy to eighty years, insisting they collected tropical cypripediums.

It often takes decades before hobbyists, professional horticulturists, and naturalists accept a scientific classification. Most growers now recognize about forty species in the genus *Paphiopedilum,* distributed from the Himalayas southeast through Indonesia. Research shows that differences between *Cypripedium* and *Paphiopedilum* go beyond dissimilar geography, temperature preferences, and the way in which their seeds attach themselves to the wall of the fruit. For example, the cells of *Cypripedium* and *Paphiopedilum* species contain different numbers of chromosomes.

Paphiopedilum species are also trap blossoms, but their unusual colors (brown and maroon blotches) indicate that some deceive pregnant hover flies. The matronly fly mistakes blackish, shiny, hairy warts on the flower for the bodies of aphids or other small insects. She attempts to lay her eggs on the warts to provision the next generation of hover maggots. As she inspects the hairy bumps, she slips and falls into the flower's "slipper." When the fly finally escapes, she is carrying a lump of orchid pollen on her back. Some hover flies do leave eggs on the orchid's black warts. Under normal circumstances the egg should hatch, and the hover maggot eats its aphid host. When a maggot hatches on the flower, it starves to death. Not even the meticulous course of mother love can withstand the deceptions of the goddess of love.

Paphinia (resembling the Paphian one) is yet another genus of tropical orchids, but this one was erected by John Lindley. It is obvious that Lindley, like Linnaeus and Pfitzer, felt that intricate and glistening orchid blossoms were more than entitled to some of the names of the goddess of love. Unlike the true slipper orchids (*Cypripedium* and *Paphiopedilum*) the lip petal (labellum) of a *Paphinia* flower never forms a hollow shoe or bucket. Instead, it resembles a lobed apron, and the margins of the petal subdivide into delicate, lacy fringes.

We recognize between ten to sixteen *Paphinia* species distributed from Central through South America. They are found on tree limbs or on boulders, but conservationists and orchid watchers note that few species form really abundant colonies. The plants produce a nodding or pendant flowering stalk, so growers recommend that species and hybrids be grown in hanging baskets to better enjoy the cascade of dangling blooms. Plants for sale often represent hybrids between South American species.

(4) DORITIS Controversy haunts *Doritis,* another genus in the orchid family. An older generation of botanists insisted that, back in 1833, John Lindley gave it the heavenly nickname of the love goddess. More recently, Umberto Quattrocchi, and

other historians of plant names, wrote that *doritis* means "spearhead." In their opinion, Lindley was obviously referring to the pointed tip of the lip petal. I must side with the older and wiser heads. By now, all readers of this book know of Lindley's preference for beautiful and lyrical names that do not draw overt attention to oddly shaped plant organs. Lindley probably wanted to confirm the simple fact that his *Doritis* belonged to the same family as Linnaeus's *Cypripedium*.

There are only two *Doritis* species, and both are found from Thailand through Indonesia. *Doritis pulcherrima* is popular in cultivation, as the flower colors vary from purple and pink to white with yellow spots. It is crossed with moth orchids (*Phalaenopsis*) to produce commercially successful hybrids. Some authorities insist that *Doritis* species are so closely related to the moth orchids that *Doritis* is best reduced to the status of yet another synonym.

(5) VERTICORDIA. Aphrodite loves myrtle, but there are more than 120 genera in the myrtle family (Myrtaceae). Using some of the names of the goddess or her employees (see §5.9), helps botanists remember which plant belongs to which genus in Australia. The genus *Verticordia* was named to show the alliance between antipodal bushes and the sacred myrtle bush of the Mediterranean. Studies of *Verticordia* have intensified, and forty species have turned into almost one hundred, concentrated in the Mediterranean-like climate of southwestern Australia. Unlike most members of the myrtle family, a *Verticordia* flower has a well-developed ring of sepals (calyx) subdivided into pretty, colorful fringes. That is why the bushes are called feather flowers and people are licensed to cut blossoming branches for the florist's trade.

(6) ASTARTE. *Astartea*, in turn, consists of seven species of shrubs that are also native to Western Australia. As you would predict, they are also members of the Myrtaceae, and closely related to *Verticordia*. *Astartea* species are often called winter pinks. Their small pink-white blossoms appear during the mild, southern winter (July and August), attracting early butterflies. Recent chemical analyses shows that the leaves of some *Astartea* are as rich in fragrant oils (myrtenol, alpha-pinene) as Europe's myrtle bush.

(7) VENUS. If a botanist feels that a new species is particularly charming he or she may name it *venustus*. My favorite is the butterfly flower (*Calochortus venustus*), a mariposa lily of California. The three white petals form a chalice, and the interior is decorated with red and pink brush strokes. Cultivated forms are available, but I wish they were hardier in my Missouri garden.

5.9 THE HOUSEHOLD OF APHRODITE

Classical artists often depicted the love goddess at her toilette. The nymph Acmena (1), was her maid, and she brought Venus's comb (2). The three

Graces, Aglaia (3), Pasithea (4), and Thalia (5), dressed and perfumed her. Pothos (6), the god of erotic yearning, followed her everywhere. She was the mother of many children by many gods, and her offspring also attended her. This included Priapus, Peitho (Persuasion), Hermione (Harmony), Hymen (god of marriage) (7), and, of course, Cupid, who fired gold or lead-tipped arrows that made all beings fall in and out of love.

The Romans believed that Cupid mended his ways when he fell in love with Princess Psyche (8) and married her in secret. Venus persecuted her daughter-in-law for injuring Cupid accidentally. Psyche became Venus's slave and was sent to do all sorts of impossible tasks, but Cupid sent different beings to watch over her. When Jupiter approved of the marriage of Cupid and Psyche, even Venus danced at her deification. Psyche was given the wings of a butterfly so she could accompany her husband on his missions.

Botany

(1) Acmena. *Acmena smithii* is a small, spreading, understory tree of eastern Australian gullies and rain forest remnants. Naming it after the maid of the love goddess shows that this species is related to the Mediterranean myrtle bush, sacred to Aphrodite (see §5.8). *Acmena*, of course, also belongs to the family Myrtaceae. Consequently, the genera *Acmena*, *Astartea*, and *Verticordia* (§5.8) are composed of Australian plants that are associated with the love goddess.

Lilly-pilly is the common name of *A. smithii*, and refers to the clusters of pill-shaped, white-purple fruit. It is gaining popularity as an ornamental tree in Australian parks and church gardens. The fruit was anthropomorphized as a supporting character in a children's novel written and illustrated by the Australian May Gibbs (1877–1969). Lilly-pilly befriends the gum nut (*Eucalyptus*) tree fairies in Gibbs's, *The Adventures of Snugglepot and Cuddlepie*. Unsurprisingly, *Eucalyptus*, with more than five hundred species, is also a member of the myrtle family.

(2) VENUS'S COMB. *Scandix pectin-veneris* (*Scandix* means "shepherd's needle"; *pectin* means "comb," and *veneris* means "Venus") is a wayside herb of Europe placed in the celery family (Apiaceae). When the flowers are fertilized, their pistils develop into long, narrow, dry fruits resembling a comb's teeth.

(3) AGLAIA. Botanists found the Graces or Charites so charming that each goddess has attractive plants named after her, but those plants are not closely related. *Aglaia*, for example, consists of about a hundred species found from India to Indonesia. Most grow as bushes and trees placed in the pride of India family (Meliaceae; see §3.3). Although some *Aglaia* trees yield useful timber, known as tasua, it is obvious that the genus name was awarded originally to species like the Chinese

perfume tree (*A. odorata*). Its small, yellow flowers scent linen and some commercial teas, just as the servant of the love goddess perfumes her mistress.

(4) PASITHEA. *Pasithea caerulea* is a charming wildflower with bright blue blossoms. It grows in the dry zones of Chile, but its bulbs are also cultivated commercially and prized by collectors. Chileans call it *azulillo* (blue lily). Placed within the daylily family (Hemerocallidaceae), *P. caerulea* represents yet another pretty flower named after graceful but minor goddesses.

(5) THALIA. As mentioned previously (see §4.3), the genus *Thalia* is another example of Linnaeus's word play. It honors both a botanist and one of the Charites. There are only seven species in the genus *Thalia* distributed in tropical South America and Africa. They belong to the prayer plant family (Marantaceae). Sold as water cannas or alligator flags, *Thalia* species are considered charming additions to bog gardens and goldfish pools. Unfortunately *T. dealbata* escapes from cultivation, clogging ponds and rivers where winters are mild. Charming is as charming does.

(6) POTHOS. The genus *Pothos* contains about fifty species of vines distributed through the Old World tropics. They belong to the jack-in-the-pulpit family (Araceae). Plants with marbled leaves are often sold as golden pothos, but devil's ivy is the most common name. If you believe the story, Linnaeus was in a naughty mood when he erected this genus. He found the name *pothos* applied to a mysterious, summer-blooming plant in the works of Pliny and was determined to use it for something special. Someone later presented Linnaeus with a specimen of an unnamed, tropical vine. The Swedish taxonomist learned that its unusually broad leaves were stitched together to make pubic aprons worn by the otherwise naked men of New Ireland (now a province of New Guinea). How could Linnaeus resist such an opportunity?

(7) HYMEN. *Hymenaea* is a genus of fifteen tropical trees from Central and South America. It is placed within the partridge pea family (Caesalpiniaceae). Linnaeus noted that the blade of each leaf subdivides into two paired leaflets. Each pair of leaflets is like a husband and wife united by the god of marriage. The trunks and branches of these trees secrete lots of resin that hardens into a product known as copal. The collection of copal is an important rural industry in Latin America. Copals are added to furniture varnishes, linoleum, and printing inks.

(8) PSYCHE. *Psychine* is a genus of only one species found in northern Africa, and it belongs to the cabbage family (Brassicaceae). The dry fruit is lobed like the wings of a butterfly or the wings of the deified princess. Flowers that form small, erect funnels (with broad petal rims); bloom during the day; and have sweet fragrances, vivid colors, and secrete nectar at the base of each funnel are most likely to be pollinated by butterflies. In the language of botany, a butterfly-pollinated flower is a psychophilous (Psyche-loving) flower.

5.10 HELIOS AND HIS SISTERS

Zeus and his brothers sent the sun Titan, Hyperion, to Tartarus in the underworld for joining the army of Atlas. However, Helios (1), Hyperion's son, never attacked the Olympian gods during the Titan war. In gratitude, Zeus gave Helios and his sisters a monopoly on celestial light. Helios succeeded his father to the sun chariot. His sister, Selene (2) (Roman, Luna) (3), became the next moon goddess. A second sister, Eos (4), is the dawn goddess, announcing her brother's imminent arrival from the east. She is also the mother of the stars and the four winds.

Botany

(1) HELIOS. For more than two and a half centuries, the sun god has been the most favored Greek deity for naming genera. At one time, seventeen genera incorporated the name of Helios: *Helianthella* (little Helios), *Helianthemum* (flowering Helios), *Helianthocereus* (flowering candle of Helios), *Helianthopsis* (looks like Helios), *Helianthostylis* (in the style of Helios), *Helianthus* (flower of Helios), *Helichrysum* (gold of Helios), *Heliocarpus* (fruit of Helios), *Heliocarya* (walnut of Helios), *Heliocauta* (red hot from Helios), *Heliocereus* (candle of Helios), *Heliomeris* (partly Helios), *Heliophila* (loving Helios), *Heliopsis* (eye of Helios), *Heliosperma* (seed of Helios), *Heliostemma* (pollen-making stamens of Helios), and *Heliotropium* (turning toward Helios). There are four interrelated reasons why this male Titan is so popular with scientists who classify plants.

First, the flower buds of many plants open dramatically early in the morning, readying sun-colored (red, yellow-orange) blossoms for pollinators that forage early in the day for their pollen or nectar. For example, *Heliocereus* (candle of Helios) is a genus of five species of climbing cacti (Cactaceae) distributed from southern Mexico through Central America. Their jointed stems scramble up tree trunks and branches, resembling waxy, green, jointed candles. The flowers are relatively short-lived, but they form magnificent, red trumpets that attract hummingbirds.

Second, the sun makes plants grow. Gardeners know that some species thrive and bloom only when they have full exposure to the sun. A genus in the cabbage family (Brassicaceae) is named *Heliophila* (sun-loving). Thirteen species come from southern Africa. They produce attractive blue flowers most luxuriously when allowed to stand in full sun.

Third, other plants are so-named because they produce a flower, flowering branch, or some other organ that looks like the yellow-orange, flat, rayed disk of the sun. That is why some genera in the daisy family (Asteraceae) celebrate Helios. The best known include *Helianthella, Helianthus, Helichrysum, Heliocauta, Heliomeris,* and

Heliopsis. The most familiar, of course, are the sixty-seven species of native American sunflowers (*Helianthus*). Hundreds to thousands of tiny flowers form a tight and continuous spiral inside a sunflower's green dish (the involucrum) that is made of curved, leaflike structures known as bracts. The more numerous tube flowers in the center make both pollen and the characteristic sunflower seeds so important to the edible oil, snack, and bird food industries. The yellow, ray petals around the edges are actually individual, sterile flowers that exist only to attract bees and other pollinators.

Fourth, some plants appear to be "obsessed" with Helios. Their leaves change position and track the sun as it rolls across heaven. They are heliotropic plants, and the story of the heliotrope (*Heliotropium*) appears in §5.11.

(2) SELENE. The moon goddess does not have as many botanical devotees as her bother. However, a number of genera are still named in her honor: *Selenia* (like Selene), *Selenicereus* (Selene's candle), *Selenipedium* (Selene's sandal), and *Selenothamnus* (Selene's shrub). *Selenicereus* is a genus of twenty species in the cactus family (Cactaceae) found through the tropical Americas. They are also climbing cacti with waxy, green joints that lash themselves to rocks or trees with little aerial roots. *Selenicereus grandiflorus* grows wild in Cuba and Jamaica, but it is popular with collectors as one of the most spectacular night-blooming cacti, with pale petals reflecting the light of the moon. Unfortunately, each glorious flower rarely lives more than a single evening. Selene snuffs out her candle as her sister Eos heralds the arrival of their brother, Helios. Growers with limited greenhouse space must stay up late to witness the opening of two or three flowers each year. In tropical El Salvador I saw a wooden fence and trellis colonized by huge specimens offering the owners fresh flowers every night. It is obvious that two American cactus experts, Nathaniel Britton (1859–1934) and Joseph Rose (1862–1928), saw a close relation between day-blooming *Heliocereus* and his night-blooming sister genus, *Selenicereus.*

Selenipedium, with four or five species, also comes from the tropical Americas (Central and South America) but belongs to the orchid family (Orchidaceae). It is another genus of slipper orchids and has a lip petal (labellum) shaped like a delicate shoe. By invoking the name of the moon goddess, the taxonomist E. Pfitzer (see §5.8) tried to show that *Selenipedium* is closely related to the love goddess (*Cypripedium* and *Paphiopedilum*). *Selenipedium chica* has the distinction of being the tallest orchid on this planet, with bamboolike canes stretching upward to a height of twelve to fifteen feet. As the goddess Selene derives from Titan stock, we expect her to be a tall girl.

(3) LUNA. *Lunaria* is a genus of only three species distributed naturally from central to southeastern Europe and is a member of the cabbage family (Brassicaceae). We know it as moonwort, honesty, or penny flower. A plant of "grandmother's garden," it is cultivated as a special source of dried decorations. The little purple flowers are not much to look at, but wait for the large, flat, penny-shaped fruits.

Because the plant usually dies after it makes seeds, the fruiting stalks are gathered and hung upside down so they stiffen straight. Then you pick off and discard the two, flat, fruit covers (valves) protecting the seeds in each flat fruit. This exposes the shiny and papery partition (septum) that looks like a silvery full moon. When a plant organ, like the blade of a leaf, grows in the shape of a crescent moon, botanists say it is lunate. As the fruit of *Lunaria* forms a full moon it is not lunate.

(4) Eos. Eos has two meanings in the language of botany. It refers to the beautiful goddess of the dawn, but it also means the east (the home of the dawn). *Eosanthe* (Eos's flower) is, or was, a rare, solitary species of shrub found on the island of Cuba. A member of the coffee family (Rubiaceae), it may be extinct, so we may never learn if it actually bloomed at dawn.

In contrast, *Eomecon* (Dawn's poppy or eastern poppy) and *Eopepon* (Dawn's pumpkin or eastern pumpkin) have Asian distributions. Are you old enough to remember when Japan was called the land of the rising sun? *Eomecon chionantha*, for example, comes from the forests of eastern China. Although a member of the poppy family (Papaveraceae), it prefers shade, and nurseries may sell it as snow poppy (the petals are bright white) or Chinese bloodroot. You may grow it as a novel groundcover under dense trees that shade out grass.

Some seed catalogs, books, and Web sites on edible plants still refer to the Chinese cucumber as *Eopepon vitifollius*. The domesticated vine grows from eastern Asia through Japan. It is a member of the cucumber and pumpkin family (Cucurbitaceae), and a lot of questionable claims are made for its fruit and root extracts, particularly for treating HIV. infection. I suspect that pickling or currying the green fruit may be a lot better then using its tinctures to treat the symptoms of HIV. Most botanists now prefer to submerge *Eopepon* within the larger genus of snake gourds, *Trichosanthes*. Various traditional remedies are also attributed to several different species of snake gourds because their bitter flesh reminds people of the taste of quinine, a medical extract from the bark of South American *Cinchona* trees. Filipino recipes often serve the cooked gourds in a shrimp paste sauce.

5.11 THE SUN'S SORROWS

Helios married the nymph Rhode, and they had one son and several daughters. He was unfaithful to his wife, enjoying the attentions of both divinities and mortals. He took Princess Leucothoe (1), a daughter of King Orchamus, as his mistress after he abandoned the nymph Clytie. How did Clytie respond? She told Leucothoe's father, and the outraged king buried his daughter alive under a sand dune. Helios removed the sand, but the girl was dead. All the god could do was sprinkle the corpse with nectar, and it turned into the first frankincense tree (*Boswellia sacra*). The precious drops of resin are Leucothoe's tears, and the tree still grows in Arabian sands. The sun god shunned Clytie. The nymph pined away until she turned into a wildflower whose leaves follow Helios, exhibiting heliotropism (2), as his chariot moves across the sky. Some said she became the African marigold (*Calendula officinalis*), but most believe she is the heliotrope (*Heliotropium*).

Helios allowed his adoring son, Phaeton, to drive the sun chariot for a day, but the youth could not control such powerful horses. He risked burning up the earth until Zeus struck him dead with a thunderbolt and Helios mastered the horses. Phaeton's body fell into the Po River. His sisters, the Heliades, gathered on the shore and mourned him. They wept until they turned into black poplar trees (*Populus nigra*). Their tears turned into resin, which fell into the sea and became gemstones. The gems became the property of the sea nymph, Electra, so the ancient Greeks called amber *elektron* or *electron* (3). Others say that the word *electron* comes from the Greek *elecktor* (the sun's glare). Phaeton's cousin, Cycnus (4), wandered the land singing sad songs in honor of Phaeton. The gods turned him into a swan, which supposedly sings once before it dies.

The Romans believed that Helios could not bear the loss of a true love and a son. The Titan resigned his position in favor of Apollo. Selene also resigned, in sympathy, leaving the moon chariot to Diana.

Botany

(1) LEUCOTHOE. As we have learned in a previous chapter, David Don liked to assign the names of mythological females to pretty plants from temperate Asia (see §4.3 and §4.5). An earlier German botanist had already named the frankincense genus *Boswellia*, but Don was free to name both the Asian and American doghobbles and fetterbushes after this other girl who turned into a woody plant. *Leucothoe* is a genus of about forty species of shrubs, but they belong to the rhododendron family (Ericaceae), not the frankincense family (Burseraceae). In fact, *Leucothoe* is a close relative of *Andromeda* and *Cassiope* (both named for Greek princesses, §6.6) as well as *Pieris* (named for the Muses, §4.3). *Leucothoe*, like *Pieris*, produces chains of small, delicate flowers that look like nodding bells or urns. When grown as garden plants, fetterbushes are also favored for their spring foliage, as young leaves are often vivid red, purple, or bronze in color.

(2) HELIOTROPISM. The Greeks and Romans were fascinated by plants whose leaves changed position while tracking the sun's chariot from east to the west. Not every plant can do it, and later botanists refer to the phenomenon as heliotropism (Helios = "sun god"; tropism = "a change in direction in response to an external stimulus"). It is all a matter of construction and water relations. Heliotropic plants

have jointed leaf stalks. The swollen joint is called a pulvinus. The ability of the leaf blade to track the sun depends ultimately on changes in water uptake (turgor) in cells within the juicy pulvinus. Plants with heliotropic leaves include commercial sunflower, cotton, soybeans, and many other legumes. Sun tracking is especially common in species found in tundras within the Arctic Circle. As summers are brief at such frigid latitudes, wildflowers must follow the sun to "squeeze" every photon out of available daylight.

(3) *ELEKTRON* OR *ELECTRON*. All amber represents fossilized tree resin, but because different gems come from different deposits, polished jewels often show considerable variation in clarity and color. Such variation reflects both the physical age of the fossil and the extinct tree(s) that made them. It is common for old deposits of amber to be eroded by rivers, which redeposit the stones in some nearby seabed. To Greeks gathering the gems in bays or on pebbly beaches, they were obviously gifts of the sea nymph Electra. True Baltic amber formed between the Oligocene and Eocene periods (twenty million to nine million years ago) and does not come from the resin of either black poplar or cherry trees (as Roman naturalists believed), or any other flowering plant. Plant remains mixed with amber fossils and comparative chemical tests prove that all Baltic amber came from the resins of cone-bearing trees, either the ancestors of modern kauris (*Agathis*) or the extinct *Pseudolarix.*

The Greeks adored amber jewelry and established trade routes with settlements along the Baltic Sea that may date back as far as 900 B.C.E. A passion for amber extended to imperial Rome. The Emperor Nero gave his favorite gladiators amber bracelets, believing it would assure their survival and victory in the arena. Indeed, a small amber carving would cost a patrician about the same amount as a full-grown male slave.

(4) CYCNUS. Often sold as swan orchids, the genus *Cycnoches* (similar to Cycnus) is distributed from Central to South America. Depending on the authority consulted, there are seven to more than twenty species clinging to the branches of tropical trees in lowland forests. In most members of the orchid family (Orchidaceae), the male (stamen) and female organ (pistil) fuse together to form a curving reproductive structure called the column. *Cycnoches* orchids are exceptions to the rule. Their flowers are either male (pollen-bearing) or female (pistil-bearing). In male flowers of *Cycnoches,* the column is elongated and exaggerated, forming the beaked head and graceful neck of a swan. The flower's petals arch backward, resembling a waterfowl in flight.

5.12 Divine Vengeance

We can see that no mortal, nymph, or satyr was safe from the anger of the Olympian gods. Hera's curse of madness and Zeus's thunderbolts destroyed many for comparatively minor sins. Other Olympians preferred to administer punishments with ironic twists. Athena was the daughter of Zeus and his first wife, Metis (see §5.2). The goddess of wisdom and weaving, Athena never tolerated anyone who took credit for her inventions or challenged her craftsmanship. She invented the plow, but when the nymph Myrmex (1) said it was her work, the goddess turned her into an ant, a thief of plowed seeds. A mortal girl, Arachne (2), challenged Athena to a weaving contest. The goddess acknowledged the superiority of Arachne's work and then changed her into a spider, the perpetual weaver.

Aphrodite's punishments were also devastating, but she did not confront mortal enemies directly. When a king and champion charioteer boasted that his mares ran faster if they were deprived of sexual intercourse, he angered Aphrodite for perverting her natural laws. She fed the mares the magical herb hippomanes (3), and it made them crazy. At the next race the mares overturned the chariot and ate the monarch alive. In another instance, Prince Hippolytus refused to worship this vindictive love goddess, so Aphrodite made his stepmother, Queen Phaedra (4), fall in love with him. Hippolytus repudiated Phaedra's offer of love. She committed suicide but not before she left a letter insisting her stepson had raped her. King Theseus, Phaedra's husband, cursed his son, and Hippolytus died in yet another chariot accident.

The male gods usually resorted to blunt action. For example, shortly after Apollo took charge of the sun chariot, he forced his attentions on the nymph Acantha (5). She scratched his face, so he turned her into a tree with spiny, skin-scratching leaves that always grows in full sun.

Or consider Ares, the war god and Aphrodite's immortal love. The pair attempted to conceal their affair from the goddess's husband, Hephaestus. Ares appointed a boy, Alectryon (6), to warn the dallying lovers of the approach of morning, but one night, Alectryon fell fast asleep an hour before the break of dawn. The sun god saw the adulterous pair and tattled on them. Ares turned Alectryon into a rooster forced to crow as night ends.

Botany

(1) MYRMEX. Unlike Myrmex, the mythical thief of seeds, many species of seed-collecting ants are beneficial to wild plants. The workers prefer to strip the seeds' shells of their juicy jackets (arils) or fatty, connective stalks (caruncles). Once the edible parts are consumed, the ants dump the gnawed but viable seeds in garbage pits located around the colony, where they sprout unmolested. The dispersal of seeds by ants is known as myrmechory. Some woodland ants of Europe, North America, and Japan are seasonally dependent on food clinging to the seeds

of spring-blooming wildflowers. Several species of forest violets, milkworts, sedges, trilliums, and trout lilies are myrmechorous.

The transformed nymph Myrmex lives on in three plant genera: *Myrmechis* (showing ants), *Myrmecodia* (ant's bulb or bell), and *Myrmecosicyos* (ant's seeds). *Myrmechis* is a genus of six to eighteen species of small, ground-dwelling orchids (Orchidaceae) distributed from temperate Asia (Japan) south into Malaysia. The flowers are tiny, and the outlines of the lobed lip petals remind some viewers of the bodies of ants.

However, since the nineteenth century, plant ecologists have noted that interactions between plants and real ants may be complex and show long-term interdependency. For example, the forty-five *Myrmecodia* species are so dependent on ants that the growing plants welcome the insects into their own bodies. Distributed tropically from Malaysia to Fiji and northern Australia, these weird, small, lumpy and often prickly plants spend their lives clinging to the branches of forest trees. It is hard to believe they belong to the same family as commercial coffee bushes (Rubiaceae). Slice open the twig-hugging tuber, and you will find it contains a series of meandering galleries like a shopping mall. This is the perfect nesting site for some tree-dwelling ants, and it engenders a mutualistic relationship. The ants colonize the apartments inside the plant—and they are messy housekeepers. Uneaten food, feces, and dead ants decay, and the plant's internal roots absorb the trace minerals. This is especially beneficial for a small plant that never grows in nutrient-rich soil.

Myrmecosicyos messorious is a member of the pumpkin family (Cucurbitaceae) from dried-up lakebeds in Africa's Rift Valley. This solitary species was not described until 1962 and is almost always found growing in association with the nests of harvester ants. As in the above case of the myrmecodia plants, the relationship between harvester ants and *M. messorious* is probably subtle and complex. We do not know whether this vine secretes nectar drops to reward protective ants or whether these insects disperse its seeds.

(2) ARACHNE. Botanists remember Arachne's punishment in two different ways. First, if a plant's skin displays thin patches of interlacing, long hairs (reminding us of cobwebs), we say that it wears an arachnoid coat. Second, many orchids produce dark-colored flowers that are spidery in appearance. *Cryptostylis arachnites, Maxillaria arachnites,* and *Oprhys arachnites* are but a few orchid species with elongated, narrow, curved, or bent petals and sepals that reminded taxonomists of long, jointed, spider legs. The tropical orchid genus *Arachnis* contains only seven species distributed through southeastern Asia and New Guinea, but their hybrids are popular cut flowers. Sold as scorpion orchids by growers in Singapore, these exaggerated blooms are reminiscent of an arachnid about to spring or sting.

(3) HIPPOMANES. Aphrodite procured a plant that drove horses mad with lust. Linnaeus preserved her deed by giving the name of the mythical plant to real trees

that continue to drive people mad with pain. Five notorious tree species are placed in the genus *Hippomane*. They belong to the poisonous spurge and croton family (Euphorbiaceae) and grow from Mexico through Central America. Most members of this family leak toxic white or yellowish milk (latex) if bruised or picked.

In particular, the innocent-looking *H. mancinella* grows along the Gulf of Mexico coastline and produces such a colorful, pleasantly scented fruit that it is often called beach apple or *manzanillo* (little apple). Sixteenth-century records of Spanish expeditions to Mexico recorded what happened when hungry sailors and conquistadors picked the fruit. Human hands stained with dripping latex erupted in severe blisters, and there were additional horror stories of male agony when they held their penises to urinate after touching the tree. Eyes rubbed with unwashed fingers suffered conjunctivitis and temporary blindness. Small wonder Linnaeus named these plants after a magical herb that inflamed an animal as big as a horse. Speaking of inflammation, I should mention that the wood of beach apple was favored for cabinetry, but woodcutters had to char the tree bark before cutting down the trunk so they could handle it. Unfortunately, this precaution had its own side effects. Sinuses and lungs were poisoned if workers accidentally inhaled the smoke.

(4) PHAEDRA. *Hippomane* is just one of many genera in the spurge family (Euphorbiaceae) that exudes toxic sap. Therefore, it is not surprising that two botanists named the American myrtlecrotons and mouse ear bushes after the most vindictive queen in Greek tragedy. Unfortunately, the genus is another victim of revision, and *Phaedra* is now known as *Bernardia*, in honor of a French botanist, Bernard de Jussieu (1699–1777). There are about twenty *Bernardia* species in warmer, drier regions of the western hemisphere, but the name change may hide their venomous nature. Some native plant lovers suggest growing myrtlecrotons as hedges in dry gardens. I vote no.

However, Phaedra was such a *femme fatale*, when dressed in her glittering jewels, it may please you to learn that her name survives in the ravishing genus *Phaedranassa* (Phaedra the queen). These six species of queen lilies come from the Andes of South America. The flowering stalk forms a parasol, and a long, sleek flower, banded with red, pink, and bluish green emerges from the tip of each spoke. They start blooming after two months of cyclical drought, so they may be potted and forced for the Christmas trade. Bulb collectors find queen lilies intoxicating, but we should also remember these plants are placed in the Amaryllidaceae with daffodils. It is a family well-known for protecting its succulent bulbs with bitter, alkaloid poisons.

(5) ACANTHA. Acantha continues to defend her honor in gardens all over the world, although she has been reduced to the status of a formal perennial groundcover. Thirty species of *Acanthus* are found from warm and dry Mediterranean Europe into the Old World tropics. Most are perennial wildflowers, never trees. If

you look at the lobes or divided borders of the leaf margins of species like bear's breeches (*Acantha mollis*), you can still see the fingernails of the nymph reduced to pointed spines.

The Mediterranean species inspired classic Greek architecture as early as the second or third century B.C.E. The true Corinthian column is slender, fluted, and beautifully ornamented with carved patterns inspired by the shape of acanthus leaves. The Romans adopted (or stole) the same design, and every time Europe or the United States experienced a "Greek revival," the Corinthian column became fashionable. Back in 1987, my wife and I visited the John Paul Getty Museum in Malibu, California. I admired the beds of live acanthus bordering the Corinthian columns.

Acantha has her own family, the Acanthaceae, with more than 4,000 species in more than 350 genera. Most are spiny, tropical vines and bushes, but they also pack their leaf cells with microscopic but inedible crystals that reduce insect attacks. That is why the leaf surface of an acanthus appears irregular or streaky to the human eye. Real plants, unlike nymphs, often employ more than one adaptation to protect themselves from unwanted admirers.

(6) ALECTRYON. There are eighteen species in the genus *Alectryon*, and most are small trees distributed on the islands of the South Pacific. *Alectryon* species belong to the litchi nut family (Sapindaceae) and may be called titoki, New Zealand oak, boonarea, or mahoe. The transformation of boy into rooster can be seen only when titoki fruits ripen and pop open. Each black seed wears a fleshy, red jacket, or aril, reminiscent of a cock's comb and wattles. Some native people eat the arils (no, they do not taste like chicken).

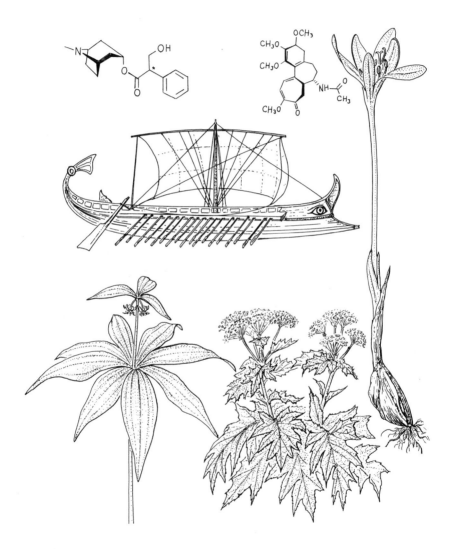

12. The *Argo* sails under constellations representing the molecules of atropine (left) and colchicine (right). On the shore to the lower left we see Indian cucumber (*Medeola virginia*). An unusually small specimen of giant hogweed (*Heracleum lantatum*) flowers in lower middle. To the right is a naked lady (*Colchicum autumnale*). Illustration by John Myers.

CHAPTER 6

⟞⟋§⟍⟝

Mortal Monarchs
and Monsters

By this, the boy by her side lay kill'd
was melted like a vapour from her sight
And in his blood that on the ground lay spill'd
A purple flower sprung up, chequered with white
Resembling well his pale cheeks and the blood
Which in round drops upon their whiteness stood.

—WILLIAM SHAKESPEARE, "Venus and Adonis"

6.1 THE FIRST KINGS

The first kings on earth were not human. King Cecrops of Attica was half man and half snake. Nevertheless, he built a great citadel called the Cecropia (1). Inachus, a river god, was king of Argos, and Pan ruled Arcadia. Pan was such a lazy and placid monarch that his impatient and impertinent subjects often blamed him for unsuccessful hunting trips and scourged the goatish god with squills (2).

Some minor goddesses became the wives of mortal kings. King Cadmus built the first version of the city of Thebes and then married Hermione (Harmony), a daughter of Aphrodite. When Cadmus grew too old to rule, the gods transformed him and his wife into sacred, immortal snakes. Sisyphus, monarch of Corinth, wed Merope (3), a child of Atlas and Pleione, but they were not fated to remain together. All of Pleione's daughters were transformed into stars and became the constellation we call the Pleiades. Merope did not remain in heaven very long. She looked down from the sky and saw Sisyphus commit so many crimes that the gods condemned him to the worst part of the underworld after he died. Merope could not stand public humiliation. She preferred inglorious self-exile and vanished from her place in heaven. No one has seen her in thousands of years.

In time, most royal families of Greece traced their aristocratic lineages to nymphs, Titans, or Olympian gods. When gods and goddesses mated with mortals, their hybrid sons were called heroes (4). These demigods usually showed superior strengths and skills and often established their own kingdoms. Romans insisted that the heroes Romulus (5) and Remus founded their city. They were twin sons of the princess Rhea Silvia. She was a vestal virgin, but that did not protect her from the attentions of the war god, Ares (Roman, Mars).

Nevertheless, within a few generations the behavior of these demigods and their children became more outrageous than that of their Olympian ancestors. An oracle warned King Laius, of Thebes, that his son was destined to kill him. The monarch pierced his baby's feet with a nail, bound them together, and exposed the infant. The shepherd who found the baby boy named him Oedipus (swollen foot) (6) and gave him to the childless king of Corinth. Oedipus, as we all know, grew up to kill his real father, Laius, and marry his birth mother, Queen Jocasta. Theban monarchs seemed destined to violent careers. Less well known is the story of the Theban princes Amphion and Zethus. They lashed their great-aunt Dirce (7) to the horns of a bull because she was mistreating their mother, the nymph Antiope. Dirce's corpse oozed so much blood that the gods turned it into a spring of water.

Botany

(1) CECROPIA. Pehr Loefling (1729–1756), a Swedish botanist who died in Venezuela, never explained why he named the genus of trumpet trees, pumpwoods, and *guaramos* after the Cecropia, but there is a probable explanation. First and foremost, a citadel is a fortress of many chambers, housing armies and sheltering citizens in wartime. Yet there is nothing particularly grand or imposing about the almost one hundred *Cecropia* species found throughout the tropical Americas. Most are small, slender, rapidly growing trees. Seeds carried by birds colonize landslides, abandoned farmland, and forests leveled by fires or storms. Only a little *Azteca* ant would think of taking refuge in a skinny *guaramo*.

However, the twigs and young branches of these trees are hollow and chambered like the interior of a fortress. *Azteca* ant queens gnaw their way in and set up their colonies. Soldier ants keep the tree free of grazing insect pests, and the workers chew off the tendrils of encroaching vines. In return, the tree produces tiny, edible, white beads exuded by skin cells located at the bases of some of the leaf stalks (petioles). The ant colony is nourished by this white food, as it is full of glycogen (an energy-rich) molecule similar to starch) and some proteins. Still, there is no such thing as the perfect bastion; *guaramo* leaves remain a favorite food of sloths (*Bradypus*). Ants cannot do much to stop this slow but steady herbivore.

The classification of the genus *Cecropia* is open to argument. At various times it has been placed with the mulberry (Moraceae) and fig (Ficaceae) families, whereas some botanists give it its own family (Cecropiaceae).

(2) SQUILLS. Who ever heard of a god who was whipped and whacked with the bulbs of common wildflowers? Squill is a name that many European naturalists give to a variety of lilylike plants that have scaly bulbs, lance-shaped leaves, and produce wandlike stalks of small flowers. You may grow striped squill (*Puschkinia scilloides*) and Siberian squill (*Scilla siberica*) to add little, bluish blossoms to your spring garden. Their bulbs are rather small, though, and could not possibly punish a god.

Therefore, this myth must refer specifically to the maritime squill. It is also known as the sea onion or red squill (*Drimia maritima*) and is placed in the hyacinth family (Hyacinthaceae). Maritime squill is common along Mediterranean coastlines and is so tough it survives summer bushfires. The reddish bulb is about the size of a fist. *Drimia* means "acrid" or "pungent." Bruise or remove the bulb's outer scales, and it weeps toxic white tears containing at least forty-five different compounds. Maritime squill provided ancient physicians with a wound disinfectant and questionable treatments for intestinal worms, constipation, bronchitis, gout, irregular heartbeat, rheumatism, and cancer. The bulbs have been farmed in the United States since 1946, because maritime squill is still a dependable rat poison. Rodents cannot vomit it up once swallowed, and they die of liver damage. I would bet that the Greek word for squill (*skilla*) and the devouring monster Scylla (see §7.6) have a common origin.

It is easy to see why maritime squill was a magic plant in Mediterranean cultures. It survived fire, always bloomed after the hottest and driest summers, offered strong medicines, and relieved homes and gardens of vermin. A plant that destroys rats must also improve the indolent and capricious behavior of the god of wild things. Belief in the supernatural power of maritime squill survives into the present day. Long after Christianity replaced the pantheon of Olympian gods, some Greeks continue to yank squills out of the dirt. The bulb is nailed to the entrances of homes to frighten off evil spirits. Pagan deities with horns and cloven hooves need not apply.

(3) MEROPE. In contrast to the diverse and successful genus *Cecropia* (above), there is only one species in the genus *Merope*. *Merope angulata* is a thorny shrub found growing in muddy and salty riverbanks of mangrove forests from southeastern Asia to New Guinea. Known locally as *limau lelang*, it has fragrant flowers and foliage and belongs to the much-loved citrus family (Rutaceae).

Queen Merope hid herself from those who remembered her husband's awful reputation as a murderer, rapist, and liar. In turn, *Merope angulata* hides itself in the dense vegetation of tropical estuaries. This wild bush grows far away from its domesticated and publicly admired relatives, including oranges, lemons, kumquats, bael, and grapefruit. *Merope* is also a close relative of *Atalantia* (see §6.4). As we will see, Princess Atalanta is another unhappy female who chooses the wrong hero.

(4) HEROES. Of course, nothing seems worse than choosing heroin, but that was not the original consensus. The heroin molecule does not occur naturally in the opium poppy (*Papaver somniferum*; see §3.1). By 1853, the invention of the hypodermic needle made it easier and safer to administer pure morphine for pain relief. Unfortunately, no one realized how addictive morphine was. By the end of the Civil War, at least forty-five thousand returning soldiers were addicted. Then, in 1874, chemists learned to alter the morphine molecule. This new and improved medicine was supposed to be an effective painkiller without addictive properties. It is called heroin because it was lauded as the "heroic solution" to morphine.

In the United States, the honeymoon with this over-the-counter wonder drug lasted well into the first five years of the twentieth century. Eventually it became impossible to ignore obvious physical addiction and violent withdrawal symptoms. The original drug manufacturers must have had considerable political clout. After all, the first American law prohibiting possession of heroin and other opiates for "nonmedical purposes" was not enacted until 1914.

(5) ROMULUS. Compared with the opium poppy, the eighty species in the genus *Romulea* are innocuous wildflowers arising from small, underground, naked bulbs (corms). Ironically, they are named after a tyrant who killed his brother, Remus, then gave his name to a city whose descendants enslaved Asia Minor, northern Africa, and most of Europe. The nomenclature is a simple matter of geography. Italian botanist Giovanni Francesco Maratti (1723–1777) was charmed by a species (probably *R. bulbocodium*) that bloomed around Rome when he named the genus. An additional seven species are distributed through much of southern Europe, northern Africa, and Asia Minor—the same regions once controlled by the Roman Empire. Today taxonomists recognize up to ninety species blooming from southern Africa northward to the Mediterranean basin. This spoils Maratti's original classification, which was based on plants restricted to old, imperial territories.

Romulea species bloom close to the ground, reminding people of crocuses. In fact, *Crocus* and *Romulea* are close relatives in the iris family (Iridaceae). It would be nice to recommend *Romulea* for gardens in the southwestern United States, but the rosy sand crocus (*R. rosea*) escaped from cultivation in California. It is spreading rapidly, yet another invasive and carpeting weed.

(6) OEDIPUS. Australia is home to several species of prickly, shrubby, nightshades (*Solanum*). Their large berries turn yellow, orange, or red when ripe, and locals call them kangaroo apples. In one species, native to Western Australia, the

kangaroo apples attach themselves to the parent plant via swollen fruit stalks (pedicels). This bush is known as *Solanum oedipus*. King Laius injured the feet of his son, the legitimate fruit of his loins.

(7) DIRCE. Why was the image of a woman tied to a bull's horns on Linnaeus's mind when he placed the new genus of North American moosewoods, ropebarks, and leatherwoods in the genus *Dirca*? These large shrubs, or small trees, continue to amuse hikers and naturalists. Their wood is so flexible and soft that you can tie their living branches into tight knots. Theoretically, one could use their branches to lash a victim to a bull's head. Tribes of Native Americans did no such thing. They stripped off the leathery bark to make ropes and thongs.

There are only two or three species in the genus. They prefer deep, shady forests, but *D. palustris* is often found on the edges of streams or swamps—reminiscent of the story of the dead woman changed into a fountain or spring. Because *Dirca* bears flowers similar to those of *Daphne* (see §5.4), it is also placed in the Thymelaeaceae.

6.2 PREFERRED PRINCES

Apollo's masculine beauty appealed to both princes and princesses. Perhaps that is why this son of Zeus was also called Philesios (loved one) (1). Prince Hyacinthus (2) of Sparta openly preferred Apollo's attentions to that of the winged god of the West Wind. One day, Apollo showed Hyacinthus how to throw a discus. The spiteful West Wind blew it back, and it struck the boy prince in the head. As Hyacinthus died, the gore from the wound turned into a wildflower. The words, "alas, alas" were written on its petals.

Handsome mortal monarchs attracted their share of possessive goddesses from heaven. Selene, the moon goddess, came down from the night sky and claimed King Endymion (3) of Elis. Zeus granted Selene's request that Endymion remain forever young but asleep. Endymion still drowses within a cave on Mount Latmus, unaware he once fathered fifty daughters on the moon goddess.

Ares, the war god, once deserted Aphrodite in favor of Eos (Selene's sister), the dawn goddess. Aphrodite placed a curse on Eos, who thereafter could not stop abducting mortal men. One time the dawn goddess carried off King Cephalus, but the monarch was destined to return to his wife, Queen Procris (4) after a much-protracted separation. Eos turned next to Prince Tithonus (5), a son of one of Troy's kings. The dawn goddess begged Zeus to give Tithonus immortality. The king of Olympus consented, but Eos forgot to ask for the boon of perpetual youth to accompany eternal life. With time, Tithonus became so weak and shrunken that all he could do was call out for Eos in a shrill voice. Tired of nursing this shriveled caricature, the goddess turned the prince into a cicada, and he flew out the bedroom window.

Handsome princes were menaces even to their own royal families. Byblis (6), a Cretan princess, fell in love with her twin brother, Caunus. He rejected her love letters and left the island to avoid her. Byblis, now always in tears, stalked her disgusted, wandering brother until she reached Phoenicia, where she turned into a sobbing spring of water.

Botany

(1) PHILESIOS. Philesios was one of those mythological names that suffered a "sex change" during the days when botanists believed that plant names should have feminine endings. Although Apollo remained a masculine deity under the name of Philesios, he became effeminate as the much-beloved *Philesia magellenica*. *Apollonias barbujana* (see §5.4) received its name because it belongs to the laurel family, and laurel trees were sacred to Apollo. *Philesia*, on the other hand, alludes only to Apollo's good looks, as its flowers form large, nodding, reddish-pink trumpets, highly favored by European connoisseurs. Modern taxonomists place *Philesia* in the family Philesiaceae, along with the Chilean bellflower vine (*Lapageria rosea*), another plant with snob appeal.

Philesia is restricted to a narrow belt of cool-temperate rain forest in the Andes of southern Chile. It grows as a shrub, but if it has a large tree to lean against, it turns into a creeper. It can be grown outdoors in the northern hemisphere provided it receives an evenly cool, moist habitat without freezing temperatures. If you cannot go to Chile, some of the nicest specimens are found in botanic gardens in Ireland.

(2) HYACINTHUS. *Hyacinthus orientalis*, named for Apollo's favorite prince, is the popular hyacinth of our spring gardens. However, like so many so-called Dutch bulbs, the wild plants are actually native to the eastern regions of the Mediterranean, not to Holland. They were originally popular as perfume sources and as ornamental pot plants in Turkey and Italy. The culture of hyacinths did not really spread to colder, wetter, northern Europe until the sixteenth century. There are three wild species in this genus, which gives its name to the family Hyacinthaceae.

Linnaeus insisted he took the name *Hyacinthus* from the works of Homer, but did he really match the appropriate plant to the ancient name used in the earliest version of this Bronze Age myth? It is possible that Linnaeus simply followed an accepted and sentimental tradition promoted by the guilds of perfume makers over the millennia. These scent sellers matched the short-lived prince with a domesticated flower long exploited for its strong, sweet odor. Frankly, our hyacinths (wild or garden variety) fail to follow one important plot thread recounted by most Greek and Latin poets. Specifically, where are the expressions of grief ("alas, alas") on flowers of either wild or cultivated *Hyacinthus*? Their petals lack any evidence of divine calligraphy in the form of blotches, lines, or squiggles.

Archaeologists, historians, and ethnographers like Sir James Frazer (1854–1941), insisted that myths about the blood of young men turning into wildflowers derived from the ancient practice of human sacrifice throughout the Mediterranean basin. A handsome youth is killed, dismembered, and buried in a field to fertilize the earth in preparation for the next grain crop. By early spring, the traditionally plowed fields are invaded by a number of weedy perennials wearing "bloodstained" petals (red or purple shades). The magenta or scarlet flowers of Asian poppies, gladioli, orchids, wild tulips, and anemones signify both divine approval and the reincarnation of the victim's soul (see §6.3).

Baumann suggests that the original myth referred to some other plant with contrasting pigment patterns on its petals or sepals. He nominates the lower, liplike petals found on some wild orchids and the corn lily, a wild gladiolus of Greece and Turkey (*Gladiolus illyricus*). These blossoms are well-dotted and streaked. In particular, the corn lily (*G. illyricus*) is a purple-flowered, spring "weed" of agricultural land and has a blotched, lower lip. It is a far better candidate for the printed lamentations of a dead prince than the blank, blue hyacinths popular at Easter time.

(3) ENDYMION. Both old garden books and some relatively recent bulb catalogs refer to the popular Spanish and English bluebells as members of the genus *Endymion*. Our domesticated bluebells are based on three or four wild species native to western Europe. Barthélemy Charles Joseph Dumortier (1797–1878), a Belgian naturalist, followed the botanical tradition of naming a popular, handsome plant after a popular, handsome figure in Greek mythology. Now favored as perennials in woodland gardens, bluebell bulbs were once dug up for their mucilage, which was used to bind books and attach feathers to arrow shafts. The bulbs also contain lots of starch, once used to whiten linen.

When *Endymion* was reduced to the status of a synonym, we lost one of the best classical allusions in botany, but save your despair. The genus was renamed *Hyacinthoides* (like Hyacinthus). Although we lost Selene's sleeping lover, botanists acknowledged that these plants were very similar to Apollo's dead boyfriend.

(4) PROCRIS. Unfortunately, French botanists of the eighteenth and early nineteenth centuries often failed to explain the name of a new genus. Philibert de Commerson (1712–1773) erected the genus *Procris* without a word of explanation, and Antoine de Jussieu was equally silent when he decided to revise the group to refer to twenty or so tropical shrubs and herbs from Africa east to southern China. We must speculate as to its origin.

Procris belongs to the noxious family of stinging nettles (Urticaceae). If you merely brush against the innocent looking, fluffy white leaves of tropical nettles (*Urtica*) you will be jabbed by microscopic hypodermic needles rich in histamine and acetylcholine. Burning, itching, and intense pain ensue. *Procris* species, however, lack these cruel weapons and may be cut and picked in complete safety. Were Commerson and Jussieu hinting that, like Queen Procris, these nonaggressive plants will not fight back when robbed by a superior force like a goddess (or a French botanist)?

(5) TITHONUS. The ten *Tithonia* species native to Mexico and Central America are fit to represent a strapping king. They belong to the daisy-sunflower family (Asteraceae). In particular, *Tithonia diversifolia* is often sold as Mexican sunflower, and its robust, erect stems offer handsome, red-orange flowering heads. Its heroic proportions remind me of some giant, unusually robust marigold. However, it never survives a hard frost and is quickly reduced to a shriveled skeleton.

(6) BYBLIS. *Byblis* continues to weep but only out of hunger. The foliage of the three species found in Australia and New Guinea are covered with mucilage glands (the princess's glistening tears). Insects that land on the plant adhere to the glands and are digested. Like Venus's flytrap (see §5.8), *Byblis* is another carnivorous genus named for a mythological female, and the plant grows in mineral-poor, peaty and sandy soils. Australians call *Byblis gigantea* the rainbow plant, as the glandular secretions glitter and refract light, like tiny prisms, when leaves stand in the sun. The genus gives its name to the family Byblidaceae, once thought to be related to the rose family, Rosaceae. More recent studies suggest it is more likely to be allied to the equally carnivorous bladderworts in the family Lentibulariaceae.

6.3 APHRODITE AND ADONIS

The queen of Cyprus boasted that her daughter, Myrrha (1), was more beautiful than Aphrodite. The love goddess took revenge by causing Myrrha to crave her father, King Cinyras. Myrrha conspired with her old nurse to make Cinyras drink a narcotic dissolved in wine. The princess hid in the bedchamber of the stupefied king each evening and did whatever she pleased with him until she was noticeably pregnant. Soberer and wiser, King Cinyras attempted to execute his depraved daughter and chased Myrrha through much of the Mediterranean. He finally caught up with her in Arabia, but Aphrodite changed Myrrha into the first myrrh tree (*Commiphora myrrha*) before Cinyras could harm her. Down came the king's sword, splitting the trunk, and a beautiful baby boy tumbled out. Aphrodite claimed the infant and named him Adonis (2).

Prince Adonis grew up to be Aphrodite's favorite lover, but he was unlucky as a hunter. Gashed by a boar's tusks, Adonis bled to death in a field of cultivated lettuce (*Lactuca*). Two miracles occurred. As Aphrodite ran to her lover's aid, she cut her foot on a bramble. Her immortal blood stained the prickles and they became the first roses (*Rosa*). Second, Adonis's corpse melted away. All that was left of him were the red windflowers (*Anemone coronaria*) (3) of spring.

For thousands of years, Greek women worshiped Adonis as the personification of vegetation drying up in the cyclical heat of a Mediterranean summer. A festival, the Adonia, occurred from mid- to late July, months after all windflowers were gone, but it still had a uniquely horticultural twist. Female celebrants carried pots of weak, hastily forced seedlings or cut flowers destined to wilt before night's end. Greek historians and playwrights insisted the Adonia was fit only for prostitutes and concubines, as it consisted of insincere mourning and drinking binges way into the night. The dead plants were tossed into the ocean or a spring the morning after, as if to return Adonis's corpse to sea-born Aphrodite.

Botany

(1) MYRRHA. In ancient times, myrrh was collected from at least six *Commiphora* species (including *C. myrrha*) growing from southern Arabia to northeastern Africa and India. The Greeks imported myrrh from what are today the countries of Yemen and Oman. This explains why in the myth Cinyras did not catch up with his daughter until they reached the Arabian Peninsula. *Commiphora* is a common genus of almost two hundred shrubs and trees found through Africa and Madagascar. A few species grow as far afield as western India and South America. They are placed in the family Burseraceae with frankincense (see §5.11). Myrrh trees hide resin canals under their bark. When it is scratched or cut, the liquid rises to the surface and hardens into dark, bitter tasting, teardrop-shaped lumps.

The resin had sacred and profane uses throughout Mediterranean civilizations. Egyptians used myrrh at several stages when embalming mummies and gluing their sarcophagi together. Myrrh perfumes and medicinal balms were so prized by Greeks and Romans, it is no wonder they gave it a supernatural origin comparable to useful and aromatic frankincense and mint (§5.2). As myrrh incense concealed the odor of burning flesh, it was popular at cremations. After murdering his wife, Poppaea, Emperor Nero was reputed to have burned Rome's annual supply of myrrh at her funeral.

Drinking myrrh dissolved in sweetened wine produced a pleasant trancelike state. Its use as a painkiller or anesthetic explains why Jesus was denied "wine mingled with myrrh" at his crucifixion (John 19.39). However, myrrh is also mentioned eight times in the Song of Songs, surely the most erotic poem in the Bible. Myrrha's nurse drugged King Cinyras. Did the Greeks believe that myrrh resin continued to express Myrrha's corruptive nature, turning the morally upright into the wantonly passive?

Garden myrrh or sweet cicely is *Myrrhis odorata*. Linnaeus found myrrhis mentioned in the herbal of Dioscorides, a military doctor under the reign of Emperor Nero. This herb still flavors various foods and liqueurs but belongs to the celery family (Apiaceae), not to the true myrrhs in the Burseraceae. Although sweet cicely had ancient medicinal uses, it was never treasured like true myrrh. Some still recommend leaves or seeds of sweet cicely in teas and syrups to treat coughs, flatulence, and indigestion.

(2) ADONIS. Omnivorous Linnaeus exploited the Adonis myth in two ways. Because Theophrastus called the windflower *anemone*, Linnaeus erected the genus *Anemone*. The name now serves more than 120 spring-blooming wildflowers found throughout the northern hemisphere, and some are garden favorites (see below). Next, Linnaeus noted that the pheasant's eye flowers of southern Europe and southwestern Asia had a lot in common with true anemones. Both groups of plants were found in the Mediterranean. Both produced raggedy-looking (deeply divided or lobed) leaves. The bowl-shaped structure of a pheasant's eye flower was similar to that of an anemone. Both flowers produced similar numbers of male and female organs. And as some pheasant's eyes produced crimson blossoms with dark centers, they resembled miniature versions of a red, crown anemone (*Anemone coronaria*). Why not give pheasant's eyes to *Adonis*?

It turned out to be a good call. *Anemone* and *Adonis* are such closely related genera that both are placed in the buttercup family (Ranunculaceae). In particular, summer pheasant's eye (*A. astevalis*), from Europe, blooms two to three months after crown anemones and makes pretty little red and black cups. It is recommended for people who think their real anemones fade far too soon. Unfortunately, summer pheasant's eye also escapes from cultivation and is now reported growing wild in eight U.S. states. Are we encouraging another troublesome plant? I am afraid so. A journal for veterinarians published a study in 2004 showing that three horses died after grazing on summer pheasant's eye hiding in pastures. The stems and leaves of all pheasant's eyes contain cardenolides. These molecules weaken the heart when consumed in sufficient quantities. It is a good rule to always make children wash their hands after picking flowers that belong to any member of the buttercup family.

(3) WINDFLOWERS. Historians and ethnologists agree that the oldest version of the agricultural myths connected to human sacrifice came from coastal, southern Turkey and the Middle East, a region that was one of humankind's earliest centers for the domestication of grasses with edible seeds. The people of these lands knew

the doomed youths by such names as Tammuz or Attis. The Greeks adopted these stories of death, fertilization, and floral rebirth as early as the seventh century B.C.E. Narcissus (see §3.6), Hyacinthus (§6.2), and Adonis offer supernatural explanations for the presence of pretty, often perennial, wildflowers in plowed fields from late winter through early spring. These plants bloomed while winter wheat and other grain crops matured. The blossoms vanished and the grain was harvested before scorching suns browned the landscape.

Visitors to northern Israel in January and February will find that both the pageant of crops and invasive wildflowers remains unchanged despite major differences in religions and technologies. In particular, crown anemones (*A. coronaria*) are still weedy celebrities. They are harbingers of cool and damp weather throughout the Middle East. I have seen wild crown anemones blooming as early as mid-January near Haifa and Bethlehem. Wild populations come in a variety of colors (blue, white, purple, or pink), but red blossoms once represented the bloodstained victim, the darling of devouring fertility goddesses throughout the Fertile Crescent.

Crown anemones proved to be so hardy that they were easily domesticated, and their garden culture spread into northern Europe. You can see the checkered flowers in Dutch or Flemish works of art painted before 1600 C.E. Shakespeare had a keen eye. Look into a crown anemone with crimson sepals, and note the blackened bases in the center of flower. This darkened area is often "chequered with white." Today, *Anemone coronaria* flowers in our gardens without any hint of cruel rituals or dead youths. Their tubers are sold as poppy anemones, anemones de Caen, or St. Brigid anemones. Biblical scripture supplanted this plant's pagan associations as Christianity conquered the Mediterranean. In fact, a long, scholarly tradition holds that the verses beginning "Consider the flowers of the field" (Matthew 6:28–30) referred to these anemones. The Hebrew word for red flowers (*nitzanim*) is too close a match for the old word, *naaman* (darling of the goddess), or Arabic, *nissan* to disregard the possibility. Whatever the case, some past authors of garden history also insisted that the inadequately identified rose of Sharon (Song of Songs 2:1) was also a red anemone.

6.4 MELEAGER AND THE FATES

Three inflexible goddesses, all daughters of Night, determine the fate of mortals. When a baby is born, Clotho spins its thread of life, and Lachesis measures its span with her rod. When each life span has run its course, Atropos (1) snips the thread, and the human falls dead. Queen Althaea (2) of Calydon was granted a vision of these Fates shortly after the birth of her son, Meleager. They warned her that her child would die as soon as one of the logs that was ablaze in the fireplace was reduced to ashes. Althaea jumped out of bed, removed the burning wood from the hearth, quenched its flames, and locked it in a chest.

Meleager grew to be a promising prince. When a giant boar destroyed much of Calydon's countryside, he assembled a party of the finest heroes of his day. The beast was killed after a protracted struggle, but then Meleager made the fatal error of awarding the flayed skin to the visiting princess, Atalanta (3) as her arrow had drawn first blood. Members of the hunting party were insulted that a woman should claim such a prize, and Meleager was forced to defend himself, killing his own uncles. When Althaea learned that her son had slain her brothers, she unlocked the chest, threw the log on the fire, and committed suicide. Meleager died as flames consumed the piece of wood. His sisters, known as the Meleagrides (4), became so hysterical in mourning that the gods changed them into squawking guinea hens (*Numida meleagris*).

Princess Atalanta, now blamed for the death of Meleager and his uncles, was embittered by the outcome of the Calydonian hunt. Putting away her bows and arrows, she declared she would marry only the man who could beat her in a foot race—and she executed all losers. Men died until the goddess of love presented Prince Hippomenes with three golden apples. During their race Hippomenes dropped an apple each time Atalanta gained on him. She stooped to scoop up each fruit, losing ground and ultimately the race, falling in love with the winning groom.

Botany

(1) ATROPOS. The Fate who cuts your life thread is well represented by the genus *Atropa*, six species of rank herbs and coarse vines in the potato or nightshade family (Solanaceae). They are found from western Europe through the Himalayas. *Atropa belladonna* is the deadly nightshade associated with homicide, sorcery, and women's cosmetics, as it is a primary source of the drug atropine. In fact, atropine and its sister poison, scopolamine, are tropane alkaloids. Certain plants manufacture these potent compounds by combining molecules of ornithine and acetic acid. Tropane alkaloids are commonly concentrated in leaf and stem cells of many members of the potato family, but an added danger of *A. belladonna* is that the seeds within its innocent-looking, tasty berries are also rich in atropine. Symptoms of atropine poisoning include blurred vision followed by excessive salivation, agitation, delirium, and death. Some historians believe that Queen Cleopatra experimented on her slaves while considering her own suicide. Extracts of deadly nightshade worked fast, but the victim died in such pain that the queen of the Nile convinced herself to switch to snake venom.

When very weak extracts of *A. belladonna*, or related species in the same family, are applied directly to mucous membranes (or rubbed into thin armpit skin) atropine and scopolamine bypass the sensitive digestive system and are transferred to the nervous system through the bloodstream. This produces a painless, trancelike state with nonfatal results. Consequently, some archaeologists who have examined papyrus scrolls and tomb paintings believe that deadly nightshade and its relatives, mandrake (*Mandragora officinarum*) and henbane (*Hyoscyamus niger*), were used by ancient Egyptian surgeons as the first anesthetic.

Belladonna means "beautiful woman," and we know that ladies of medieval and Renaissance Europe placed tinctures of *A. belladonna* in their eyes to make their pupils dilate, giving their faces a bewitchingly languorous look. Unfortunately, any modern eye specialist will tell you that these enchantresses must have felt miserable, as the effects of a single application last for days, causing blurred vision and pain upon exposure to daylight. On the subject of witches, moreover, Church records implicate atropine extract from these wayside plants as the active ingredient in the infamous "flying ointment" of the witches' sabbath. Women were said to have mixed the plant extracts with animal fat and used the salve to grease a staff or broomstick. They then rubbed their vaginas with the greasy stick. This resulted in a trancelike state, lasting for hours, producing hallucinations both of flight and sexual intercourse (perhaps the true origin of the self-satisfied witch's cackle).

(2) ALTHAEA. Few medicinal herbs produce effects as different as *Atropa* and *Althaea*. The Greek word *althaea* also meant "healer" in the works of Theophrastus. *Althaea officinalis* was the root that produced the original source of marshmallow, which now has been replaced by commercial gelatins. Marshmallow was originally used as a folk medicine instead of a sweet treat. Roots were prized for their gooey mucilage and were converted into a stomach-soothing potion known as a demulcent. This is the only logical association between the original genus of marshmallows and Queen Althaea, who saved or healed her baby son. Linnaeus kept the classic name to erect the genus of marshmallows, accommodating a dozen species in the hibiscus family (Malvaceae) native to Europe and northern Asia.

Renamed *Alcea officinalis*, this herb is still offered in seed catalogs, although it has long escaped from cultivation and is a naturalized weed in swamps and grassy estuaries of North America. Unfortunately, most modern taxonomists now see no obvious difference between *Althaea* and Linnaeus's genus of hollyhocks, *Alcea* (an old Greek word for mallow). *Althaea* became a synonym and was plunged into the larger genus with fifty species.

(3) ATALANTA. *Atalantia* is a genus of eleven species of shrubs and small trees in the citrus tree family (Rutaceae). They inhabit forests from India to the Philippines. Because the fruits of some species have yellowish-orange rinds, horticulturists call

them Venus's apples or golden apples to remind us of the more expensive fruit Atalanta picked up during her race. The fruits of *Atalantia* species are anatomically similar to those of citrus trees (the hesperidium; see §5.3) and should never be confused with a true commercial apple (*Malus* ×*domestica*), which belongs to the rose family (Rosaceae). Ironically, there is little interest in eating Atalanta's golden fruits in Western societies. However, some species adapt well to tropical gardens and are often clipped into topiaries or formal hedges.

(4) MELEAGRIDES. Meleager's shrieking sisters return as *Fritillaria meleagris,* a species of spring-flowering bulb native to Mediterranean Europe and Asia Minor. All *Fritillaria* species belong to the lily family (Liliaceae), but flowers produced by wild populations of *F. meleagris* wear distinctive, checkerboard or scaly patterns of brownish-purple, magenta, and cream, which mimic the intricate, mosaic patterns on guinea hen feathers. This also explains such common English names as guinea hen flower, checkered lily, and snakeshead. The petals wear the plumage patterns of Meleager's sisters, following their hysterical metamorphoses.

6.5 PRINCE PERSEUS

An oracle told King Acrisius of Argos that he would be killed by his grandson. He promptly locked up his only child, the Princess Danae (1), in a dungeon with brass doors. No prison ever stopped Zeus, who dripped through an opening as a shower of golden rain and impregnated the princess. Danae had a baby boy named Perseus. Acrisius now locked mother and infant in a chest and threw it into the sea. The tides swept the chest to the island of Seriphos. Danae and Perseus survived the trip, and Polydectes, the king of Seriphos, then fell in love with Danae.

Perseus grew up opposing his mother's marriage to Polydectes. The king decided to trick Perseus and pretended to court Princess Hippodamia (2) of Elis. Acrisius cunningly asked Perseus to contribute to the bride price. "I have no money, Perseus replied, "But to see you married to Hippodamia I will bring you whatever you want, even the head of Medusa" (3). "That would make the most impressive gift," said Acrisius. "I accept your offer."

Medusa was one of the three Gorgon (4) sisters. They were so hideous, humans and animals turned to stone if they looked at them. Polydectes was convinced he would never see Perseus again, but Athena, Zeus's most loyal daughter, was listening. The goddess of wisdom took Perseus to the island of Samos to see the only extant statues of the Gorgons, and he learned to tell them apart. At first, all three idols appeared identical. They were winged, their mouths had boar's tusks, and each Gorgon's tongue (5) struck out. However, Perseus soon noted that Medusa's statue had snakes instead

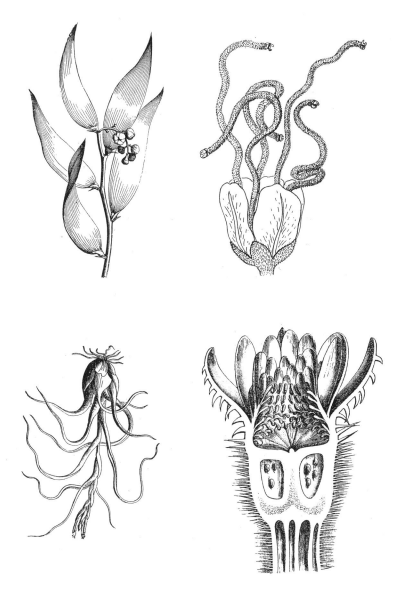

13. Plants named after the mother of Perseus and the monsters in his myth. Top left, a flowering stem of poet's laurel (*Danae racemosa*) showing a terminal stalk of female flowers (from Baillon). Top right, a much-magnified flower of *Medusanthera richardsiana* with its snaky stamens drawn by author/illustrator John P. M. Brenan (*Kew Bulletin*, 1952). Bottom left, a flowering plant of *Tillandsia caput-medusa* grows upside-down (from *Paxton's Flower Garden*). Bottom right, a cutaway of the flower of the gorgon plant (*Euryale ferox*) shows the many prickles on the skin and the fox nuts developing in the ovary. The illustration was taken from Adolf Engler and Karl Prantl *Die Naturlichen Pflanzenfamilien* (1887–1909). All illustrations reproduced with the permission of the library of the Missouri Botanical Gardens.

of hair. The scalp of the idol of Euryale (6) depicted flaming thorns. No one knows what Perseus saw when he looked at the statue of Stheno.

Athena gave Perseus a polished shield so he could see Medusa's reflection without looking directly at her. Then the goddess of wisdom sent him to the Stygian nymphs to obtain winged sandals, a sickle that would cut through Medusa's bronze neck, a purse that could hold her poisonous head, and a helmet of invisibility.

Botany

(1) DANAE. Shrubby *Danae racemosa* grows wild from Iran to Syria. Although some people call it poet's laurel or Alexandrian laurel, it is not a member of the bay laurel family (Lauraceae) and is best placed with the butcher's brooms (Ruscaceae). Poet's laurel is recommended as a hedge in warmer and drier zones. As the fruiting stems remain stiff and green long after cutting, they are much used by European florists.

Linnaeus must have noted obvious similarities between his specimens of butcher's broom (*Semele androgyna*; see §5.6) from the Canary Islands and the poet's laurel bush from the Middle East. Both plants have tiny, whitish, unisexual flowers, and they both make bright, reddish-orange berries. By naming the two genera after two princesses loved and abandoned by Zeus (Semele and Danae), Linnaeus emphasized that these plants shared much the same reproductive features even though they were well isolated by sheer distance.

(2) HIPPODAMIA. Compared to Danae, Hippodamia was the more magnificent princess in Greek mythology. To win her hand, men competed with Hippodamia's father, King Oenomaus, in chariot races. The king beheaded at least a dozen losers. Hippodamia finally married Prince Pelops after her father died in a racing "accident" (Pelops cheated).

Likewise, the genus *Hippodamia* was once one of the most magnificent genera in the gloxinia family (Gesneriaceae), found from southern Mexico through Central America. Whereas most gesneriads are relatively small and compact wildflowers or epiphytes (see *Napeanthus*; §3.4), species placed in the old genus, *Hippodamia*, were trees more than thirty-five feet high with trunks almost five feet in diameter. Botanists were also delighted with the curved, tubular, orange and yellow flowers. Unfortunately, *Hippodamia* is now a synonym for the genus *Solenophora* (tube-bearing, referring to the flowers). This new name conceals the regal stature of eleven species of tropical trees.

(3) MEDUSA. So much for the beautiful; we now descend into the unceasingly monstrous imaginations of plant taxonomists. Let's proceed from the common to the increasingly rare reflections of Medusa that botanists see in the sexual organs

of flowers. For example, the genus *Medusanthera* (Medusa's anthers) refers to the many twisted, snaky-looking pollen boxes (anthers) in each flower. There are about five species in this genus, distributed from Malaysia through the islands of the western Pacific. They belong to the Icacinaceae, the tropical family of churnwoods.

A similar feature has influenced the naming of *Medusandra richardsiana*, a tree of Cameroon's forests in western Africa. *Medusandra* means Medusa's men, or Medusa's stamens, and also refers to the pollen-making boxes (anthers) tipping each male organ (stamen) in the flower. The anthers in these flowers are snaky-looking things too, but they have an extra trick. They release their pollen grains by means of unique, curving valves. Botanists consider this mode of pollen release so bizarre that most place the tree in its own family, the Medusandraceae. The International Union for the Conservation of Nature warns that *M. richardsiana* is a vulnerable species, as 30 percent of its distribution has vanished in logged forests and woodlands cleared for farmers' fields. The tree is important to African wildlife, because its fruits feed baboons and parrots.

Finally, Medusa refers to both a mythical monster and any free-swimming, bell-shaped jellyfish. If you go to the Seychelles islands in the Indian Ocean, you may see protected groves of the native jellyfish tree (*Medusagyne oppositifolia*). *Medusagyne* means Medusa's woman and refers to the female organ, the pistil, in the center of each flower. The five stinky, white petals on each flower form the "bell" of the jellyfish. They curl backward, exposing a large pistil bearing seventeen to twenty-five necks (styles) forming the elongated "tentacles" of the jellyfish or the gorgon's crown of serpents. Once again, botanists found this bizarre species unique and gave it its own family, the Medusagynaceae. Much of the flora of the Seychelles was so devastated by human settlement that naturalists once believed that jellyfish trees were extinct. Not a single live specimen was found from 1903 to 1970. A dozen wild survivors have been found and nurtured since then. All jellyfish trees, grown in botanical gardens all over the world, are derived from the seeds of these remaining plants.

(4) GORGON. If a new species of plant looks especially grotesque, or if its leaves or floral parts are twisted and snaky, it may be named *gorgonea, gorgoneum,* or *gorgoneus*. For example, *Aonium gorgoneum* comes from the Cape Verde Islands and is a member of the succulent stonecrop family (Crassulaceae). Each woody stem is topped with a bizarre "lollipop" of orange-green, fleshy leaves.

Earlier, I noted that the grotesque and odorous flowering stalks in the philodendron family (Araceae) inspired Heinrich Wilhelm Schott. He delighted in naming new genera after hideous but classical creatures (see §4.9). It should come as no surprise that he named a genus *Gorgonidium* (worthy of a Gorgon). Five species come from South America. As might be expected, each flowering stalk consists of a luridly colored, sinister hood (spathe) packed with a cob of smelly flowers (spadix).

(5) GORGON'S TONGUE. Why do orchid flowers command so much attention? Much of their glamour lies in their petals, the ring of organs called the corolla. In the vast majority of flowering plants all petals found in the same corolla are identical in size, shape, and color. Each orchid flower has only three petals, but one of those petals usually differs in size, shape, and color compared with the other two lateral petals. Physical differences between the two lateral petals and the solitary, irregular petal are dramatic. Centuries past, some botanists compared the odd petal to a lip, so they called it the labellum. More imaginative naturalists thought the labellum resembled an exaggerated and protruding tongue. Tongue orchid is a common name found in field guides to the wildflowers of the Mediterranean and Australia. Members of the genera *Serapias* and *Cryptostylis* are called tongue orchids in English.

Friedrich Carl C. Lehmann (1850–1903) was something of a polymath. Acting as the German consul in the South American republic of Colombia gave him plenty of time to collect and study the tropical orchids. In 1897, he described a plant with flowers bearing small lip petals that looked like furry yellow buckets. Lehmann noted that the bucket margins ended in fine fringes (like wispy, coiling snakes of different sizes). The tips of the lateral petals also ended in a few snaky threads. Lehmann named the new genus *Gorgoglossum* (Gorgon's tongue).

It is a wonderful name, but it could not be retained. The German consul did not realize he was describing a species that belonged to a genus described almost three decades earlier. His gorgoglossums were members of the genus *Sievekingia*. The genus *Sievekingia* (named to honor a former mayor of Hamburg, Germany) was described back in 1871. Following the rules of taxonomy, the older name took precedence. It is not enough to invent the cleverest name for a new genus. You have to be the first to describe it. Taxonomists continue to dispute the genus *Sievekingia*. Some insist there are at least fourteen species distributed from Costa Rica to Bolivia. Some say there are only four.

(6) EURYALE. Forget orchids for a minute. If you live in a warm climate and have a big goldfish pond, why not grow your own gorgon? *Euryale ferox* (*ferox* means "ferociously prickly") is the prickly water poppy or gorgon plant found in waterways from China west to India. It belongs to the water lily family (Nymphaeaceae). Like the thorny head of the mythical Euryale, gorgon plants wear long sharp prickles on large, floating leaves and emergent flower stalks. Fortunately they will not burst into flames. If you harbor this monster, you will be rewarded with beautiful purple flowers in warm weather. Ancestors of this plant had a much wider distribution. Fossil flowers of an extinct water plant resembling *Euryale* were found in clay deposits in New Jersey believed to be at least ninety million years old. The Chinese call *E. ferox* the fox nut and have eaten the seeds and mud-dwelling stems for more than three thousand years.

6.6 THE DEEDS OF PERSEUS

Once armed by the Stygian nymphs, Perseus flew to the northern land of the Hyperboreans, where he found all three Gorgons asleep. Using the much-polished shield, he identified Medusa in its reflection. Perseus beheaded her and then placed her head (1) in the purse on his belt. The hero hid from the two remaining sisters by wearing the helmet of invisibility.

Perseus toured the Middle East and the southern Mediterranean in his winged sandals. While soaring above the port city of Joppa, he saw a beautiful naked woman chained to a rock on an island. Princess Andromeda (2), was about to be devoured by a sea monster to placate angry gods. Androm-eda's mother, Queen Cassiopeia (3), once bragged that her daughter was more beautiful then the nereids (see §3.4). These sea nymphs complained to their master, Poseidon, who sent the beast to destroy both port and princess. Perseus took out his sickle and killed it first.

Andromeda promised to marry Perseus, and he flew with her to Seriphos. King Polydectes and his toadies were banqueting when Perseus entered un-announced. "Did you bring what you promised?" said the king, with a sneer. Perseus opened the purse, averted his eyes, and held up Medusa's head. The king and his retinue turned to stone. Most poets insist that Perseus returned all the supernatural devices to the gods and gave Medusa's head to Athena. A few say that when Perseus became king of Argos he buried the horrible head in the central marketplace (*agora*), hoping that continuous trampling would make it lose its power. The poisonous mandrake (*Mandragora offici-narum*) (4) grew out of the gorgon's head, sprouting through the packed dirt.

Medusa was pregnant when Perseus beheaded her, and the winged horse, Pegasus, leapt out through her severed neck. The miraculous stallion flew free until it was bridled and tamed by Bellerophon. This hero used Pegasus as a mount to kill the fire-breathing chimera (5), a daughter of Echidna who was part lioness, part nanny goat, and part snake.

The Greeks believed that the Fates are implacable. Perseus did indeed kill his grandfather, albeit accidentally, thus fulfilling the original oracle (see §6.5). The hero took part in a sporting event held in the kingdom of Larissa, unaware that Acrisius was among the spectators. The discus thrown by Perseus spun out of control and fell on his grandfather. Acrisius never knew that his grandson was registered as an athlete at the Larissan games.

Botany

(1) MEDUSA'S HEAD. Botanists are so obsessed with monsters that they found a dead Gorgon in a member of the bromeliad or pineapple family (Bromeliaceae). Most

bromeliads are air plants or epiphytes that spend their lives clinging to twigs and branches. Inspect the trees, telephone poles, fences, and roofs of houses from southern Mexico through Central America, and you are likely to find specimens of *Tillandsia caput-medusa* (*caput* means "head").

The dry fruits of this plant release plumed, wind-dispersed seeds that become entangled in twigs or wires. Once it sprouts and matures, *T. caput-medusa* hangs upside down like the Gorgon's head dangling exposed from the belt of Perseus (a favorite image of Western artists). The swollen, bulbous, scurfy leaf bases resemble scaly heads. Their long, narrow, and coiled leaf tips look like serpents. Wild specimens should be left alone. The leaf bases are hollow and colonized by species of stinging ants that rush out to protect their homes on the slightest provocation. As in the myth, Medusa's head keeps some active, evil power following decapitation.

(2) ANDROMEDA. We now return to the pretty princesses. While still a graduate student, Linnaeus enjoyed a long collecting expedition in Lapland. One day he was beguiled by a small, flowering shrub in a bog. The encounter between man and bush provoked the most whimsical and romantic passages recorded in any field journal.

14. Sketch from the famous Lapland notebook in which Linnaeus compared a graceful, pink-flowered shrub to the Princess Andromeda. With the permission of the Council of the Linnean Society (London).

I noticed that she was blood-red before flowering, but that as soon as she blooms her petals become flesh-colored. I doubted whether any artist could rival these charms in a portrait of a young girl or adorn her cheeks with such beauties as are here and to which no cosmetics have lent their aid. As I looked at her I was reminded of Andromeda as described by the poets, and the more I thought about her the more affinity she seemed to have with the plant; indeed had Ovid set out to describe the plant mystically he could not have caught a better likeness. . . .

She is anchored far out in the water, set always on a little tuft in the marsh and fast tied as if on a rock in the midst of the sea. The water comes up to her knees, above her roots; and she is always surrounded by poisonous dragons and beasts—i.e., evil toads and frogs—which drench her with water when they mate in the spring. She stands and bows her head in grief.

Visual metaphors followed. Linnaeus drew a picture at the bottom of the journal page contrasting the naked Princess Andromeda, threatened by a dragon, with a flowering twig, shading a harmless newt. Years after the trip, he named the new species *Andromeda polifolia.*

Gardeners who like plants from cold, Eurasian latitudes call this species marsh andromeda or bog rosemary. It belongs to the rhododendron or heath family (Ericaceae). This means that *Andromeda* is a close relative of *Pieris* bushes (see §4.3). Unfortunately, the American horticultural industry confuses identification by selling *Pieris* species as andromedas. The continued misuse of this common name is a problem for people landscaping rock gardens and shrub collections. Fortunately, Andromeda's mother comes along next to clear up the mess.

(3) CASSIOPEIA. Inspired by Linnaeus's use of classical mythology, David Don gave us the genus *Cassiope,* also in the rhododendron-heath family (Ericaceae). Whereas *Andromeda,* the "daughter" genus, grows in Lapland and Russia, *Cassiope,* the larger "mother" genus, consists of a dozen species, with the majority distributed through the Himalayas. *Cassiope* species are found as far west as Alaska, where they are often called mountain heathers. It is easy to confuse *Andromeda, Cassiope,* and *Pieris.* They are all evergreen shrubs that produce nodding, urn-shaped flowers tinted white to deep pink. To discriminate between the genera when purchasing plants, compare their leaves for obvious differences in size, shape, thickness, and colorful luster. *Pieris* bushes have the largest, longest, glossiest leaves with young, scarlet foliage.

(4) MANDRAKE. In this uncommon version of the myth, a toxic plant rises from Medusa's head. An odd ecological truth is reflected in this outrageous tale. Mandrakes remain common, wayside plants through much of northern Israel, including the stony ground around Jaffa (Joppa). I have seen how these herbs thrive along roadsides and in the center of dirt paths where the soil is well trampled. Goats and sheep leave them alone. Why?

Both *Mandragora* and poisonous *Atropa* belong to the infamous nightshade family (Solanaceae). Mandrake roots, leaves, and seeds are rich in the tropane alkaloid hyoscyamine, a molecule similar in structure and strength to atropine (see §6.4). No wonder the ancient Greeks associated the toxic mandrake with the devastating face of the Gorgon. Fermented mandrake root was purportedly the preferred murder weapon of Cesare Borgia (1475?–1507), one of Lucrezia Borgia's brothers, who was also the son of the corrupt Pope Alexander VI. The Borgia family was reputed to use poisons when discreet homicides were preferred.

(5) CHIMERA. The monstrous chimera was depicted as another hodge-podge of animal parts. A plant chimera is a hodge-podge of tissues. The best-studied examples are ornamental plants with variegated leaves (some grasses, philodendrons, clown figs, coleus, or lettuce trees, for instance). Green and white or green and yellow are the most common colors of chimera foliage. When mutations occur irregularly but frequently in the stem's shoot tip (known as the apical meristem), new leaf cells inside the same leaf contain different amounts of genetic material. Normal cells in the leaf turn on chlorophyll and appear green. Abnormal cells in the same leaf cannot make chlorophyll, so no green color develops, and we see yellow pigments or no color at all (white). Collectors of African violets (*Saintpaulia ionantha*) favor flower chimeras. In most cases, the petal rims are colored differently from their centers, and the blossom looks like a five-pointed pinwheel.

Some growers encourage mutation by spraying the plant with dilute solutions of colchicine (see §6.10). The cells that make up the tender young growth in the shoot absorb the powerful molecule. This increases the frequency of genetic errors during cell division, because chromosomes contaminated with colchicine have trouble separating during division. A second way to make a chimera is to graft two different plant species together. New shoots appear where the two cut ends are joined, and these new sprouts weave together the cells of both parent plants.

6.7 THE CONCEPTION, BIRTH, AND YOUTH OF HERACLES

Zeus believed both gods and mortals needed a champion to protect them from monsters and cruel rulers. This required a great act of procreation. When King Amphitryon of Troezen rode off to war, Zeus told the sun god not to shine for three days. Zeus disguised himself as Amphitryon and spent the extended night in bed with the king's wife, Alcmene (1). He departed as Amphitryon returned triumphantly from battle to celebrate his victory with his queen.

Nine months later, Alcmene had twin boys named Iphicles (son of Amphitryon) and Alcaeus (son of Zeus), but Zeus knew his child. He carried little Alcaeus to Olympus and placed him on the breast of sleeping

Hera. The infant suckled happily, gaining a god's strength, until Hera awoke and angrily brushed him away. Excess drops of milk dripped into the night sky, producing the Milky Way. A few trickled down to earth and dyed a red lily (2) pure white. The gods admired this new flower, exclaiming that its petals were paler than Aphrodite's limbs. The goddess of beauty grew jealous and stuck a large, green, phallus-shaped pistil in the center of the flower, spoiling its looks.

As for the baby, he was renamed Heracles (Roman, Hercules) (3), "the glory of Hera." With his supernatural strength and his brass-bound club of olive wood, friends and foes called him *claviger* (club bearer) (4). He was tutored by Chiron, and while still a student, Heracles introduced mankind to the curative properties of spikenards (*Nardostachys grandiflora*) and wild sarsaparillas (*Aralia*) (5).

Botany

(1) ALCMENE. A woman who spends three days in bed with a god and then gives birth to twins must be tough. Perhaps this is what the German horticulturist and explorer Ignatz Urban (1848–1931) had in mind when he gave this queen's name to a genus of tropical American trees in the custard apple family (Annonaceae), instead of some delicate wildflower. The point is moot, as *Alcmene* was reduced to a synonym and all former species now belong to the genus of lancewoods (*Duguetia*).

(2) LILY. Botanists and archaeologists agree that the myth of the flower turning white must refer to the Madonna, Bourbon, Annunciation, or European Easter lily (*Lilium candidum*). Yes, this Christian emblem has a long pagan history. Five thousand years ago both *L. candidum* and the equally white sea daffodils (*Pancratium*) were associated with the mother goddess of Crete. The Greeks said it was sacred to Hera. But it was only five or six centuries ago that Renaissance artists started placing Madonna lilies in the hand of the archangel Gabriel, to depict the Annunciation. In between these eras, Egyptians used the flowers to make perfume. Greek herbalists insisted that lily oil removed wrinkles when added to ointments or salves. It still takes more than 250 pounds of flowers to yield little more then a quarter of a pound of lily essence.

(3) HERACLES. Linnaeus found a plant named *Heracleum* (Hercules the healer) in the works of Theophrastus (370–287 B.C.E.). Plainly amused by the story of a baby who balloons into the biggest and strongest hero, the Swedish botanist gave the name *Heracleum* to the giant hogweeds and cow parsnips now placed in the celery family (Apiaceae). In temperate parts of the world most members of this family are dainty herbs, but there are exceptions to the rule, such as giant fennel (see §4.10). Just as Heracles towered above men, many of the sixty species of hogweeds

distributed through Eurasia and North America are whoppers compared with celery, dill, parsley, coriander, and other culinary herbs. Hogweeds may grow more than ten feet high, and the span of their flowering parasols can be up to two feet across. In eastern Europe the seeds flavor alcoholic drinks. These plants contain some powerful compounds. Although sheep and pigs eat them without effect, the sap causes blistering if it spatters on human skin and is exposed to ultraviolet rays.

(4) CLAVIGER. The power of plants is also reflected in their ability to influence the often whimsical imaginations of botanists. Some plant taxonomists found the club of Hercules in some of the oddest plant structures, growing far from Greece. For example, some members of the ginger family (Zingberaceae) often form a tight, thick club of flowers at the tips of their stems. They look like a menacing knobkerry. Consequently, we have *Costus claviger*, one of many "wild gingers" from South America, popular in tropical greenhouses and gardens.

Hercules's club is another name for the southern prickly ash (*Zanthoxylum clavaherculis*), a small tree in the citrus family (Rutaceae). It is native to southern woodlands of the United States, from Virginia east to Oklahoma. Linnaeus, who named the species, was probably amused by the menacing appearance of the bark, as the tree sports some fearsome-looking spines and bizarre, corky warts.

(5) ARALIAS. Following the European tradition, American naturalists gave of their native aralias the common name of Hercules's club. These plants are now treated as members of the celery family (Apiaceae), making them relatives of both the hogweeds (*Heracleum*) mentioned above and the cure-all, ginseng (*Panax*; see §5.6). Chippewa Indians pounded stems and leaves of American spikenard (*Aralia racemosa*) into a rag or piece of cloth and applied it directly to the skin as a poultice for coughs and fractured bones. Hercules's club (*A. spinosa*) is a large, prickly shrub once used extensively by American herbalists to induce vomiting. It is also called angelica tree and devil's walking stick, depending on your faith in purgatives.

6.8 THE LABORS OF HERACLES

Hera waited until Heracles became a father before cursing him with madness. He killed his own children and two of his nephews, believing they were enemies attacking the city. Recovering his sanity, Heracles went to the Delphic Oracle and asked what he must do to pay for his crimes. "Put yourself in the service of your enemy, King Eurystheus of Tiryns," was the reply. Heracles served Eurystheus for twelve years, completing twelve mighty labors.

Eurystheus wanted the hero dead or lost, so he sent him to the most dangerous places on and under the earth. For example, Heracles killed two of Echidna's monstrous children for his first and second labors. The Nemean lion fell to Heracles, despite its weapon-proof hide. The hydra (1) was a giant, venomous, multiheaded snake, living in the Lernaean swamps. It could sprout new heads, so Heracles lopped off the old ones then seared the neck stumps before they could regenerate. For his ninth labor Heracles entered the dangerous kingdom of the Amazons, a conquering race of warrior women, and took the golden girdle of Queen Hippolyta (2). He killed the queen, grabbed her double-edged axe, and used it against her followers with grim success.

Becoming desperate, Eurystheus commanded Heracles to go to the earth's end and bring back the golden apples of the Hesperides (see §5.3) for his eleventh labor. First, Heracles shot an arrow over the garden wall and killed Ladon, the dragon, wrapped around the apple tree. Ladon, another child of Echidna, was Hera's favorite servant. The queen of heaven placed his body in the sky, and we know it as the constellation Draco (3). The hero knew that the Hesperides would still refuse to give him any fruit, but they would never reject their own father. Heracles relieved Atlas of his burden temporarily and held up the sky while the Titan entered the garden and visited his now generous daughters.

Eurystheus had only one more opportunity. For the last labor, the king insisted that Heracles go to hell and bring back Cerberus (4). This giant, three-headed hound was another child of Echidna that Hades kept at the gates of his kingdom to prevent the escape of homesick ghosts. Once Heracles crossed the Styx, the goddess Persephone welcomed him as her honored half-brother. Even Hades tolerated his nephew and offered a compromise. "You can borrow my pet provided you do not hurt him with your weapons." When Heracles put the three necks of Cerberus in a chokehold, the dog submitted to a chain. However, it had been a long time since the hound had seen the sun, and it vomited upon exposure to the upper air. The mess grew into the aconite (5), the most poisonous plant in Greece and a favorite of witches.

Freed from his labors, Heracles competed for and won the hand of Princess Dejanira (6). She gave him four sons and a daughter to replace his lost children. Although Heracles remained on good terms with Chiron, a new race of centaurs (see §6.9) proved troublesome to mankind. When the centaur Nessus attempted to rape Dejanira, Hercules killed him with an arrow dipped in the venomous blood of the hydra.

Botany

(1) HYDRA. The genus *Hydrilla* (little hydra) consists only of *H. verticillata*, an underwater plant native to ponds and slow creeks in Europe and Asia. It is not poisonous

like its namesake and was once considered excellent food for goldfish or used to decorate aquaria. This waterweed belongs in the Hydrocharitaceae with *Egeria* (see §3.5). Unfortunately, when *Hydrilla* was released into Florida's waterways in the 1960s, it responded with equally monstrous growth. The plants formed dense mats with stems up to twenty-five feet in length. They branched as frequently as the hydra's heads, jamming outboard motors. Stem fragments rooted in sand or mud, increasing their distribution. *Hydrilla* remains at large as a pest; it is also blamed for smothering native vegetation and reducing the numbers of fish that prefer open water.

(2) HIPPOLYTA. The seventeen species in the genus *Hippolytia* display an Amazon's toughness. These wildflowers have woody rootstocks and often live at high, dry altitudes on mountains from Pakistan east through China. Instructions for maintaining them in rock gardens often include growing them in gravel. They are members of the daisy family (Asteraceae). Alpine and rock gardeners like their dense, silvery gray foliage and numerous, tight, yellow flowering heads (the queen's golden girdle). *Hippolytia* is a close relative of the tansy and pyrethrum daisies (*Tanacetum*) and probably packs some of the same chemical weapons against marauding insects.

(3) DRACO. Ladon faired far better in astronomy and botany than his three brothers (Cerberus, the Nemean lion, and the hydra). This dragon is honored both in the night sky and in six plant genera. We have *Dracaena* (female dragon), *Dracontium* (in Draco's image), *Dracontomelon* (dragon's melon), *Dracophyllum* (dragon's leaf), *Dracopsis* (dragonlike) and *Dracunculus* (little dragon). Let's consider two groups of trees named for the tree-guarding monster.

Dracaena draco is the dragon's blood tree of the Canary Islands. A member of the maguey family (Agavaceae), dragon's blood trees leak a deep, reddish resin used in special varnishes and, at one time, for engraving photos. They grow slowly, rarely putting out a new branch more than once every decade. The oldest surviving trees on the islands are approaching their fourth centuries. The longer a tree lives, the more likely it will weep resin, like a dragon bleeding to death from invisible arrow wounds.

Dracontomelon belongs to the mango family (Anacaridaceae), not to the true melons in the family Cucuribitaceae. The eight species of dao, mon, or argus pheasant trees live in the forests of southeast Asia and New Guinea. They are prized as "luxury timbers" that are used for expensive veneers, furniture, and traditional canoes. In Vietnam and Laos, some women continue to burn seeds of the dao tree (*D. dao*) and then paint the soot onto their teeth. Black, not white teeth are beautiful in Kammu culture. You would think that a genus named dragon's melon would produce enormous toxic fruits. This is not the case. Most trees bear fruit the size of commercial plums. They are eaten with relish by people in New Guinea and by orangutans in Malaysia. The name appears to reflect the massive trunks of some species. Some grow more than one hundred feet in height and are covered with scaly, multicolored bark, like a dragon's back.

(4) CERBERUS. Although botanists apply monster names to new plants with tongue-in-cheek, few are quite as ironic as *Cerbera*. While comparing flowers, Linnaeus recognized that sea mangoes and pong pong trees were closely related to European dogbanes (*Apocynum*). *Apocynum* means "without dogs," because dogbane was used to tip arrows or poison baits to get rid of unwanted canine packs. Naming a new genus after a monstrous hound standing guard over unhappy ghosts gives persecuted puppies the last laugh. Linnaeus must have heard stories about victims in India, southeast Asia, or the tropical islands of the Pacific, who died after eating bits of pong pong seeds, leaves, or tree sap. Some poor souls swallowed it to prove their innocence in a trial by ordeal. Others used it to commit suicide.

We now understand that the trees are rich in the molecule cerberin. It is a steroid hooked up to a sugar molecule (a cardiac glycoside), and its consumption changes the rate at which calcium enters the chambers of the heart. Fatal symptoms resemble heart attacks. Seeds of the suicide tree (*C. odallam*) have a bitter taste, but that can be masked in spicy cuisines. It is suspected that five hundred people in Kerala, India, died of suicide tree poisonings between 1989 and 1999. Three-quarters of the victims were young women, suggesting they were unwanted wives murdered by their husbands' families.

(5) ACONITE. The West has its own heart-stopping history of plant-based murders, represented by the autumn-blooming monkshood (*Aconitum*) in your garden. The common name refers to the cupped top sepal that forms a hood, or monk's cowl, over the other organs in the flower. If you prefer old Hollywood werewolf movies, you can call the same plant wolfsbane. In either case, here's another excellent example of an ancient culture's ascribing a unique origin to a powerful herb. There are an estimated hundred species of *Aconitum* in the northern hemisphere (most grow in China), and they belong to the buttercup family (Ranunculaceae).

The active toxin in the taproot is the alkaloid aconitine. Once released in the bloodstream, it causes irregular heartbeat. Breathing slows until it stops altogether. Drop for drop aconitine is more lethal than strychnine or cyanide. The Greeks believed the plant's roots ate through marble (they do not). These wildflowers were probably the oldest known source of arrow poisons in Europe and temperate Asia. Prince Paris of Troy was accused of dipping his arrowheads in aconite before shooting one into the heel of Achilles (see §7.3). Hunters in the Himalayas brought down wild pigs with aconitine-tipped darts. Greeks on the island of Chios were reputed to use it in a potion to put old, sick men out of their misery.

(6) DEJANIRA. After so much monstrosity and destruction, it is nice to return to another pretty princess. We have seven species of South American wildflowers

in the genus *Deinara*. It is placed within the gentian family (Gentianaceae). Thanks to the myth of Chiron (see §3.7) and the healing centaury plants, gentian-loving botanists milked Greek mythology for the names of people who had run-ins with the race of half men/half horses (§6.9). Dejanira despised Nessus, but *Deinara* flowers resemble European *Centaurium* nonetheless. The myth of medicinal gentians dies hard. Brazilian pharmacologists experimented recently with extracts of *Deinara* leaves and roots to kill malaria parasites without much success.

6.9 THE CLOUD WOMAN

Ixion, of the Lapiths, inherited his kingdom, and criminal nature, from his father, King Phlegyas (an arsonist who burned the temple at Delphi). In turn, Ixion burned his new father-in-law to death in a charcoal pit, as he did not want to pay the bride price. Nevertheless, this cruel, young monarch was a much-favored grandchild of Zeus. While only a mortal, Ixion was welcomed on Olympus and dined on ambrosia and nectar. He repaid his divine grandfather by attempting to seduce his immortal step-grandmother, Hera.

When Hera complained to her mighty husband, Zeus picked up a passing cloud, molded it into a likeness of his wife, and breathed life into it. The nebulous decoy visited Ixion while he was drunk, and the man made love to her. Nephele (1), the cloud woman, gave birth to Centaurus, a bestial man who mated with mares. Ironically, Ixion became the grandfather of an equally ungrateful new race of centaurs who were as treacherous and lustful as he was. Ixion was succeeded by his legitimate son, Peirithous, who made the mistake of inviting his "half-horse cousins" to his wedding. The centaurs became drunk and attempted to rape the bride, bridesmaids, and various boys. The Lapiths fought them off, but subsequent warfare lasted for years until Heracles killed most of the centaurs with his poisoned arrows.

Hera commanded that King Athamas of Boeotia marry Nephele. They had three children, but Nephele, made in proud Hera's image, scorned her mortal husband. Athamas took Ino, Semele's sister (see §5.7), as his concubine and even agreed to raise Semele's child, Dionysus. Nephele floated back to heaven and told Hera. The queen of Heaven punished Athamas with the curse of madness. He killed one of his sons, believing the boy was a deer, and dismembered the corpse. Ino committed suicide, but Zeus, grateful for her attempted protection of Dionysus, turned her soul into a sea goddess. Athamas's two surviving children fled on the back of a winged, golden ram provided by Zeus. The ram flew east, but Helle (3), the daughter, could not hang on and fell to her death in sea straits since named the Helles-pont. The ram carried Phrixus, the son, to Asia. In gratitude, the boy sac-rificed the animal to Zeus, hanging its golden fleece in a sacred grove. Athamas eventually regained his sanity but was banished from Boeotia. He founded a new city on the island of Sicily, where Mount Athamas and the country Athamania (4), were named in his honor.

Botany

(1) NEPHELE. The haughty queen lends her name to the genera *Nephelaphyllum* (Nephele's leaf), *Nephelium* (in Nephele's image), and *Nephelochloa* (Nephele's grass). These genera have one thing in common. At some stage of their life cycles, some part of each plant looks as fluffy as a cloud. This includes the fruits of rambutan (*Nephelium*) in the soapberry family (Sapindaceae). The leathery rinds wear soft, curving spines colored pink, red, or yellow. When they hang from a tree in heavy, ripe clusters, they look like massed cumuli at sunset. There are thirty-five species of these trees, native to Indonesia and Malaysia. *Nephelium lappaceum* remains the most common backyard rambutan. Many people like the fruit's sweet-and-sour pulp, but a friend of mine who grew up in Singapore compared walking on paths strewn with fallen fruit to "stepping on the bodies of dead mice."

(2) LAPITHS. By now, some readers can predict botanical "hook-ups" with certain plot threads and recurrent characters. At one time, the word *Lapithea* served as another common example of a plant taxonomist's naming a new genus in the gentian family (Gentianceae) after people who interacted with centaurs (see §3.7 and §6.8). *Lapithea* referred to a genus of pink wildflowers found in North Amer-ica. It is now just a synonym hidden within the accepted genus of rose pinks (*Sabatia*).

(3) HELLE. Likewise, yet another member of the orchid family (Orchidaeae) is named after a pretty princess. *Elleanthus* (Helle's flower; the "H" was dropped) con-tains at least seventy species in the tropical Americas. Most of these plants attach themselves to tree branches or rocks. The leafy stems are long and slender, and the purple, red, or yellow flowers form dense and vivid clusters at each stem tip. Note that the stems of some *Elleanthus* species often hang downward when at peak bloom. Perhaps these lovely miniature bouquets, dangling precariously from tree limbs, re-minded Carl Borivog Presl (1794–1852), a botanist from Bohemia, of Helle falling from her seat on the ram's back.

(4) ATHAMANIA. The Mediterranean is rich in fragrant herbs that belong to the celery family (Apiaceae), and this region is where we find fifteen *Athamanta* species. Linnaeus erected the genus and named it *A. sicula* (*sicula* = "dagger-shaped fruit"), which continues to grow in central Sicily, where Athamas reigned. The leaves and

the hard, dry, single-seeded fruits of candy carrot (*A. cretensis*) continue to flavor liqueurs. Other wild species are said to have edible roots, but that is no surprise, as they are related to true carrots (*Daucus carota*) and parsnips (*Pastinaca sativa*).

6.10 JASON AND THE ARGONAUTS

King Pelias usurped the throne of Iolcus from his half-brother, Aeson, and murdered most of Aeson's children. Only one infant survived. Aeson smuggled him out of the palace and sent him to live, in secrecy, with the centaur Chiron. The boy, renamed Jason by the wise centaur, reentered the city after he grew up, confronted Pelias, and claimed the throne for himself. Of course, Pelias did not recognize his half-nephew, and he asked this upstart challenger, "What would you do if a total stranger appeared before you and demanded your kingdom?" Jason, unaware that his answer was inspired by Hera, replied, "I'd send him as far away as possible until he found the golden fleece" (see §6.9).

Pelias accepted the offer with unusual enthusiasm, commissioning the building and provisioning of a ship called the *Argo*. He allowed Jason to select the crew of Argonauts, but the sly king was also unaware of his nephew's unique education. As a pupil of Chiron's, Jason could rely on loyal alumni. They included Prince Meleager (§6.4), Heracles (§6.7), Nauplius (1) the navigator, and many more. Jason was uninterested when Orpheus (2), the master musician, volunteered to join the crew. He changed his mind when Chiron prophesied that Orpheus's songs would settle disputes and defeat supernatural threats. With so many powerful allies and the patronage of Hera, the success of Jason's voyage was never in doubt.

They sailed to the land of Colchis (3), an Asian country by the Black Sea in the Caucasus mountain range, where Prometheus was chained and tortured daily. Drops of the Titan's gore fell to earth and turned into magical, autumn-flowering herbs. The sacred grove of Phrixus was located there, but the precious fleece was now guarded by a sleepless dragon. King Aeetes of Colchis had no intention of giving up the fleece. He challenged Jason to tame and yoke two fire-breathing, bronze bulls. Medea (4), the eldest daughter of Aeetes, was an accomplished sorceress. Hera bribed Cupid to shoot his arrow and make Medea fall in love with Jason. The princess protected her new lover with a salve made from the magic herbs that grew from the blood of Prometheus. Jason was not burned when he yoked the bulls. Medea then put the dragon to sleep with yet another potion so her new lover could take the fleece. The Argonauts retreated, pursued by the Colchian fleet, but soon escaped thanks to more of Medea's stratagems.

Some Argonauts never returned home. Iphitus and Mopsus died. Hylas, the squire of Heracles, was kidnapped by naiads. When the handsome boy bent down to fill his pitcher at a pool, the nymphs dragged him into their underwater grotto. Butes fell overboard but was rescued by Aphrodite, who spirited him away to her sacred mountain, Eryx. They had a daughter named Erycina (5).

King Pelias was not overjoyed when Jason presented him with the fleece. Instead, the vain old monarch succumbed to Medea's promise that she could restore his youth. Her boiling cauldron turned an old ram into a lamb. Crocuses sprouted where drops of the elixir fell to earth. Pelias died when he allowed his own daughters to cut him into pieces and toss him into the boiling pot.

Botany

(1) NAUPLIUS. The *Argo*'s navigator and shipbuilder had an unusually aquatic heritage. Nauplius's father was the sea god, Poseidon. His mother, Amymone, knew the location of underground springs that gave Argos fresh water through hot, dry summers. Artists depicted her carrying a pitcher of water. Visit the rocky coastlines of most Mediterranean islands and countries, and you will often find a little, annual wildflower in the daisy family (Asteraceae). This is *Nauplius aquaticus*. As its seeds appear to remain viable after soaking in seawater, the plants disperse naturally around the region and journey far further than their namesake.

Taxonomists now recognize eight species in the genus *Nauplius*. Some grow on Mediterranean mountain slopes, but others are restricted to the Canary Islands, far out in the Atlantic Ocean. The *Argo* sailed east to Asia, so Nauplius would never have seen the *Nauplius* species of the west. *Nauplius sericeus* is a low-growing bush with silvery leaves and pleasantly scented flowering heads favored in Mediterranean-style gardens.

(2) ORPHEUS. This is the last example of how tales about men and centaurs (see §3.7, §6.8, and §6.9) may influence classification within the gentian family (Gentianaceae). Some classic artwork and story fragments insist that Orpheus was a favorite pupil of Chiron, surpassing his hoofed professor on the lyre. Linnaeus, you will recall, gave us the genus *Chironia* (§3.7). Ernst H. F. Meyer (1791–1858), a director of the botanical garden in Konigsberg, Germany, tipped his hat to Linnaeus when he named *Orphium frutescens.* Meyer was trying to point out that this bushy perennial was closely related to the genus *Chironia.* Both Christmas berries (*Chironia*) and the sea rose (*O. frutescens*) grow in southern Africa. Both are members of the gentian family and related to *Centaurium* (§3.7). Also known as sticky flower, both petals and leaves of *O. frutescens* release complex secretions, but the function(s) of such

chemicals is not understood. It is quite a handsome plant when covered with glossy, pink-purple flowers and rewards its owners with blossoms in the middle of summer.

(3) COLCHIS. Linnaeus found *Colchicum* (from Colchis) in a version of the *Materia Medica* by Dioscorides, the doctor who treated soldiers loyal to the Emperor Nero. However, translations of Egyptian magical formulas, written far earlier than Dioscorides's treatise, suggest that the plant has been part of humankind's pharmacy for the past 3,500 years. The corms (a type of "naked" bulb) produced by the sixty-five *Colchicum* species, distributed from the Mediterranean basin east to India, are natural factories of the drug colchicine. We now know that colchicine is not unique to *Colchicum*. Other members of the family Colchicaceae, including garden favorites like the gloriosa lily (*Gloriosa*) and the star of Bethlehem (*Ornithogalum*), make the same molecule.

The earliest healers probably used *Colchicum* corms or seeds to treat symptoms of arthritis or rheumatism (note that Medea rubs her salve on Jason's limbs). It remains a respected and specific treatment for gout to the present day. Some pharmacists credit Benjamin Franklin (a noted gout sufferer) with popularizing colchicine in the United States. Because the molecule does not break down if the corm is killed and dried, crude colchicines could be shipped around the world over many months. Powerful plants have a long history of abuse. *Colchicum* never outlived rumors that it was a suicide root. Slaves of cruel Greek masters were reputed to eat it to escape further suffering. Medea, in turn, never outlived her reputation as a poisoner.

It is easy to see why root collectors thought it was a magic plant, something that sprouted from the blood of the trickiest Titan to defy the gods. The life cycle of *Colchicum* species reverses that of other bulbous herbs. Lush foliage appears in late winter only to die weeks before the summer heat. The flower buds do not appear and bloom until autumn. People refer to the voluptuous clusters of smooth, pink-and-white flowers as naked boys or naked ladies. *Colchicum autumnale* is also sold as meadow saffron, but that is a dangerous misnomer, as all parts of the plant contain some colchicine, and no one should ever consider using the pistil for culinary purposes. The bulbs are so genetically hardwired to bloom after hot, dry summers that you can wrap one in a damp towel, plop it on a table or windowsill and it will flower massively without benefit of soil.

(4) MEDEA. Depending on the source, Medea is reputed to have killed her husband's uncle, her children, a king of Corinth, Princess Glauce, and Glauce's father. The cup of wine that she mixed with aconite (see §6.8) failed to poison Theseus, however. It is hard to maintain a perfect score. Ironically, Linnaeus named a North American woodland herb, *Medeola virginiana*, purportedly to honor Medea's good medicines and white magic. To her credit, in some versions of this myth cycle

Medea cured Heracles of madness, rejuvenated Jason's father, and restored the beauty of the worn-out nymphs who raised and followed Dionysus.

Indian cucumber (*M. virginiana*) grows in moist, hardwood forests and has crunchy, underground stems that purportedly taste like cucumber. Some American Indians made teas of the leaves and berries to treat convulsions and spasms. Eating the plant was believed to purge the body of poisons because it stimulated urination. Colonial herbalists and apothecaries recommended cucumber root for swollen limbs (dropsy), a condition that occurs when the heart no longer throbs fast enough to rid the body of excess fluids. In time, digitalis derived from foxglove (*Digitalis*) proved far more effective for the same purpose, and cucumber root became an increasingly infrequent and odd remedy used by rural Americans.

Was Linnaeus being sarcastic when he named a modest and benign herb after a forceful and ruthless princess? Colleagues and friends insisted he had an ill-tempered, demanding wife. Perhaps the renowned taxonomist preferred powerful and determined women. However, we must note the similarities between the lilylike flowers of Indian cucumber and *Colchicum* (see above). Most taxonomists continue to place *Medeola* in the lily family (Liliaceae), and that allies it to the Colchicaceae based on shared structures of fruit architecture, pollen grains, and recent information taken from genes in their smaller cell bodies (mitochondria and chloroplasts). Amateur psychiatry is fun, but Linnaeus was always comparing reproductive organs in flowers, and he must have noticed that the neck (style) of a *Medeola* pistil divides into three slender "arms," just as the neck of a *Colchicum* pistil does. After all, Medea is the princess of Colchis.

(5) ERYCINA. Some scholars insist that Erycina is yet another name for Aphrodite. Therefore, the genus *Erycina* follows the gallant tradition of naming beautiful orchids after the various incarnations of the love goddess (see §5.8). Collectors of tropical American orchids treat *Erycina* as a "rare and choice" genus, consisting of only two species native to Mexico. Their flowers are supposed to smell like fresh-cut grass. Pleasing hybrids are made by crossing *Erycina* with species that belong to the closely related genus of dancing doll orchids (*Oncidium*).

15. The Greeks must have escaped from the wooden horse after it was dragged into Troy's arboretum. Top right depicts flowering branches of *Protea cyanaroides*. Top left shows fruiting twigs of the jujube (*Zizyphus lotus*). A date palm (*Phoenix dactylifera*) grows in the lower left-hand corner. Illustration by John Myers.

CHAPTER 7

ᴇᴈᴐ

Troy and Its Aftermath

In the close, under-arm of a tropic
house, dripping from the end of a leaf,
a tendril swells into a drop of grief—
a dragon's bib, hinged lid; a waxy lip,
where gnat and ant and beetle slip
into a speckled tankard full of sleep. . . .

—EDWIN WILSON, "Nepenthes"

7.1 THE ORIGIN AND GROWTH OF TROY

Some say that colonists from Crete settled the country around Troy. Others
say the first pioneers came from Athens in Greece. All agree that Teucer (1)
was the first king of the region, long before Troy's walls were built. Teucer
welcomed Dardanus, a son of Zeus and Electra, to his land. Dardanus
built a kingdom called Dardania and passed it on to his son Erecthonius.
Tros and Ilus were sons of Erecthonius, and they built settlements near
Dardania. Eventually the city of Troy (Tros) merged with the kingdom
of Dardania and the town of Illium (Ilus). Troy was guaranteed fresh water
when King Tros married the nymph Callirhoe (2), daughter of the river
Scamander.

Laomedon, a son of Ilus, was the next ruler of Troy. He employed Poseidon and Apollo to build impregnable walls around the city, but arrogant
Laomedon cheated both gods of their pay. The two deities allowed Heracles to destroy the city. Heracles killed Laomedon and all his sons, except
for Prince Priam. To restore the terrible losses to his royal family, Priam
had many children by various wives and concubines. Queen Hecuba (3),
his primary consort, gave him nineteen sons. Just before the birth of her
son Paris, Hecuba dreamt she gave birth to a stick that burst into flaming
snakes. The fiery serpents burned Troy and the surrounding land to ashes.
Seers warned her to kill the newborn, but she exposed the baby on Mount
Ida rather than watch him put to death. Little Paris was found and adopted
by a peasant.

Botany

(1) Teucer. *Teucrium* is another classical name that Linnaeus fished out of the herbal of Dioscorides. As in the earlier cases of *Artemisia* (see §5.4), *Gentiana* (§3.6), and *Juglans* (§4.1), the ancient root collectors, herbalists, and orchard owners named powerful and popular plants after powerful and influential monarchs and deities. Of course, the original descriptions of these plants in Greek or Latin texts were so incomplete that taxonomists like Linnaeus often gave the original, classical name to a completely unrelated plant genus—for example, *Pothos* (§5.9). Linnaeus decided that in this instance Dioscorides was describing the herb germander (*Teucrium chamaedrys*). There are about a hundred *Teucrium* species in the mint family (Lamiaceae). They grow wild through much of Europe, and there is an ancient tradition of making tea out of the bitter leaves in an attempt to treat blood diseases, fevers, whooping cough, and skin eruptions. Germanders are still used to make alcoholic tonics to stimulate appetites, as is gentian root (§3.6).

There was never much American interest in germander. When rural folk wanted to make a bitter tea or throat lozenge, they were far more likely to collect a variety of related weedy species in the mint family. These herbs are still known, collectively, as horehounds (*Marrubium, Ballota,* or *Lycopus*). Homemade cough syrups made by mixing boiled-down solutions (decoctions) of horehound with honey remained the standard remedy in Ozark Mountain kitchens until the early 1950s.

(2) CALLIRHOE. Attempts to domesticate the American wine cup, *Callirhoe involucrata*, began in the nineteenth century. These perennial wildflowers make attractive ground covers in dry beds or on slopes with sunny exposures. They have fan-like leaves and burgundy-colored blossoms. British-born botanist Thomas Nuttall explored the original prairies where these wildflowers grew. However, he never explained why he decided to name this very American genus of eight species after an Asian nymph who became a queen. I imagine he wanted to point out that wine cups are members of the hibiscus family (Malvaceae). That made them cousins of both the "marshmallow queen" (*Althaea;* see §6.4) and the dell nymphs (*Napaea,* §3.4). Because *Althaea* and *Napaea* were names erected by Linnaeus, Nuttall was paying tribute to "the Master."

I also suspect that *Callirhoe* was Nuttall's attempt at finding a classical name that could also function as a pun. American pioneers who built their farms on the tall grass prairie loved these little plants and called them poppy mallows. The petal cup of *C. involucrata* makes the flower look superficially like a miniature, magenta-colored poppy. *Calli* is Greek for pretty. *Rhoeas* is the classic Greek name for a field poppy. *Calli-rhoeas* (*Callirhoe*) hides the common name inside the classical allusion.

(3) HECUBA. In Greek mythology, poor Queen Hecuba turns into a vengeful, black dog after the destruction of Troy, the murder of two of her surviving children, and

the execution of her favorite grandson. *Hecubaea* was a genus of two Mexican species in the daisy family (Asteraceae). The flowering stalks have blackish-red hairs. Candolle named it to show it was closely related to the sneezeweeds in the genus *Helenium*. Just as Hecuba became the unwilling mother-in-law of Helen of Troy (see §7.2), the genus *Hecubaea* was once deemed closely related to *Helenium*, the genus of sneezeweeds. By the twentieth century, however, most specialists working on the daisy family felt that the black pelt on the stalks of the two Mexican wild-flowers was insufficient to keep them separated from the sneezeweeds. The genus *Hecubaea* was reduced to a section within the bigger genus, *Helenium*, adding a fresh insult to mythology's most humiliated queen.

7.2 THE JUDGMENT OF PARIS

Meanwhile, Priam and Hecuba's abandoned son Paris grew up and became a cowherd. When bulls fought, he awarded each winner a garland of flowers. His reputation as an impartial judge spread to Olympus. When the Olympian gods attended the wedding of the mortal king Peleus and the sea nymph Thetis, the goddess Eris (Discord or Strife) spoiled the reception by leaving a golden apple on the table shared by Hera, Athena, and Aphrodite. "For the fairest" was inscribed on the fruit. Naturally, all three deities reached for the same prize. Hera, Athena, and Aphrodite appeared to Paris and insisted that he decide who was entitled to the apple.

Each nude goddess attempted to bribe him when it was her turn to be judged. Hera offered riches and a great kingdom. Athena promised victory in every battle. "Wouldn't you like to posses the most desirable queen in the world?" Aphrodite whispered. "She is Helen (1) of Sparta, but some call her Lacaena (2), as she is of the Laconian tribe." "And why is she so desirable, my Lady?" Paris asked. "Because she is a demigoddess. Her mother was the magnificent Queen Leda (3). Her father was Zeus. He took the form of a swan, the most beautiful of birds, when he made love to Leda."

The apple was awarded to Aphrodite. A short time later, Paris was revealed to be a son of Priam. The old king was delighted to learn of his son's survival and appointed Paris to lead an expedition to Greece to reclaim a kidnapped relative. When this Trojan prince visited Sparta, he left with its queen. Helen's husband, King Menelaus, appealed to his brother, King Agamemnon of Mycenae. They formed an army of Greek city-states and declared war on Troy. The war would never have happened if Paris had remained faithful to his first love. She was the fountain nymph Oenone (4), daughter of the river god Oeneus. Paris forgot her the first time he saw Helen's face.

Botany

(1) HELEN. The usual story, told by generations of plant taxonomists, is that Linnaeus found a reference to a medicinal herb named after Helen of Troy while reading the works of Theophrastus. As noted above (see §7.1), the Greeks and Romans named putatively powerful plants after powerful figures in mythology. Linnaeus suspected that Theophrastus was referring to a common Mediterranean wildflower, known as the elecampane. He named it *Inula helenium*. Elecampane is a member of the daisy family (Asteraceae), and its root has an old history as a potherb, a candy, and as an ingredient in various tonics to treat intestinal worms, bronchitis, stomachaches, and other ailments.

To show that elecampane had close relatives all over the world, Linnaeus named the North American sneezeweeds *Helenium* (in the image of Helen). Today we recognize about forty *Helenium* species. Ironically, the name of the most spectacular queen in Greco-Roman mythology honors some of the least spectacular members

16. Plants named for the founder of Troy and Queen Helen. Left, a flower of germander (*Teurcrium*) showing how the stamens and pistil tip protrude from the tube made by the fused petals. Right, the flowering head of the elecampne (*Inula helenium*). Both illustrations come from Baillon and are reproduced with the permission of the library at the Missouri Botanical Garden.

of the daisy family. Some sneezeweeds are pretty, though. Like most daisies, the flowering head of a sneezeweed has a ring of polished, yellow ray flowers. The interior of the head is made of smaller tube flowers tinted yellow to brownish purple. *Helenium autumnale* is a garden-friendly sneezeweed, and selective breeding has brought out nice red-orange streaks on the ray flowers. Despite the common name, sneezeweeds do not cause hay fever.

(2) LACAENA. Orchid expert John Lindley was also unimpressed with Linnaeus's earlier attempt to immortalize Helen of Troy in botany. How could any mundane daisy ever represent the face that launched a thousand ships? Fortunately, the beautiful queen of Sparta had a nickname, unused by Linnaeus. Lindley was particularly captivated by the beauty of flowering orchids native to Mexico and Guatemala. He honored them with the names of mythological females like Lycaste (see §5.7) and Erycina (§6.10).

His genus *Lacaena* is small (only two species) but choice. The Helen of Troy of orchids prefers to grow on rich humus or rotting, fallen trees found in misty, cloud forests from Mexico to Nicaragua. *Lacaena spectabilis* is the more popular plant in cultivation, and it is easy to understand why. It produces a beautiful chain of glistening white and violet spotted blossoms. The lip petal is an exquisitely dappled, angular spoon. Lindley seems to be saying to the viewer, "Now, here's a flower that measures up to the reputation of Leda's daughter."

(3) LEDA. Happy is the man who is allowed to turn his hobby into his career. Charles B. Clarke (1832–1906) worked for the British Empire as a bureaucrat and school inspector in India as a means to fulfill his real passion, collecting exotic plants. He retired to Kew Gardens in 1887. His genus *Leda* was published a year after his death. You would presume that Clarke, following the traditions of Linnaeus or Lindley, would apply the name *Leda* to a new orchid or a member of the daisy family. Instead, the ten *Leda* species found in the Malaysian archipelago are placed in the acanthus family (Acanthaceae; see §5.12). If Clarke had a good reason for breaking the "orchid-daisy chain," he took it to the grave.

He left no written explanation why these tropical plants reminded him of Queen Leda. It is obvious he was following Lindley's suggestion that the name of a new genus should be nondescriptive, lyrical, and easy to remember. Let me add one personal observation. Most members of the Acanthaceae produce white- to cream-colored flowers. When they are pressed, the beaked tube of petals (corolla) folds up and resembles the head of a folded, paper swan.

(4) OENONE. Helen and Leda are well remembered. In contrast, poor Oenone was first abandoned by Paris in antiquity and then dumped by botanists early in the twentieth century. As she was a nymph of flowing, drinkable water and the daughter of a river god, it is entirely appropriate that the genus *Oenone* was erected

to classify half a dozen species of small, river-dwelling herbs (rheophytes). It belonged to the Podostemaceae, a family restricted to aquatic sites in South America and tropical Asia. Although they are flowering plants, "podostemes" have such low, simple growth that they are often mistaken for lichens or aquatic ferns. Their flowering stalks usually push up above the water's surface. By the midtwentieth century, most botanists failed to find anything unique in the genus *Oenone* (and also *Ligeia*; see §7.6). Its species were added to the much larger genus *Apinagia* (from a river near the Brazilian town of Apinages), native to South America.

7.3 THE TROJAN WAR

A Greek fleet assembled at Aulis but was unable to sail to Troy owing to an unrelenting gale. Calchas, a priest and prophet, warned King Agamemnon there would be no friendly winds until the monarch sacrificed his beautiful daughter, Iphigenia (1). The vindictive goddess, Artemis, demanded a life for a life, because Agamemnon had killed her sacred goat. Iphigenia's father handed her over to the priests, and she replaced the usual animal victim. The Greek fleet was thus able to depart; it landed on Troy's coast and besieged the city for a decade. In the tenth year, Greek fortunes declined. Achilles (2), the greatest Greek warrior, refused to fight after King Agamemnon deprived him of his favorite captive girl. King Priam's son Hector exploited the resulting weakness in the invader's lines, killing many Greek warriors including Patrocles, the best friend of Achilles.

Now filled with anger, Achilles returned to the battlefield in new, impregnable armor. He killed Hector and then despoiled and dragged his corpse behind his chariot. Weeks later, Achilles killed many of Troy's Amazon and Ethiopian allies. Eventually, however, Paris fatally wounded Achilles by shooting a poisoned arrow into the Greek warrior's naked heel. Even though Achilles had given the Greek troops a miraculous herb to close wounds, it proved ineffective against his own injury. The greatest mourner of Achilles was his mother, the sea nymph Thetis. Her many sisters, including Nesaea (3), Galatea, Glauce, and Clymene, accompanied her and mourned for seventeen days.

No one wanted the wonderful armor of Achilles as much as his cousin, the mighty Ajax (4). Agamemnon denied Ajax this gift, although Ajax was one of only two soldiers to rescue the dying Achilles from the battlefield. Ajax went mad. Podalirius (5), a Greek surgeon (and son of Asclepius; see §5.5) diagnosed the demented fire in the warrior's eyes but did nothing. During the night, Ajax killed a herd of cattle and tortured a pair of rams believing that he was taking revenge on Agamemnon, Menelaus, and their followers. When morning came, Ajax saw his mistake and committed suicide out of shame. A new flower grew from his blood. Its petals were spotted with the words *ai ai* (alas, alas).

Now deprived of their greatest warriors, the Greeks resorted to subterfuge and built the giant, hollow, wooden horse, stocking it with soldiers. The Greek army pretended to leave the country and went into hiding. The Trojans, in gratitude, took the wooden horse into the city believing it was a prize left by their enemies. That night, the Trojans celebrated until they were exhausted. The soldiers in the horse escaped through a trapdoor and opened the gates of Troy. The Greek armies entered, killing most of the Trojans and sacking the city. King Menelaus reclaimed his wife, Helen. The war ended with the ritual execution of another innocent. Princess Polyxena (6), daughter of King Priam, was one of the last victims. The Greeks sacrificed her at the tomb of Achilles to appease his ghost.

Botany

(1) IPHIGENIA. There must have been something about small, lilylike wildflowers with bright white or vividly colored petals that brought out the romantic side of Carl S. Kunth. Remember, he also gave us the equally adorable genera *Periboea* and *Simethis* (see §3.6). In fact, Kunth placed *Iphigenia* in the lily family (Liliaceae) with *Periboea* and *Simethis*. We now know that the passive princess of Mycenae can defend herself. By the end of the twentieth century, *Iphigenia* was moved to the family of colchicums (Colchicaceae). Biochemical studies showed that, like *Colchicum* (§6.10), the nine *Iphigenia* species manufacture the dangerous colchicine molecules. *Iphigenia* plants have a distinctly Asian distribution, and their seeds and bulbs are still valued in the traditional medicines of China and India.

(2) ACHILLES. In contrast, the leaves of common, wayside yarrow (*Achillea*), especially *A. millefolium*, remain a traditional medicine through the Mediterranean basin. Yes, ancient herbalists believed that yarrow stopped bleeding if its leaves were placed in an open wound. This dangerous folk remedy is classified properly as a vulnerary and is not recommended. There are more than eighty-five *Achillea* species in the daisy family (Asteraceae). Most are native to temperate zones in the northern hemisphere. Other cultures found medicinal virtues in the strong smelling foliage. Some North American tribes made teas of the leaves to treat colds and stop diarrhea. They also made compresses out of hot wet leaves because they also believed yarrow relieved inflamed, infected wounds. Some Bedouins of Syria still believe that diabetics feel better after eating the bitter flowering heads.

Yarrows are enjoying new popularity in European and American gardens even though few of us grow herbs for the sake of dubious remedies. Domesticated yarrows are now cultivated as bushy, summertime perennials for sunny borders. Some breeds produce colorful, candy-striped heads.

(3) Nesaea. Applying the name of a sea nymph (nereid) to fifty-six species belonging to the loosestrife or henna family (Lythraceae) is a bit of a stretch. In Greek mythology, Nesaea ruled her own island. Although some *Nesaea* species are found on the islands of Australia and Sri Lanka, plenty more inhabit the continents of Africa and South America. Furthermore, nereids are aquatic nymphs, but they inhabit saltwater. My examinations of collections in the herbarium of the Missouri Botanical Garden showed that *Nesaea* species prefer to root in mud or sand drowned by freshwater. Labels on sheets emphasized that the plants were collected in canals, seepages, and along creek banks.

You have probably seen *Nesaea* if you keep tropical fish and prefer to decorate aquaria with living plants. Their cut stems usually root after they are anchored in gravel. As a boy, I recall pet shops selling *Nesaea* in tight bunches. You may know them better as stalkflowers or orange hygro. *Nesaea crassicaulis* appears to be the most popular species for fish tanks these days. It offers leaves tinted with velvety orange or red, provided it is grown under a strong lamp.

(4) Ajax. *Consolida ajacis* grows wild in Greece but is distributed naturally through the Mediterranean from southern France eastward through the Aegean Islands into Albania. Gardeners of "old-fashioned flowers" call it rocket larkspur, annual delphinium, or doubtful knight's spur (fatal doubts killed this Greek knight). A member of the buttercup family (Ranunculaceae), rocket larkspur is such an internationally popular garden annual that it has escaped from cultivation in North America and Australia.

Like the commercial hyacinth (see §6.2), rocket larkspur is supposed to bear a written message of despair. Also like the commercial hyacinth, it is hard to find lines or dots on living flowers of rocket larkspur. Breeds of rocket larkspur come in shades of blue, purple, pink, and white, but photos, and my past attempts at horticulture, fail to show signs of calligraphy on the living petals. However, you get a nice surprise when you dry rocket larkspur for winter floral arrangements. Black streaks and squiggles become prominent toward the bases of some petals and sepals. Ajax mourns his fate after death withers him.

(5) Podalirius. The belief that plants will offer cures in war and peace spreads far beyond yarrow and *Iphigenia* (see above). It was entirely appropriate for an older generation of botanists to name plants after Podalirius. The genus belongs to the pea and bean family (Fabaceae), and such plants have a long history in apothecaries. *Podalyria*, in particular, is a genus of twenty-two species of bushes native to southern Africa. Some have silvery leaves and such pretty flowers that they are often

called sweet-pea bushes or water blossom peas. Ironically, the traditional healers of Africa have never shown much interest in these plants.

However, in the late eighteenth century some plant taxonomists thought that *Podalyria* was a much larger genus, well-represented in the northern hemisphere. *Podalyria* was a name given to wildflowers and trees bearing pea blossoms found all over the world. French botanist André Michaux (1746–1802) named the American false indigo (*Baptisia tinctoria*) *Podalyria tinctoria*. Unlike the sweet-pea bushes of Africa, the false indigo of the United States was used extensively as a laxative, as a liver stimulant, and as a treatment for typhoid. It was an important component of poultices placed on mouth ulcers or sore nipples. At least one American physician took the name *Podalyria* a little too literally and said it was effective against dementia (another false hope). By the twentieth century, most legume taxonomists finished separating *Baptisia* and *Sophora* (found in Europe, Asia, and North and South America) from the purely African *Podalyria*. The sweet-pea bushes of southern Africa were allowed to keep the name of the mythical doctor, even though they have no known curative properties.

(6) POLYXENA. Kunth was such a predictable "old softie" that this section will end where it began—with another genus he named after a much-persecuted princess. Two bulbous *Polyxena* species come from the Cape of Good Hope. They offer masses of small, light blue, mauve, or white tubular flowers. Known as Cape hyacinths, *Polyxena* belongs to the hyacinth family (Hyacinthaceae). When blooming from April through June (autumn in the southern hemisphere), these wildflowers offer the dainty and modest charm that Kunth routinely associated with minor females in Greek mythology.

7.4 KINGS RETURN TO GREECE

Despite their overwhelming triumph, few Greek generals enjoyed an easy return home. The fleet commanded by King Menelaus was blown off-course, and he and Helen spent eight years touring Mediterranean ports before returning to Sparta. Helen mourned Troy's destruction until she arrived in Egypt. There, Queen Polydama offered the sad demigoddess remarkable hospitality. "I have something that will banish all your cares," said Polydama. She gave Helen the magic cup, Nepenthes (1). Helen drank from it and forgot Troy.

While in Egypt, Menelaus was befriended by the sea nymph Eidothea (2). She could not tell him why he had so much trouble returning home and suggested he capture and consult her prophetic father. Eidothea's father was the shape-shifter, Proteus (3), who tended Poseidon's flocks of seals.

Menelaus disguised himself in a seal's skin and hid on the beach where Proteus took his afternoon nap. The king pounced on the god. Proteus tried to escape by changing himself into various animals, running water, and a tall tree but Menelaus would not let him go until he received an explanation for the continual detours that prevented his homecoming. "Your brother, Agamemnon, was murdered by his wife upon his return to Mycenae. Propitiate the gods and honor your brother's phantom if you ever want to return to Greece," Proteus declared. Menelaus released the sea god, and followed all his instructions. He and Helen returned to Sparta without additional delays.

Not all kings were as lucky. The return of Acamas to Greece was long delayed by storms. His beloved, the Athenian Princess Phyllis (4), died of heartbreak without ever seeing his ship in port. The gods turned her corpse into a blossoming almond tree (*Prunus dulcis*). King Phoenix (5) fought with

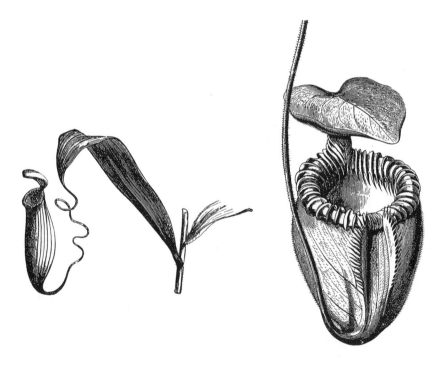

17. The illustration on the left shows how a pitcher-shaped trap develops at the tip of a tendril leaf of *Nepenthes distilatoria* (from Baillon). On the right is a close-up of the tankard trap of *N. villosa* (*from Paxton's Flower Garden*). Reproduced with the permission of the library of the Missouri Botanical Garden.

the Greeks at Troy and served as tutor to Achilles. Some say Phoenix introduced the first date palms to Greece when he returned from the Asian coast. Ironically, Phoenix lost his life and kingdom to Neoptolemus, the only son of Achilles.

Botany

(1) NEPENTHES. This section is devoted to curiosities and ancient associations. For example, Queen Polydama's "cup-of-sorrows" is on display at almost every botanical garden boasting a living collection of tropical novelties. Most of the seventy species in the genus *Nepenthes* grow as vines in the wet forests of Madagascar and Sri Lanka, east through Indonesia and northern Australia. Each simple leaf can develop a grasping tendril at its tip. This living rope allows the vines to hoist themselves up tree trunks and boulders.

A tendril often develops a fat bud at its tip. Within three weeks the bud inflates and develops into a half-lidded pitcher, or tankard, containing a mixture of water, acids, and enzymes. Insects drown in the cup and are digested for their mineral content. The eroded soils of tropical rainforests are notoriously low in nitrogen, phosphorous, and potassium, so essential to plant life. Luring, killing and "eating" a bug supplements diet deficiencies when roots are unable to locate essential elements underground.

Taxonomists give *Nepenthes* species their own family, Nepenthaceae, even though these vines play the same carnivorous game as *Dionaea* (see §5.8) and *Byblis* (§6.2). However, a recent article by John Moran, in *Natural History* magazine, suggests that *Nepenthes* species evolved far more novel ways of taking nourishment than we ever imagined. One species wears hairy tissue on the outside of its pitchers, and this attracts termite prey. A second encourages tree frogs to lay their eggs in the pitcher's brew. Some *Nepenthes* are vegetarians. They grow on the forest floor, and their cups accumulate and digest fallen leaves and twigs. Moran suggests that *Nepenthes lowii* functions as a combination juice bar and public toilet. Tree shrews drink nectar, secreted by the rim of the pitcher, but then these little mammals defecate into the leaf tankard. Shrews eat insects, so their feces are nitrogen rich.

Is there any magic in *Nepenthes*? Asian forest dwellers told Moran that the liquid in the cup of one species would cure baldness. He applied it to his own naked scalp without success. When I take my students on field trips to the Climatron of the Missouri Botanical Garden, I always stop under a tree festooned by a particularly vigorous *Nepenthes* vine. Nothing brings down the house like tipping out the contents of an old pitcher, thereby exposing a half-digested cockroach.

(2) EIDOTHEA. A name based on a mythological figure may symbolize the reality of continental drift and fossil records. In the mid-1990s, two Australian botanists,

A. W. Douglas and Bernard Hyland, named a new genus *Eidothea*. These large, newly discovered trees were restricted to a few sites in dense tropical forest in northern Australia. Douglas and Hyland named the genus after the nymph Eidothea to show that these trees belonged to the macadamia nut family (Proteaceae, see the entry for Proteus, below). As we will soon see, *Eidothea* is linked with the beautiful sugar bushes (*Protea*) of southern Africa.

Douglas and Hyland named the new species *Eidothea zoexylocarya* (living woody nut). Each massive fruit contained a single seed surrounded by a thick, hard, protective layer. These living fruits were almost identical to fossil fruits (*Xylocaryon lockii*) described in 1883. The petrified remains were dug out of rock from the Australian gold mining district in the temperate, southern state of Victoria. They had lain there for millions of years, long after the original rain forest had vanished as a result of a drying, cooler climate. Obviously, the ancestors of the new *Eidothea* tree were old and established citizens of the island continent.

Robert Kooyman, an Australian authority on the ecology of tropical vegetation and its restoration, discovered a second *Eidothea* species in northeastern Australia in 2000. The new tree was named *Eidothea hardeniana* to honor taxonomist Gwen Harden, of the Royal Botanic Gardens in Sydney. Some foresters now call this tree the nightcap oak, as the species appears to be restricted to the Nightcap Ranges of New South Wales. Trunks of *Eidothea hardeniana* yield an attractive hardwood reminiscent of the timbers produced by European oaks (*Quercus*). However, true oaks and the nightcap oak are placed in separate families and are not close relatives.

With the great help of Peter Weston, a curator at the Royal Botanic Gardens of Sydney, and Robbie Kooyman, I visited the hidden grove of nightcap oaks a few years ago. They were mighty canopy trees, and a couple rose more than a hundred feet high. Their fruits were not dainty little acorns. Like the fossils from Victoria and the living *E. zoexylocarya*, the fruit of each nightcap oak was the size of a cannonball wrapped in an unusually rough and tough rind. Weston and Kooyman set up a ladder, and I climbed up into a smaller "nymph." The tangled, gray, spicily fragrant flowers attracted metallic green Christmas beetles by day and blackish-brown darkling beetles by night. The flowers failed to secrete nectar, but the hard-shelled insects gorged on pollen. A report published by the Environment and Conservation Ministry of New South Wales in 2004 revealed that the maturation and transformation of a little hairy pistil into a massive, golden cannonball fruit took a full year.

How could such a huge tree avoid detection by generations of trained botanists for so long? That is the nature of Australian plant classification, I'm afraid. For more than two centuries, too few plant taxonomists have been available to catalog the overwhelming diversity of new Australian plants. Many of the tropical forests

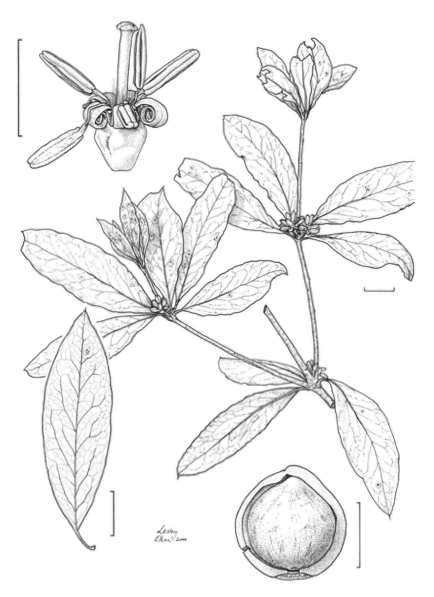

18. A flowering branch of Australian nightcap oak (*Eidothea hardenensis*) with a close-up of the nectarless flower and a much reduced depiction of the massive, single-seeded fruit. Illustration by Lesley Elkan. Copyright is held by the Royal Botanic Gardens of Sydney and Domain Trust.

in the north and much of the scrublands in the west of the continent remain underexplored. The door is always open for the next, new Aussie genus to be named after a Greco-Roman figure.

And how did the two huge species of *Eidothea* trees come to inhabit their obscure corners of antipodal rain forest? The answer to that question lies in the following section on *Protea* and the Proteaceae.

(3) PROTEUS. European attempts to explore and colonize southern Africa in the seventeenth and eighteenth centuries introduced Western civilization to plant and animal diversity unknown north of the equator. In particular, early naturalists were astounded by the contents of temperate South African heath-lands. They appeared to be crammed with bushes bearing large, tough, colorful funnels, torches, and brushes. On closer inspection these huge "flowers" were revealed to be unusually dense and hard branches consisting of masses of tiny flowers (florets) encircled by colorful, scaly leaves (bracts). The architecture of these compound blossoms was so variable that Linnaeus named the genus *Protea*, after the shape-shifting god.

British colonists in South Africa noted that the flowering heads of *Protea* species secreted lots of sweet nectar and called them sugar bushes. Their bracts and florets live a long time after they are cut, and domesticated varieties grown commercially in Africa, California, Hawaii, and Australia formed the nucleus of a thriving, international florist's trade. As generations of botanists tackled southern African diversity, they came to understand that *Protea* had to be subdivided into smaller, distinctive genera, all grouped together in the same family, Proteaceae. Collections made by botanists on other continents showed that the Proteaceae was primarily a southern family. Today wild members of the Proteaceae are found in dense forests, open heaths, and bushlands of Africa, South America, Australia, and New Zealand.

Fossil evidence indicates that the Proteaceae is such an old family of flowering plants that ancestral trees and bushes existed before the complete separation of all the geological plates and land bridges in the southern hemisphere. Both sugar bushes and Nightcap oaks appear to be orphans of the supercontinent of Gondwana. Similarities in flower structure, pores on the pollen grains, seeds, and wood anatomy continue to link "daddy" *Protea* in dry, southern Africa to daughter *Eidothea*, in her damp Australian bower. The fossil record also indicates that the ancestors of this family of woody plants originated in wet and warm forests more than seventy million years ago. Time and continental drift has not been equally kind to the two genera.

Daughter *Eidothea* could not adapt to the drying and cooling of Australia as it drifted north. They became extinct in the south part of the continent and survive only in tropical remnants in the north, where they grow closer to the equator and benefit from generous annual monsoons. The same thing has happened to all rain forest members of the Proteaceae that call Australia home. They are relicts surviving in antipodal refuges. Father *Protea,* on the other hand, adopted an adapt-or-die policy. Most of the 115 species in this genus tolerate soils that dry out in summer and produce most of their new growth during the wet, rather cool winter. They are robust bushes, not mighty trees. *Eidothea* towers over her father, but only two species remain in small populations that require protection and conservation protocols.

(4) PHYLLIS. The vegetation on Gondwana became isolated as the supercontinent separated. During warmer epochs some plants rafted northward as their plates realigned. In particular, the ancestors of some African species spread into the Atlantic islands of Macronesia (the Azores and Canaries). That is where we still find two species of shrubs in the genus *Phyllis.* The inexplicably named bastard hare's ear (*Phyllis nobla*) is unique to laurel forests on the island of Madeira.

As usual, Linnaeus could not resist another classical tale about a woman turning into a tree. *Phyllis* is placed in the coffee family (Rubiaceae), whereas edible, commercial almonds (*Prunus dulcis*) belong to the rose family (Rosaceae). Linnaeus knew very well that commercial almonds and bastard hare's ears shared little in common. He insisted he named the new genus of bushes from Madeira after Princess Phyllis because the dried branches he examined retained foliage similar in size and shape to the leaves found on domesticated almond trees. Yes, it is a pretty thin explanation, but I think it proves that even the bombastic master of plant taxonomy could be swayed by a pretty myth. As we will see next, when Linnaeus decided to formalize the genus *Phoenix,* he did so as a serious historian of economic botany, not as a mere fan of fables.

I must pose a question before tackling the genus *Phoenix.* The sad story of Acamas and Phyllis is the last myth in this book in which a character turns into a plant. Did you spot the trend in the rhizotomi's ancient tradition of naming plants after mythical figures? Nymphs and mortal women appear more likely to expand into trees or woody vines (see §3.7 [Philyra], §5.4 [Daphne], §5.7 [Carya], §5.12 [Acantha], and §7.4 [Phyllis]). Mortal men and demigods dwindle into herbs and wildflowers (§3.5 [Crocus], §3.6 [Narcissus], §5.5 [Paeonius], §5.7 [Orchis], and §6.2 [Hyacinthus]). The stories of the first clump of reeds (§3.5), the cypress tree (§3.7), and mint (§5.2) are exceptions to the rule.

(5) PHOENIX. Historically, the Greeks and Romans associated date palms with King Phoenix, just as they associated gentians with King Gentius and centaury plants with the centaur Chiron (see §3.7). All Linnaeus had to do was formalize the name associated with this tree in old herbals. However, Greek mythology recognized three monarchs named Phoenix. The first fought at Troy and was the tutor of Achilles. The second Phoenix became a king in Asia. The third was the putative

father of Adonis, instead of intoxicated old Cinyras (§6.3). It was not until the end of the eighteenth century that plant taxonomists insisted that ancient orchard keepers and oasis owners honored the Phoenix who was a veteran of the Trojan War. A much more likely explanation is that the rhizotomi first associated the date palm with the Asian ruler Phoenix. He was both the ancestor of the Phoenician people and a son of King Agenor. The Greeks believed date palms came originally from Phoenicia, a country once located along a coastline that now encompasses much of modern Syria south through parts of northern Israel.

Whatever the precise origin of the name, there are at least seventeen species in the genus *Phoenix,* and they belong to the palm family. Although one species grows wild in Crete and Turkey, most extend their natural distributions eastward into tropical Asia and then southwest into Africa. Dozens of passages in the Bible refer to date palms, and the woman's name *Tamar* probably means date palm. These trees became so identified with Jewish civilization that, after the destruction of Jerusalem by Titus in 70 C.E., the Emperor Vespasian minted a coin showing a grieving woman seated under a date palm. This commemorated Rome's merciless retaking of the colony they called Palestine.

All commercial date plantations are derived from *P. dactylifera* and are probably descendants of palms first domesticated more than six thousand years ago. In comparison, the toddy palm (*P. sylvestris*) comes from India and is exploited for the sugar made from its boiled-down sap. During the eighteenth and nineteenth centuries, the original recipes for alcoholic, hot toddy drinks called for palm sugar, not bee's honey. The oldest civilizations around the Mediterranean esteemed dates as the first source of wine. The fruit's flesh is nearly 70 percent sugar and ferments easily, especially when fresh and juicy. In comparison, grape-based wines became the preferred drink in Greece less than four thousand years ago. This probably explains why Dionysus was the last god to join the Olympian pantheon (see §5.7). Small wonder that the Greeks associated the date palm with another influential monarch.

A date palm is either a male tree (producing only pollen flowers) or a female tree (producing only fruit). To ensure maximum yield, growers first cut off the pollen-rich flowering stalks on male trees. The date farmer has the option of manually shaking the stalk's pollen onto opening flower buds on a female tree. In most cases, though, the male stalk is tied directly to a branch on a female tree. Gravity and breezes spread the sperm-filled grains. By the eighth century B.C.E., the Assyrian civilization was so well versed in the sex life of dates that the procedure was depicted on stone carvings on their palaces. Winged, eagle-headed, wind gods were shown carrying male branches to female trees. This makes me wonder. Phoenix is also the name of a fabulous, long-lived bird in Mediterranean mythology. The

Greeks thought the phoenix was a giant, reddish-gold eagle that lived in the east. Did the name of the fanciful bird and the mythical monarchs develop from a trade in date wine between Greeks, Assyrians, and Phoenicians?

7.5 THE INTERRUPTED VOYAGE OF ODYSSEUS

King Odysseus (1) had the ill luck of stopping at almost every Aegean island inhabited by hostile natives and/or powerful, possessive deities. Despite his cunning, it took him a decade to return to his kingdom on the island of Ithaca. Storms pushed his ship off-course, and Odysseus docked on a promontory along the Libyan coast where the inhabitants ate lotus fruit (2). When some Greek sailors ate the lotus, they forgot their mission and had to be dragged back to the ship.

Libya was a pleasant diversion compared with their next stop on the island of the Cyclops. This was a new race of one-eyed giants, sons of Poseidon and the nymph Thoosa. Uncouth, shaggy shepherds, they were only distant nephews of Gaia's original three artisans (see §3.2 and §4.5). Odysseus, accompanied by some sailors, made the mistake of entering an occupied cave. They ate cheese and drank milk stored by the owner, Polyphemus. When the Cyclops returned, he barred the mouth of the cave with a rock and ate several feta-stuffed Greeks. The monster spared Odysseus, temporarily, when the hero made him drunk on wine that the Greeks had brought from the ship to barter for food. Once Polyphemus fell into a drunken stupor Odysseus and his remaining men blinded the Cyclops (3) with a smoking, wooden stake, heated in the creature's own hearth.

The following day, sightless, aching Polyphemus opened the mouth of the cavern to allow his herds out to pasture. He could not know that the Greeks had tied themselves to the undersides of his giant rams and ewes. The Cyclops searched vainly for his tormentors. It was not until the ships were safely out to sea that Polyphemus heard a mocking voice. "Now monster, tell everyone what Odysseus, son of Laertes, has done to you." This was a terrible mistake. When Polyphemus learned the name of the man who blinded him, he cursed Odysseus in the name of his father, Poseidon. The god of the sea heard his son and found cruel, new ways to prolong the Greek king's return to Ithaca.

The next island belonged to Aeolus, Keeper of the Winds. He presented Odysseus with a bag of winds, but the sack lacked the gentle west wind, Zephyrus (4). This winged god could have blown the ship all the way home in complete safety. Instead, Aeolus told Odysseus to use each gale one at a time, releasing them only if the ship needed to change course suddenly.

The crew did not discover the sack until they were in sight of the island of Ithaca. Believing it contained treasure, they freed all the winds at once, blowing the ship far off-course once again. Odysseus and his men found themselves on the Italian shores of the Laestrygonians, a race of cannibals descended from Lamia (see §5.6).

Botany

(1) ODYSSEUS. Austrian taxonomist Otto Stapf (1857–1933) lived much of his life in pleasant, landlocked Vienna. He must have admired Odysseus for his ability to survive on inhospitable coasts. There are only two species in the genus *Odyessea*, but they are distributed along the shores of the Red Sea and range as far south as the tropical coastlines of southern Africa. These steek grasses, in the grass family (Poaceae), tolerate saltwater and have such tough root systems that they can bind sand dunes. Like the wiliest of Greek warriors, steek grasses are armed and prepared. Their leaves end in spiny tips.

(2) LOTUS FRUIT. As we will see, a few botanists delighted in naming species after the plants and creatures Odysseus encountered on his extended travels. A common, thorny shrub of the Mediterranean is named *Ziziphus lotus*, as it bears sweet fruit. This bush is related to the French jujube or Chinese date (*Z. jujuba*) of Eurasia and the mistol fruit (*Z. mistol*) of the Andes. Chinese dates remain popular in China, and I tasted them on two occasions during my first trip to Beijing in January 2007. They were used to make a sweet, hot fruit soup. They were much tastier when their flesh was pressed into savory little cakes and served as a side dish to accompany Mongolian hotpot.

Numerous biblical scholars insist that the thorns and briers in the book of Isaiah (7:19, 9:18, 55:13) also refer to *Ziziphus* bushes. Christian folklore hints that the infamous crown of thorns came from branches of *Z. spina-christi*. There are at least eighty-five *Ziziphus* species distributed through tropical countries, and they belong to the buckthorn family (Rhamnaceae).

(3) CYCLOPS. *Acacia cyclops* is a wattle bush from Western Australia now growing wild in California. It is a bulky shrub, but no giant compared to many other Australian wattles. Examine one of its ripe, open pods, however. As in most legumes, each seed wears a stalk of placental tissue, known as the funiculus. This stalk allows the seed to cling to the inner ridge of the pod's wall. The funiculus of an *A. cyclops* seed is so long and exaggerated that it curls around the shiny, black seed like a fleshy, red frame. Here is the bloody, smoky, blackened eye of Polyphemus. When the pod splits apart, the seeds continue to cling to the ridge of the fruit wall. A seed's bright, red frame attracts birds that pick off and eat the funiculus while dispersing and dropping the hard-shelled seed.

(4) ZEPHYRUS. Ancient Greeks believed the west wind was an erotic and virile spirit. In one myth he impregnates a harpy (a female bird demon), and she gives birth to talking horses. Some versions of the myths insist that Zephyrus fathered Cupid, courted Hyacinthus (see §6.2), and, most important of all, married a mortal queen who became the goddess of spring. Consequently, Zephyrus is as responsible for bringing flowers out of the earth as is Flora (§7.7).

Three bulb-making genera of wildflowers share this wind god's name. They are *Zephyra*, *Zephyranthella* (little flower of Zephyr), and *Zephyranthes* (Zephyr's flower). Rain lilies, atamasco lilies, and zephyr lilies (*Zephyranthes*) remain in cultivation as tender bulbs. More than seventy species are distributed through the southern half of the United States and down through South America. They are usually placed in the daffodil family (Amaryllidaceae).

Many zephyr lilies bloom for a few days following a rainstorm after having survived a prolonged summer drought. It seems as if they have been resurrected by the west wind's moist, warm breath. Most zephyr bulbs cannot tolerate frozen ground and are kept in windowsill pots over the winter. An older generation of potted plant growers called *Z. candida* the coffee can lily. It was such a prolific plant and so tolerant of cramped containers that no one wasted money buying clay pots for these vigorous bulbs. When repotting, remember that these lily bulbs are as toxic as those of daffodils. Never allow them to become the unexpected treats or toys of children or pets.

7.6 ODYSSEUS AND THE WOMEN

Odysseus and his surviving crew fled the Laestrygonians. Upon reaching the island of Aeaea, he sent some sailors on a foraging party. Only one man returned, with a fantastic story that a beautiful woman had transformed the crew into pigs. The hero took the path to the woman's house and met the god Hermes on the way. The divine messenger handed Odysseus a little plant with a black root and a white flower. "This is moly (1). It is the only thing that can protect you from the magic of Circe (2)," said Hermes.

As expected, Circe's attempt to bewitch Odysseus was unsuccessful, and he threatened her with his sword. The sorceress became far more hospitable after disenchanting the sailors. She shared her bed with Odysseus for a year. The enchantress also insisted he visit the kingdom of Hades to consult with prophetic spirits. The phantom of the great seer Tiresias gave Odysseus an important warning ("Do not let your men harm the cattle of the sun god when you visit the island of Sicily") and an even more critical piece of information: "In your long absence, your kingdom of Ithaca fell into the hands of greedy, foreign princes. The gods will let you take your revenge on them upon your return."

Circe also warned her lover of additional threats in the Aegean before he deserted her. "If you want to listen to the beautiful music of the Sirens (3), have your men tie you to the mast and make them stuff their ears with wax," she advised. As the ship sailed past the Sirens' island, the three bird-like sisters, Ligeia (4), Leucosia, and Parthenope sang their seductive song. They expected the men to fall under their spell and crash their ship on the rocks. It did not happen. Odysseus could not break his bonds, and his men heard nothing.

Thanks to Circe's sound advice they also escaped certain destruction by avoiding the whirlpool woman, Charybdis. This monstrous female lived at the bottom of the sea and sucked down all vessels that sailed over her. Unfortunately, staying away from the whirlpool meant sailing far too close to Scylla's rock. Scylla was once a beautiful nymph pursued by the merman, Glaucus (5). The sea god's fish tail and his bluish-green hair made him repulsive to Scylla but attractive to Circe. When Glaucus rejected Circe's advances, the sorceress took revenge and poisoned Scylla's favorite bathing pool. Glaucus's adored nymph was transformed into a sedentary creature with six heads mounted on six elongated necks. As Odysseus's ship sailed past Scylla's rock she snatched half a dozen sailors.

Now starving, Odysseus and his crew landed on Sicily, where the sun god kept his cattle. The men disobeyed their captain and killed and ate some cows. Helios complained to Zeus. The king of Olympus waited until the ship departed Sicily and then destroyed the craft with a thunderbolt. Only Odysseus survived, lashed to pieces of timber. He drifted to the island of Ogygia. There the hero was revived and claimed by the nymph Calypso (6). She lived in a verdant, well-watered grotto and kept her Greek warrior for seven more years. Athena forced Calypso to free Odysseus. He sailed off on a raft only to be capsized by Poseidon, in revenge for blinding his son (see §7.5). Odysseus swam to the island of Drepane, where he was befriended by Princess Nausicca. Her parents sent him back to Ithaca in a new ship.

Disguised as a beggar, Odysseus surveyed his palace and saw terrible things. Suitors were trying to marry his wife, Penelope (7), while they gobbled up Ithaca's resources and abused the palace maids. Penelope remained faithful to her husband's memory but could not turn away such powerful princes. Revealing himself only to his son, father, and a few loyal servants, Odysseus reclaimed his bow and shot all his rivals.

Botany

(1) MOLY. Scholars speculated on moly's identity for centuries. Some thought it was a smelly, wild species of rue (*Ruta*). Others believed it was a cyclamen (*Cyclamen*) with nodding white flowers and a plump, black tuber. In addition, an existing body of European folklore insisted that garlic or onions neutralized the evil magic of Mediterranean witches who supposedly stole a man's blood to put him under their power. Linnaeus could not resist naming a wild onion *Allium moly*, although the bulb had a distinctly brown skin and bore yellow flowers. He was as prophetic as Tiresias. Think of the decades of vampire movies exhorting the prophylactic power of garlic. Moreover, I have grown *Allium moly* in my garden for a decade and never suffered a single supernatural attack.

(2) CIRCE. Linnaeus also read about a magic herb called the *kirkaia* in the works of Pliny the Elder. He decided to give the name to a plant the Germans still call *hexenkraut* (witch's cabbage). One wonders what anyone found magical about the seven or so species in the genus *Circaea*. They are distributed through the northern hemisphere and belong to the fuchsia family (Onagraceae). To the best of my knowledge, no one has ever been poisoned or has experienced visions after eating *Circaea* stems or fruit.

Yet Circe's reputation still influences other common names of plants in the genus. American wildflower books continue to call *C. lutetiana* enchanter's nightshade. Purists insist it should be called enchantress's nightshade. Harvard botanist David Boufford watched goats in a meadow in China. They ate everything except *C. cordata*. Perhaps its smell repels some animals in the same way that so many humans are repelled by the stench of freshly bruised garlic.

(3) SIRENS. The genus *Syrenia* addresses ten species of wildflowers found from eastern Europe into Siberia. The name *Syrenia* (with a *y* instead of an *i*) was designed deliberately to make the reader think of both the three Sirens and the nymph Syrinx (see §3.5). It is a silly name, as it has absolutely nothing to do with myths about any of these minor goddesses. The genus *Syrenia* belongs to the mustard and cabbage family (Brassicaceae), not the family of reed grasses (Poaceae) associated with Syrinx. The plants are not found in Greece or on any Aegean island. *Syrenia* species do not root in water, on rocky islands, or by the seaside. Eating the leaves or seeds will not make you as pretty as a nymph or improve your singing voice.

It was Ihsan Al-Shebaz, curator of the Brassicaceae at the Missouri Botanical Garden, who told me the real reason why the Austrian-born physician and plant taxonomist Willibald Swibert Joseph Gottlieb von Besser (1784–1842) selected the name *Syrenia*. Besser wanted a name that would remind plant taxonomists that that these wildflowers were closely related to Siberian wallflowers (*Erysimum*). *Syrenia* is nothing more than a cynical, unconnected, and badly constructed anagram of *Erysimum*.

Remember the rules for naming living things back in chapter 2. You cannot give a new genus or species a legitimate scientific name by stringing gibberish together and Latinizing it. You must start with a word that means something and then convert it into Latin or Greek. That is why Rafinesque's names of nonexistent nymphs were discredited and dumped. Both the Sirens and the nymph Syrinx are good classical names. The word *Syrenia* looked and sounded enough like *Erysimum* to please Besser, and it satisfied the rules of taxonomy. The botanical community was content . . . for a while.

Besser was too clever by half when he pointed out that his *Syrenia* was so similar to the Siberian wallflowers. Al-Shebaz points out that past studies on the DNA of plants belonging to the cabbage family showed that syrenias fit inside the much larger genus *Erysimum*. *Syrenia* is now regarded as another synonym by most Western taxonomists. A few botanists and pharmacologists, scattered among the cities in what was once the old Soviet Empire, continue to treat *Syrenia* as the valid name of the genus, however. They perform chemical analyses on these plants to look for useful molecules.

(4) LIGEIA. Later generations of artists rejected Homer's description of feathered nymphs and painted the Sirens as fish-tailed. *Ligeia*, like Oenone (see §7.2) was a genus in the tropical family of river herbs, the Podostemaceae. Like *Oenone*, *Ligeia* became a synonym for *Apinagia* in the twentieth century.

(5) GLAUCUS. If the protective, waxy cuticle on a plant's foliage gives its green leaves or stems a grayish or bluish sheen, then they are said to be glaucous. This form of coloration is particularly common in regions where mild climates encourage the long-term survival of foliage made by evergreen trees and shrubs. In this environment, individual leaves live for years, provided that their thick coat of wax slows down the harsh rate of summertime evaporation inside leaves. The bluish pigments also reduce damage by screening out harsh, ultraviolet rays. Cells inside the leaves still contain green chlorophyll, but when seen through the tinted cuticle, the overall effect gives the plant a grayish or bluish cast.

Glaucous foliage is worn by thousands of species of woody plants native to the Mediterranean basin (southern Europe, northern Africa, and the Middle East). However, the Mediterranean climate occurs in coastal pockets all over the world. The leaves of many trees and shrubs native to Australia, southern California, Chile, and South Africa are also glaucous in coloration. They all grow under similar conditions, with dry and hot summers followed by cool and wet winters. This explains why Australian gum trees (*Eucalyptus*) and wattles like *Acacia cyclops* (see §7.5) do so well in between San Francisco and Los Angeles. Look at the glaucous foliage the next time you buy fresh eucalyptus stems at a florist's shop.

(6) CALYPSO. Few North American orchids have been so well loved by naturalists as the two species in the genus *Calypso*. Both produce flowers with curved lip petals that resemble pink, white, and yellowish sandals. They are called fairy slippers in older wildflower books. I have felt ecstatic every time I have seen them blooming in Minnesota, Montana, and Oregon. Fairy slippers like wet, mossy seeps on shady, forested slopes, reminiscent of the nymph's lush grotto described by Homer.

(7) PENELOPE. Queen Penelope remained faithful to her husband's little island of Ithaca. *Penelopeia suburceolata* is unique to the little island of Hispaniola. In the Dominican Republic, this long, slender vine scrambles up trees to a height of eighteen feet or more. Collectors find stems of *P. suburceolata*, bearing orange flowers and small leaves with toothed margins, twirled around air ferns that also crowd a tree's branches.

Penelopeia is related to pumpkins and squash in the family Cucurbitaceae. This family is most appropriate for honoring the most cautious and dutiful queen in Greek mythology. Pollen-making stamens (the princely suitors) are never found in the same flower as the pistil (Queen Penelope). Most plants produce male and female flowers on the same vine. In Homer's epic, Queen Penelope avoided her 112 suitors by excusing herself from the banquet hall. She stayed in her chamber all day, weaving a shroud. When night fell, she remained in her room, unraveling the same garment. Penelope's ruse kept her free of serious but unwanted proposals for three years. Likewise, each pistil of *Penelopeia* stays in its own chamber, made of a funnel of petals, isolated from male flowers on the same stem.

7.7 NESTOR AND HIS MOTHER

Nestor, king of Pylos, was a grandfather when he fought with the Greeks at Troy. Ironically, he was the only postwar general who returned to Greece without delay. No one threatened to kill or dethrone him upon his return. Some say his happy fate was a divine reward for the piety, justice, and eloquence Nestor expressed in the face of war. Perhaps the gods owed Nestor a favor, because on two occasions children of Zeus massacred his family. When Nestor's grandmother, Niobe, bragged that her children were superior to Apollo and Artemis, these two gods killed Niobe's brood, with the exception of Princess Meliboea and Prince Amyclas. These two children had prayed to Leto, the mother of Apollo and Artemis, for protection. The gods spared them, but Meliboea turned green with fear. For the rest of her life, she was called Chloris (green shoot) (1).

Chloris was married to her uncle, King Neleus of Pylos, and had twelve sons, Nestor among them. Heracles held an old grudge against Neleus, as the monarch once refused to purify the hero after Heracles murdered a man in one of his fits of madness. Heracles later killed Neleus and eleven of his sons when they met on opposite sides of the battlefield. Nestor escaped extermination because he was too young to fight and was still receiving an education in a distant kingdom. Widowed, Chloris was claimed by Zephyrus, the west wind. He rejuvenated her, and she became the goddess of flowers. When Zephyrus breathed on Chloris each spring, petals dropped from her mouth and flowers grew in her footsteps. The Romans renamed her Flora (2) and celebrated her festival, the Floralia, from the last days of April through the first few days of May.

Botany

(1) CHLORIS. She may be the goddess of flowers, but Chloris is still remembered, largely, for her green complexion. Nothing symbolizes renewal to many people as much as a pasture filled with freshly sprouting, glossy, emerald, grass shoots (tillers). These verdant tufts make us forgive the useful family of grasses (Poaceae) for its failure to offer any pretty or conspicuous flowers. You would be incorrect, though, if you assumed that *Chloris* was named after grasses that push up out of defrosting winter soil. There are at least fifty species in this genus, and most belong to the tropics, or at least to regions enjoying long, warm seasons. Ranchers in the southern hemisphere often favor these finger and windmill grasses as pasturage. Rhodes grass (*C. gayana*) came from Africa, but its many cultivated forms have been introduced all over the world.

(2) FLORA. Any book or publication that attempts to identify and describe the native and introduced plant species found growing within a natural boundary or political perimeter is known properly as a flora. Floras are usually big and thick books because they cover vast territories, including entire islands (say, the flora of Crete), states and provinces (say, the flora of Manitoba) and entire continents (say, the flora of North America). Some floras are highly specialized and focus on certain plant families (the cactus flora of Arizona) or growth habits (the trees found west of the Mississippi River).

Until the first half of the twentieth century, all organisms made of cells with protective walls were regarded as plants. Consequently, the diversity of bacteria in a human gut is still called a microflora, and we refer to the fungi infecting rotting wood as the mycoflora. Most studies now agree that cell walls made of cellulose (plants), chitin (fungi), peptidoglycan (some bacteria), or silica (diatoms) divide major groups, instead of unifying them. Plants, bacteria, fungi, and various algae are now placed in different taxonomic kingdoms (see chapter 2).

The goddess Flora attended to all plants. Therefore, a real flora remains distinct from a field guide. Field guides fail to account for all the diversity in a region, emphasizing only the species most likely to be encountered by visitors. When you attempt to use a field guide to make your identification, all you can do is try to match a live specimen with a colored drawing. These drawings almost always lack the finer details (number of organs in the flower, types of hairs on the stem) required to make a precise identification. In contrast, a good flora contains diagnostic keys that allow you to identify specimens from either living or dried plants. The growth habit, vegetative organs (stems and leaves), and reproductive structures (flowers and fruit) of each species are described briefly, but accurately. You do not flip through hundreds of pictures. You read a line in the key and, if it fails to match your specimen, the next line tells you to skip over to another section in the key.

We talk about the flora and fauna of a region. If Flora was a goddess who became a book, then who was Fauna? The Romans believed she was a good and unusually modest goddess (Bona Dea). Fauna encouraged the fertility of farm animals and protected their babies. Some identified her with Rhea. A fauna book is to the animal life of a region what a flora is to plants. Many animal genera and species are named after mythological species, but that is another cycle of stories.

Epilogue

A Plant for Persephone?

See what simplicity
This nymph begins her golden days!
In the green grass she loves to lie,
And there with her fair aspect tames
The wilder flow'rs and gives them names. . . .

—ANDREW MARVELL, "The Picture
of Little T.C. in a Prospect of Flowers"

In this computerized age, there have been radical calls to replace the Linnaean system of double Latinized names with something shorter and more to the point. Some taxonomists recommend giving each species a number or a combination of numbers and codes. Each code would represent the physical feature(s) that makes the original description of each species unique (bfl = big flowers). A colleague of mine recently pointed out the problem with this proposed system of digital taxonomy. It is perfect for a computer's memory but hard on human minds and tongues. Do you have trouble remembering your license plate number or state and federal codes for taxes and social security? Consider what would happen if the names of hundreds of thousand of species, thousands of genera, and hundreds of plant families were codified.

Industry will build smaller portable computers for us, but few of us want them joined perpetually at our hips. Computers are the best of consultants on big projects in the museum and laboratory, but do we really want them to become our extra brain lobes because we are unable to recall jumbles of numbers and letters? Plans to codify and digitalize all forms of biological diversity seem far more complicated then the simpler, older system of two names for each species. We need mnemonic devices to classify today and recall tomorrow. Scientific names based on diverse cultural references offer some of the most useful tricks for stimulating human memory. It is refreshing to know that taxonomy still needs men and women familiar with belles lettres as much as it requires minds trained in empirical logic.

Friends have also asked me whether the field of molecular biology threatens the more literary world of taxonomy. In fact, taxonomists have recognized the sheer importance of comparing species on a gene-by-gene basis for most of the last decade of the twentieth century. A molecular approach to classification has become the most dependable tool to understand how so many "species twigs" interconnect within the branches of the great "shrub of life." Scientists extract, analyze, "read," and compare information-recording molecules inside the cells of living things. Genes inside a cell's nucleus give us lots of information, but so do other microscopic sites, including the ribosomes and mitochondria. Botanists are particularly lucky because they can prospect for molecules in places unavailable to those studying animals or fungi. We can extract additional information from chloroplasts, the powerhouses within plant cells. One day this will give us several evolutionary pathways that will teach us how plants developed systems to make sugars out of water, carbon dioxide and sunlight.

Molecular taxonomy then, is simply the newest device for understanding the boundaries that separate and connect species. As a tool, it does not aim to erase Linnaeus's protocols for describing a species or Darwin's theories about how new species evolve with time. Indeed, most molecular taxonomists start their research in museums studying traditional pressed or pickled or skinned specimens. They must learn to identify the definitive physical structures of each species before they go off into the field to make fresh collections. After all, no curator will ever allow them to grind up parts of precious type specimens just to extract remnants of DNA or RNA.

A case in point: Professor Luo Yi-bo, a colleague in Beijing, wanted to know if any of the lady's slipper orchids (*Cypripedium*) in North America are closely related (sister species) to slipper orchids in southern China. He asked me to collect specimens of showy lady's slippers (*C. reginae*) that bloom toward the close of our Missouri spring. I took a plant press, as usual, but I was also armed with a little pair of scissors, some small, self-locking plastic bags, and a sac of silica gel. After driving for more than four hours from St. Louis to the Ozarks, Retha Meier; her husband, Larry; and I found our orchids. We snipped off a bit of each plant's fresh, green leaves, put each piece in its own bag, and then covered the specimens with the beads of silica gel. The leaf fragments were allowed to dry out for ten hours before they were placed in a courier envelope and sent to China.

How did we know that we were sending Luo showy lady's slippers instead of yellow lady's slippers (*C. parviflorum*)? Both species are found in the state of Missouri, and both flower in spring. Like all good taxonomists, we did our homework in the usual way before attempting any collections. We consulted herbarium sheets in the Missouri Botanical Gardens. Standard reference books also taught us which physical structures (plant height and the size, shape, and color of petals) make identifications dependable. After snipping leaves we collected and pressed a whole, flowering stem from the same site as a voucher specimen to store in a herbarium cabinet. If other taxonomists ever doubted our identifications, they could look at a sheet of one of the plants that provided us with DNA while it was still alive. They could run our specimen through the standard diagnostic keys in a flora (see §7.7) to validate our work. In other words, to make use of the new molecular science we had to start with the same Linnaean rules and museum and library tools known by every field botanist since the eighteenth century. There are no substitutions.

Not only are the traditional techniques still relevant in this genomic age, so is our binomial system of nomenclature. Will the language of taxonomy always retain its lyrical charm and scholarly pride in offering us new names derived from Greco-Roman myths? I am not so sure. Most of the scientific publications published by botanical gardens and research institutes these days indicate that botanists do not renew their poetic licenses. Yes, ongoing funding for botanical expeditions and scientific revisions guarantees the discovery and description of new species. However, when it comes time to select a name for a new plant, few botanists feel inclined to shop for words in the great works of Homer or Ovid. Unless something changes, *Eidothea* (see §7.4) may be the last genus of flowering plants named after a goddess.

I hope this is not the case, but we must remember that most plant names based on myths are more than a century old. As revision is a primary goal of the science of taxonomy, we are forced to conclude that many more pretty and easy-to-recall names will vanish as technological advances make it easier to reclassify genera and species. Previous chapters in this book show that some names are reaching the end of their shelf life, because plant taxonomy is a contentious sport as well as a rigorous science. You cannot stop a revision because you prefer old names. Good revisions are a necessity; they clarify complicated relationships within a lineage of closely related populations. Which of these populations are best regarded as discrete species and which species are so closely related that they are best clustered within the same genus? Ultimately, some beloved names must become synonyms, and only the most passionate historians of science will remember them.

Let us also remember that there was never a time in which allusions to myths dominated the naming of new plants, their organs, or their growth cycles. Books and journals devoted to the history of botany list the publications of hundreds of plant taxonomists from the eighteenth century until the present day. Only a comparative handful of these scientists repeatedly exploited word opportunities found in classical poems and epics. Recall, too, that according to the rules of taxonomy, any preexisting word, in any language, can be "Latinized" and popped into the binomial system. With so many to choose from, why should a latter-day taxonomist turn to the names of heroes, monsters, and divinities long abandoned by popular culture? Furthermore, as taxonomists in the Middle East and Asia are brought up on different stories, they have every right to assert national claims and may select names from poems depicting completely different pantheons. That is a happy prospect, in my opinion. If this book revives and stimulates a fresh interest in naming new species after mythical figures, I hope that taxonomists harvest tales told in India, China, Japan, Iran (Persia), sub-Saharan Africa, Australia, and many other cultures. After all, Linnaeus and his followers combed only a few ancient texts written by poets and herbalists.

Molecular taxonomy has produced an age of shifting alliances between plants we thought we knew so well. Interpreting this new information changes the very position of twigs on the great shrub of life. A valid, old species may be transferred to a new genus. A valid genus (*Paeonia*) may be given its own family (Paeoniaceae), and then it joins a different order (Saxifragales), thereby divorcing garden peonies from buttercups and delphiniums (see §5.5). How can scientific names based on mythical figures be of any importance to this world of research? Reclassification will never detract from the sheer beauty of plants, however, so now is a good time to invoke the wise spirit of John Lindley (see §2.6). Do you remember Lindley's advice? Do not rely too much on shape, anatomy, or natural architecture when coining a new genus name. Physical structures may not occur consistently when you discover more species that turn out to be closely related.

Suddenly, the musings of a proper Victorian botanist seem almost prophetic in our molecular age. Playing the immodest role of a modern-day Lindley, I argue that erecting future names based primarily on shared physical structures or even geography may accidentally imply false connections and evolutionary histories. Of course, you must use physical features when you want to identify a plant in the field or on a herbarium sheet. If you are describing a new genus or species, though, perhaps it is better to list its physical features thoroughly, as usual, but then baptize it with a neutral but attractive name from the classics. Such a name will show the taxonomist's appreciation for the new plant, especially if it is also a subtle metaphor. A well-selected name based on a classical allusion has the advantage that it may also hint at the plant's wild habits (for example, sweet aroma, a preference for riverbanks, leaf drop in autumn) or how humans exploit it over time (for instance, food, medicine, murder weapon).

Why not follow the lead of some of the finest scientists and wittiest naturalists of the eighteenth and nineteenth centuries when we attempt a revision? My colleagues at the Missouri Botanical Garden continue to revise the fuchsia family (Onagraceae) using molecular techniques. The family includes the genus *Circaea* (enchanter's nightshade; see §7.6). Evidence offered by information molecules suggests that it is much better to divide large genera in the fuchsia family into smaller, discrete ones. Let me remind these taxonomists that Circe had a sister named Pasiphae, a brother named Aeetes, and a son named Telegonus.

We can plunder any pantheon we choose, provided we understand the urgency of the situation. Culture wars are nothing new, but there must be something better than these never-ending rants exchanged between a few people who claim to represent the proreligion and the proscience lobbies. The only thing worse than a demagogue who insists that science ultimately betrays decency and faith is some posturing pundit who insists that every religion ultimately ruins civilization. There is nothing I can do or say that will change the opinion of those who cling to the narrowest interpretations of scripture. As a botanist, though, it may be possible to offer a younger generation of taxonomists another option before they become cynical and hardened after one too many misguided attacks on their profession.

No artist, political scientist, jurist, historian, anthropologist, or psychologist would agree that religions ruin everything. To the contrary, history shows that religions served, and continue to serve, all of these professions as sources of inspiration. Let's acknowledge that religion can work as a positive and creative stimulus within science. If you are concerned about offending the pious (and it is a real concern) stick with deities that no one worships anymore. Linnaeus, Lindley, Don, Miller, and Nuttall made the same choice when they erected new genera and species. They were praised, not persecuted for their inventiveness.

Botanists have yet to take up my challenge, but I am optimistic. While writing this book, I discussed the contents with a colleague who is both an entomologist and a Jesuit. He specializes in the classification of tiny, parasitoid wasps with big, bulging eyes. These insects do not build mud or paper nests. There are no queens or worker castes. A pregnant female finds a nice, fat inchworm and injects her eggs into the caterpillar. As the wasp's grubs hatch out, they gobble the inchworm's internal tissues. The victim resembles an Egyptian mummy by the time the new winged generation of parasitoids emerges and abandons their dead host.

Before he joined our faculty, Father Fortier worked extensively with men and women who belong to tribes native to the Pacific Northwest of the United States. He said he wanted to continue to honor the cultures of Native Americans and their relationships with their land. He asked me to lend him my copy of Michael Jordan's *Encyclopedia of Gods,* and that developed his interest in their folklore. A few weeks ago he told me he was preparing a revision of a group of braconid wasps. Some were new species, and a few would be named after spirits found in the religions of Native Americans. *Aleiodes mannegishii* alludes to trickster spirits in the stories of the Cree nation. The Mannegishi are a tiny race with six fingers on each hand. A braconid is a small insect and, like all adult wasps, has a six-legged body. The Cree believed that the faces of the Mannegishi lacked noses and had big eyes (much like the heads of parasitoid wasps).

So many more names from Greco-Roman mythology almost beg to be used as well. Demeter's daughter, Persephone, represents the annual return of the spring season and the agricultural cycle of edible grains (see §5.2). The name Persephone (Greek) or Proserpina (Roman) is not given to any living group of plants at the present time. That's a wasted opportunity in my book. Why not let Proserpina serve as a new genus of grasses? Better yet, Persephone stays in the underworld through the winter. Why not give her name to a wildflower with a cold-dormant tuber or bulb?

GLOSSARY

ADNATION. The fusion of different organs in the same flower. For example, when stamens become adnate to the central pistil, they form a compound organ called the column.

ALKALOIDS. A large class of defensive chemicals manufactured by many angiosperms and some fungi. The skeleton ring(s) of an alkaloid molecule consists of carbon atoms and at least one nitrogen atom.

ANDROECIUM. The ring or rings of male organs (stamens) in a flower.

ANGIOSPERM. A plant identified by female reproductive organs that make seeds inside the closed and chambered ovary of a carpel or a pistil.

ANNUAL. A herbaceous growth habit in which the plant matures during a single growing season and is also genetically programmed to die after it blooms and sets seed. An herb that takes two growing seasons to store enough resources to reproduce and die is often called a biennial.

BERRY. A fleshy fruit containing more than one seed. In most berries, the seeds are housed in two or more chambers.

BRACT. A modified leaf that protects an immature flower bud or an entire branch of maturing buds. Some bracts are small and scalelike, whereas others form large, colorful flags or hoods around stalks of relatively inconspicuous flowers (*see* spathe). In gymnosperms, the bracts often form hard shingles and protect the seeds in spirally arranged cones.

BULB. An underground, perennial stem with a compact, globular or teardrop shape. Bulbs protect their growth shoots with layers of scaly or papery leaves (the brown "wrappers" on an onion or tulip bulb).

BUSH. *See* shrub.

CALYX. The ring or rings of sepals in a flower that usually form the young, protective bud case.

CARPELS. Female organs in a flower that make up the central ring known as the gynoecium. Each carpel contains one or more unfertilized seeds that must wait patiently for the sperm inside a pollen grain. When carpels fuse together, they form a compound organ called the pistil.

COALESCENCE. The fusion of two or more organs in the same ring in the same flower. For example, when the sides of all the petals in the same corolla coalesce, they form a continuous funnel or bell.

COLUMN. A compound reproductive organ found in the center of the flowers of most orchids, milkweeds, trigger plants, and some other blossoms. A column is a pillar or knoblike organ consisting of one or more male organs (stamens) fused to a female organ (pistil).

CORM. An underground perennial stem with a compact, globular, teardrop or torpedo shape. Corms lack protective, scaly leaves and are either naked or wear a thin layer of fibers, known as the tunic.

COROLLA. The ring or rings of petals in a flower.

CORONA. A continuous and round rim, tube, or wispy halo produced by the corollas of some flowers.

COTYLEDON. One or more leaflike organs that remain attached to the embryo inside a mature seed. In most plants, the cotyledons vanish or shrivel up within a couple of days after the seed sprouts and the young stem shoot produces its first, true, foliage leaves.

DEMULCENT. A herbal remedy made of gooey plant mucilage that is supposed to soothe the throat or stomach.

DIOECIOUS. Having exclusively either all male (pollen-making) flowers or all female (seed-making) flowers on each plant in the same population. In Linnaean terms, husbands (male flowers) and wives (female flowers) live in two different and isolated houses (male or female plants).

ENDOCARP. One or more layers of tissue inside a fruit that surround one or more mature fertilized seeds. Some endocarps are soft and fibrous, whereas others are hard and stonelike (as in the pit of a peach or plum).

EPIPHYTE. An herb or small shrub that spends its adult life attached to the limb or trunk of a larger, woody plant. Epiphyte roots usually function as attachment organs. They do not penetrate the host tree or rob it of stored water and food.

ESSENTIAL OILS. Fragrant and spicy molecules often found in flowers, ripe fruit, leaf glands, resins, and tree bark. They are so light in weight that they explode into airborne particles at room temperature. They are not essential to the life of the plant, but they do become an "essence" in the air. Reduced to liquids at lower temperatures, they have a greasy feel, but they are not true oils and usually belong to a large class of molecules known as terpenes.

EXOCARP. Mature fruit skin or peel consisting of one or more layers of tissue.

FLOWER. A much-reduced branch consisting of one to several rings, spirals, or both rings and spirals of modified leaves in which unfertilized seeds are locked inside bottle-shaped ovaries.

FORM (forma). Infrequent but recurrent genetic-based differences noted among members of a population all belonging to the same species. Forms occur with predictable mathematical frequency in a generation owing to natural rates of mutation or the expression of a recessive gene. For example, plant species that produce purple flowers will almost invariably have one or more populations in which we can find one individual bearing pure white flowers.

FRUIT. A mature ovary that consists of one or more chambers containing one or more fertilized seeds.

GENUS. Every species (*see* species) has two names (the binomial). The genus name is always given first (*Rosa* [genus] *centrifolia* [species]). Think of the genus name as a surname (Cohen, Jones, Lopez, or Smith) linking together closely related species sharing a common, genetic origin (Myra Cohen, Frank Cohen, Lisa Cohen, Edward Cohen). Consequently, we recognize almost a hundred species of rose bushes in the genus *Rosa* (*R. carolina, R. chinensis, R. damascena, R. multiflora, R. rugosa*, and dozens more).

GONDWANA. The ancient, southern supercontinent that once contained the conjoined tectonic plates of Antarctica, South America, India, Africa, Madagascar, Australia, and New Zealand. The major plates started separating toward the end of the Jurassic period, more than 135 million years ago. India rafted northward, collided with Eurasia, and "sent up" the Himalayas.

GYMNOSPERM. A plant that makes seeds but lacks flowers. An immature gymnosperm seed is usually attached to a little scale that leaves the seed exposed to the open air when it is old enough to receive incoming pollen. Many gymnosperms arrange seeds in pairs on the same scale. In turn, the scales are arranged in spirals forming cones that are protected by hard, shinglelike bracts.

GYNOECIUM. The central cluster of carpels in a flower or a large, compound pistil.

HABIT. The growth form taken by a plant when it reaches reproductive maturity. Habits are either woody or herbaceous.

HELIOTROPISM. When leaves and some stems change their angle or position to track the sun's rays as the earth revolves on its axis, they are said to be heliocentric. Most heliocentric leaves have a pulvinus.

HERBACEOUS. A genetically programmed growth habit in which the primary stem fails to lay down wood cells (xylem) in reinforced rings. Herbaceous habits are either annual or perennial.

HERBAL. A book of lore describing plants reputed to have medicinal virtues.

HERBARIUM. A museum for plants in which most specimens are pressed, mounted on labeled sheets, and stored in cabinets. Large, hard fruits are usually cross-referenced and stored in boxes. Large, fleshy fruits or flowers with thick, succulent tissues may be pickled and stored in bottles or vials.

HESPERIDIUM. A specialized berry found in some members of the citrus family (Rutaceae). Each fruit usually consists of a thick and fragrant exocarp, a mesocarp that subdivides into segments (each segment is filled with many juice sacs), and an endocarp of hollow hairs (pith).

HOLOTYPE. A labeled specimen, stored in a museum, once used to describe a new species. The published description of the new species is ultimately based on the characteristics found on the holotype specimen.

HYBRID. The offspring between two species. Some hybrid plants are known to backcross to one or more of their parent species. When this occurs over several generations, the combined population of parent species, first-generation hybrids, and back-crosses are known as a hybrid swarm.

HYPANTHIUM. A continuous floral cup, bell, or sleeve-shaped tube formed by fusing the sepals to the petals and then fusing the same petals to the stamens.

INVOLUCRUM. A disc or bowl made of many curving, interlocking bracts. They make a platform supporting hundreds or thousands of small flowers arranged in a continuous spiral. Most members of the daisy family (Asteraceae) arrange their tiny flowers in involucra. Some field guides or wildflower books refer to the involucrum as a head inflorescence.

LABELLUM. The lip petal of an orchid. Orchid flowers typically have three petals. Two lateral petals are identical to each other. The shape, margins, and sculptures found on a labellum are usually distinct from the lateral peals. The labellum lies directly opposite the column and often serves as the landing platform for pollinating insects.

LAURASIA. This is the great, northern supercontinent that once included the North American and Eurasian tectonic plates. Laurasia's fragmentation occurred relatively late in geological history, with major plates separating early in the Tertiary period, sixty-five million to seventy million years ago. It explains why the flora of eastern Canada and the United States resembles much of the vegetation of northwestern Europe and why Japan, Korea, and eastern China share similar botanical treasures (primroses, peonies, heaths, and slipper orchids) with Vancouver and the Pacific Northwest of the United States.

MEDITERRANEAN HABITAT. A complex of environments often located on the west coast of continents. They experience hot, dry summers and cool (not freezing), wet winters. Shrubs are the dominant woody life form, and most fresh leaf and stem growth occurs during the winter. Most of the Mediterranean basin consists of interlocking Mediterranean habitats, but the same climate and similar soil patterns are also found in southern California, Chile, western Australia, and at the Cape of Good Hope.

MESOCARP. The middle layer of tissue in a fruit. In fleshy fruits, the mesocarp consists of loosely attached cells that often contain lots of water, sugars, starches, or oils.

MONOECIOUS. Having two different kinds of unisexual flowers (male and female) on the same plant. Husbands (stamens) and wives (carpels) live in the same house (the same stem or branch) but occupy different rooms (the flowers).

NECTAR. A watery secretion enriched with sugars and other nutrients.

NECTAR GUIDE. Sharply contrasting colors on flower skin indicating the location of nectar secreted by a nectary.

NECTARY OR NECTAR GLAND. A gland that develops on the surface of plant skin that secretes nectar during some stage of the plant's life cycle.

ORCHIS SYSTEM. *See* tuberoids.

OVARY. The chambered base of a carpel or pistil containing one or more unfertilized seeds.

PARASITE. A plant that penetrates the stems or roots of another plant and then attaches itself to the host's conducting tissues and robs it of water and, in some cases, sugars. Parasites typically have special invasive organs instead of true roots of their own.

PERENNIAL. An herb that lives more than one or two growing seasons because its primary stem retreats into a state of dormancy when physical conditions become unfavorable. In temperate zones the long-lived, primary stem often lives underground, taking the form of a bulb, corm, tuber, or rhizome.

PETAL. A flat, sterile organ in a flower that is often broad, colored, and scented. Petals make up the ring or rings known as the corolla.

PISTIL. The central, female organ in a flower formed by the fusion of two or more carpels.

POLLEN. Living grains that contain one or more sperm cells. Stamens make pollen, encasing each grain in a double-layered wall.

POLLINATION. The deposition of pollen grains onto the receptive stigma or stigmas of a carpel or a pistil. Although some flowers are self-fertile and pollinate themselves, most require a pollinator to move grains from stamens to pistils.

POLLINATOR. Forces of nature (air currents, water currents, or gravity) or animals (insects, birds, bats, or small wingless mammals) that transport pollen to the receptive tips of carpels and pistils. Animal pollinators usually visit flowers in search of edible rewards, including nectar, pollen, edible oils, starch bodies, and other substances.

PULVINUS. A swollen joint on a leaf stalk (petiole). When the pulvinus is filled with water (turgid) it allows the flattened leaf blade to track the sun.

PURGATIVE. An irritant, and often violent, herbal remedy given to induce rapid evacuation of the bowels. Purgatives stimulate natural, wavelike muscular contractions (peristalsis) that move food through the digestive organs. They were given to people in the hope of cleansing the body of accumulated poisons. Purgatives used to expel internal parasites (flukes and worms) were often called vermifuges.

RESINS. Fragrant and sticky fluids concealed in special, interconnecting, ductlike cells beneath the bark or in the young wood of many trees and shrubs. When collected resins harden naturally upon exposure to the air, they are called copals. Resins may protect woody plants from some diseases and boring insects (moth or beetle larvae).

RHIZOME. A jointed, often branching, primary stem that grows in a horizontal pattern. When a rhizome grows underground, it produces lateral buds that develop into secondary aerial stems or leaf clusters. These new organs grow upward and penetrate the soil's surface.

RHIZOTOMI. The ancient root collectors of Greece and the Grecian colonies found throughout the Mediterranean basin. Their combined lore about how to identify plants, where to find them in season, and their virtues as medicines were compiled in texts known as herbals.

SEPAL. Flat, sterile, and often leaflike organs that make up the calyx in a flower.

SHRUB. A plant with a woody habit, erect or creeping, consisting of many branching, secondary stems but with no obvious central trunk.

SPADIX. A fleshy or scaly stalk of small, often unisexual flowers resembling a miniature corncob, reptile's tongue, or animal's tail. A spadix is usually hooded or partially sheathed by a spathe.

SPATHE. A bract that is so large it can form a sheath around an equally large branch of flowers. Spathes are particularly common in the palm (Arecaceae) and jack-in-the-pulpit (Araceae) families. The spathes of jack-in-the-pulpits are more than protective structures. Their color and shape help attract and detain pollinators that visit the interior cob of small flowers (the spadix).

SPECIES. One or more populations in which the individuals share the same life cycle. Taxonomists give each species a double name (the binomial). Each binomial starts with the genus name (*see* genus) and ends with the species name.

STAMEN. The pollen-making organ in a flower. Most stamens consist of a solitary and sterile stalk (the filament) that ends in a swollen, lobed pollen box (the anther).

STIGMA. The specialized, glandular tip of a carpel or pistil that receives, accepts, and processes incoming pollen.

SYNONYM. A previous name of a genus or species now replaced by a new name. A scientific name (binomial) may become a synonym for several reasons including invalid publication, inattention to valid characteristics found on the holotype, or failure to account for overlapping rates of variability between closely related populations.

TONIC. An herbal remedy believed to stimulate sluggish bodily functions. Tonics were believed to increase the appetites of sick people if swallowed or to encourage hair growth if rubbed on a bald scalp.

TREE. A plant with a woody habit (usually erect) that consists of a single primary stem (trunk) strong enough to support the weight and drag of one or more smaller, secondary stems (branches).

TROPANE ALKALOID. A special class of alkaloids (*see* alkaloids) made primarily by members of the nightshade family (Solanaceae). The plant cell combines molecules of acetic acid and ornithine, producing a toxin that is often fatal if swallowed even in dilute solutions.

TUBER. A swollen, irregularly shaped, underground stem protected by a layer of bark. Tubers are usually packed with storage starch. Aerial stems emerge from dimpled buds (eyes) embedded in the bark.

TUBEROID. Paired, underground storage bags connected below the seasonal stems and roots of some perennial herbs (especially soil-dwelling orchids). Tuberoids resemble a pair of mismatched testicles, and their internal tissues combine stem and root characteristics.

VALVE. A discrete segment that protects developing cells or seeds. When valves dry out, they separate along proscribed weak points known as sutures. Valves in a dry fruit (pod) release seeds when they open. Valves in a stamen release pollen grains.

VARIETY. Small, physical differences noted between plants isolated in different populations over the natural range of a species. Zoologists are more likely to use the word *subspecies* to indicate the small but consistent differences between populations of the same animal species.

VINE. Climbing and twining plants producing stems that are so elongated they are unable to grow upward without using other things (trees, boulders, walls) for support. Vines may be herbaceous or woody. A woody vine is known properly as a liane.

VULNERARY. A traditional remedy in which a fresh or dried piece of a plant is placed in an open wound.

WOOD. When water-conducting cells (xylem) are laid down in continuous, interconnecting layers over several growing seasons, they form a reinforced and internal skeleton within stems and roots. In most plants with woody habits the xylem layers are produced by a thin, living cylinder of tissue known as the vascular cambium.

Selected and Annotated Bibliography

Biographies of Botanists

Blunt, Wilfrid. *The Compleat Naturalist: A Life of Linnaeus.* New York: Viking Press, 1971.

There are more recent and detailed biographies of Linnaeus, but this "scrap-book" version is so well illustrated, it really gives you a feeling for the man's life and the impact he had on his students and the scientific community in general. The two chapters on Linnaeus in Lapland may become personal favorites, as they leave the reader with an impression of what a graduate student can do in an alien landscape armed with the simplest tools.

Evans, Howard. E. *Pioneer Naturalists: The Discovery and Naming of North American Plants and Animals.* New York: Henry Holt, 1993.

The genus and/or species names of many American plants honor early explorers and natural historians. Howard Evans (1919–2002) provides a biographical sketch of each naturalist with engaging titles like "Nelsons's Larkspur" and "Woodhouse's Toad." The ill-fated Constantine Rafinesque is represented by a big-eared bat. Evans was a prolific author who wrote many natural history books for nonscientists. He deserves to be rediscovered.

Stearn, William T., ed. *John Lindley (1799–1865): Gardener-Botanist and Pioneer Orchidologist.* Bicentenary celebration ed. Suffolk, UK: Antique Collectors' Club in association with the Royal Horticultural Society, 1999.

John Lindley is such an important figure in the history of botanical science that it is a shame I had to abbreviate his life and accomplishments. Fortunately, this book was published to celebrate his birth, now more than two hundred years ago. Ten botanists and historians of science take a serious look at the Lindley legacy and his contributions to the study of orchids, fossil plants, and economically important plants. The reproductions of nineteenth-century color plates of tropical orchids are magnificent.

GRECO-ROMAN RESOURCES

Baumann, Hellmut. *The Greek Plant World in Myth, Art and Literature.* Portland, OR: Timber Press, 1993.

Obviously a labor of love, Baumann examines most aspects of nature worship in the extinct religion of pre-Christian Greece. Wild and domesticated plant species are associated with appropriate myths and religious rituals. Color photographs make it easier to understand passages in stories, plays, and lyrics. The author supplies a color photo of a pressed, dried flower of rocket larkspur and shows how to pick out the *A* and the *I*. You will also find a dramatic shot of a maritime squill nailed to a doorway.

Detienne, Marcel. *The Gardens of Adonis: Spices in Greek Mythology.* Translated by Janet Lloyd. Princeton, NJ: Princeton University Press, 1994.

The author disagrees with the standard interpretation of the Adonis myth—that the death of the hero symbolized the withering of crop plants during the hot, dry, Greek summer. To prove his point, Detienne compares the lore and use of aromatic plants and spices in classical Greek culture versus the tending and harvest of grain crops. Although I do not find the overarching argument convincing, I appreciate Detienne's discussion of unfamiliar myths and for providing translations of ancient commentaries on the natural histories of bees, birds, and plants.

Farrar, Linda. *Ancient Roman Gardens.* Gloucestershire, UK: Sutton Publishing, 2000.

How often is a specialized history book both informative and fun? Farrar accounts for the plants that Romans grew for pleasure and profit. The Roman taste for topiary, odd tools, small statues, water effects, and novel inventions (imagine a ceramic container for fattening dormice) rivals modern English gardens in complexity and whimsy.

Graves, Robert. *The Greek Myths,* 2 vols. London: Penguin Books, 1957.

Robert Graves linked hundreds, or perhaps thousands, of myth fragments, derived from dozens of sources. His two volumes remain the most accessible reference books for reconstructing stories with multiple plots and changing casts of characters. For example, Graves offers four different Creation myths. He gives three different reasons as to why Theseus decided to abandon Ariadne on the island of Naxos. Most scholars disagree with Graves's obsessive argument that true Greek myths symbolize the displacement and subjugation of a goddess-based religion (officiated by female priests) for a brotherhood of gods (controlled by inflexible male priests). There are odd omissions. Graves listed all the possible names for the Sirens but forgot to name all nine Muses. Be forewarned also that Graves excludes all Roman myths (for example, Cupid and Psyche, Janus, Pomona, and Vertumnus).

Hesiod. *The Works and Days, Theogony, The Shield of Herakles.* Ann Arbor: University of Michigan Press, 1987.

Most scholars go back to the Greek poet, Hesiod (seventh century B.C.E.) for the standard Creation myth and the genealogy of the gods and goddesses. *Theogony,* in particular, provides most of the names of the minor characters (nymphs, winds, Fates, monsters) derived from Titan parents. The poem suggests that honors attributed to some goddesses declined with time. Hesiod revered the protection of Hecate, whom later poets reviled as an underworld goddess who practiced black magic.

Hollingsworth, E. Buckner. *Flower Chronicles: The Legend and Lore of Fifteen Garden Favorites.* 2nd ed. Chicago: University of Chicago Press, 2004.

Buckner Hollingsworth (1892–1979) was fascinated by the uses of popular garden flowers long before they were grown solely for ornament. She spent at least seven years reading some of the oldest books on mythology, herbal remedies, cookery, heraldry, cosmetics, and archeological treatises. While the chapters discuss the use of the plants in the United States, England, and China, readers will also learn what Greco-Roman societies thought of irises, roses, peonies, primroses, lilies, and other flowers. The Romans, for example, believed roses were effective in the treatment of rabies. Hollingsworth's chapter on the saffron crocus is a good place to begin before attempting to enter the world of ancient Crete as unearthed and described by Sir Arthur Evans.

Jordan, Michael. *Encyclopedia of Gods: Over 2,500 Deities of the World.* New York: Facts on File, 1993.

Members of the Greco-Roman pantheon are described and may sometimes be compared and contrasted with the deities of Semitic, Polynesian, Norse, Chinese, and Hindu civilizations. When there is sufficient information, the author provides the reader with known periods of worship, cult centers, art references, and literary sources for each god. Jordan is especially helpful when he explains the origin and attributes of the original Latin gods (Neptune, for example) before their worship was merged with Greek idols (Poseidon).

Ovid. *Metamorphoses.* Oxford World's Classics. Oxford: Oxford University Press, 1986.

A. D. Melville provided the English translation for this paperback edition, which is fun and easy to read. The footnotes are especially useful, because heroes and divinities often have more than one name. The index makes it easy to track down recurrent characters, like Circe or Minerva, within the epic. This is where most people go to find the more obscure myths associated with Roman deities. The reader is left with the distinct impression that Ovid was particularly interested in the unnatural history of nymphs.

Thornton, Bruce S. *Eros: The Myth of Ancient Greek Sexuality.* Boulder, CO: Westview Press, 1997.

The author uses myths and dramas to argue that pre-Christian Greek societies were not cultures of eroticism and male experimentation. The Greeks lived in fear of Aphrodite and her servant/son. These deities ruined mortal careers, destroying prosperity and reputations. The text provides a number of unfamiliar versions of standard stories and comments briefly on seductive plant scents.

Zimmerman, John E. *Dictionary of Classical Mythology.* New York: Bantam Books, 1971.

This dictionary lists characters in Greek and Roman myths. Extensive cross-referencing makes the complicated genealogy of gods and heroes much less bewildering. Like most classical scholars, Zimmerman was interested primarily in the role of mythological figures in classical allusions. The author gives the titles of plays and poems, written in Greek or Latin or English, in which these characters make their entries and exits.

PLANT CLASSIFICATION (TERMINOLOGY AND NOMENCLATURE)

Gledhill, David. *The Names of Plants*. Cambridge: Cambridge University Press, 2002.

This is an excellent place to begin if you come home from a nursery with a plant tagged only with a scientific name. It translates most species names, so you can discriminate between *ermersus* (rising out of the water), *emerus* (an Italian name for vetch legumes), and *emeticus* (makes you vomit). I wish the author had included more genus names, but Quattrocchi (see below) takes care of that.

Mabberley, David J. *The Plant Book: A Portable Dictionary of the Higher Plants*. 2nd ed. Cambridge: Cambridge University Press, 2002.

All genera and families of ferns, cone-bearing trees, and flowering plants are listed alphabetically. The author gives you the number of known species in the genus, the natural distribution of the genus, and, when available, interesting bits of information about their life cycles, commercial and traditional. Mabberley's book is particularly helpful, as he also lists genera that were reduced to synonym status within the past five to ten years. He cross-references the old synonym with the new genus name or combination. *The Plant Book* is the quickest and easiest reference to updated names. A new volume came out in 2006. However, Mabberley will not tell you what the genus name means or how it was derived. For that, you need Quattrocchi (2002), see below.

Porter, Cedric L. *Taxonomy of Flowering Plants*. 2nd ed. San Francisco: W. H. Freeman, 1967.

Plenty of fine textbooks on plant taxonomy and systematics remain in print. However, I must recommend this golden oldie to the novice, even though it contains an outdated system of classification. The merits of this book include its brief biographies of plant taxonomists and its historical summary of plant classification before DNA analyses. There is also a fine introduction to plant collection and herbarium protocol. Within only a page and a half, Porter explains how a new species is described using the Type Method. Fine pen-and-ink diagrams reviewing plant anatomy and morphology are easy to follow.

Most of the families described in the book remain valid even though their classes and orders have changed. Representative flowers of each family receive two kinds of drawings. The first is an architectural "floor plan" that simply shows the numbers of each organ present and how they are connected to each other. The second drawing of the flower offers a more realistic, longitudinal section, depicting the relative lengths and positions of the organs.

Quattrocchi, Umberto. *CRC Dictionary of Plant Names*. 4 vols. Boca Raton, FL: CRC Press, 2002.

Bulky but necessary, these volumes translate each plant genus and tell you who described them. Without Quattrocchi it would have taken many more years to write my book. The author lists both current genera and old synonyms. Some names (for example, *Janusia*) are missing, but no explanation is provided.

Schultes, Richard E., and Arthur S. Pease. *Generic Names of Orchids: Their Origin and Meaning*. New York: Academic Press, 1963.

Another collector's item, but orchid fanciers and growers would benefit if it were reprinted and updated. Orchid taxonomists bicker constantly over the classification of their plants. Many new genera were erected after 1963, while old genera were reduced to synonyms. When descriptive names are used, the authors break down the Greek words for you and refer to appropriate parts of the plant's anatomy. The book is always charming, as it is well illustrated with nearly two centuries of botanical plates and the portraits of famous botanists.

Shosteck, Robert. *Flowers and Plants: An International Lexicon with Biographical Notes.* New York: Quadrangle Press, 1974.

If you prefer to start with common names, this may be the place for you. The author alphabetizes more than eleven hundred common names and provides a scientific name to the right of each common entry. One or two paragraphs discuss the derivation of the common name and add information on the life cycle or its history as a garden plant. The trouble, as always, is that so many plant species have more than one common name. About a third of the species are accompanied by nice line drawings located in the book's margins.

Stearn, William T. *Botanical Latin.* 4th ed. Portland, OR: Timber Press, 2004.

Available since 1966, this is the standard reference work used to write a valid, publishable description of a new genus or species. Almost every English-speaking plant taxonomist owns a copy. The reader is taught how to conjugate and abbreviate. Stearn provides you with the terminology needed to describe the colors, forms, surface textures, leaf-folding patterns, and growth directions of plant organs.

Practical Botany and the Natural History of Plants

Bernhardt, Peter. *The Rose's Kiss: A Natural History of Flowers.* Chicago: University of Chicago Press, 2002.

I offer this book as a "modest alternative" if you have problems understanding passages describing flowers. I explain the function and arrangement of organs in a blossom, what happens if they fuse together, and how floral sexuality changes from species to species. There are also chapters about how animals pollinate pistils and some evolutionary history based on the reconstruction of fossil blossoms.

Duke, James. *Handbook of Medicinal Herbs.* 2nd ed. Boca Raton, FL: CRC Press, 2002.

Every year, some student or staff member asks me to recommend an appropriate book on medicinal plants. The request makes me shudder. Does the world need another weekend shaman or wannabe sorceress? Most modern herbals are plagiaristic and rarely give you the full story about side effects. This is the only American herbal I trust. Duke always does his homework, combing through centuries of dubious research. I personally recommend all of his books for both their scholarly research and dry sense of humor.

Langenheim, Jean H. *Plant Resins: Chemistry, Evolution, Ecology, Ethnobotany.* Portland, OR: Timber Press, 2003.

If you are interested in the history of Mediterranean civilizations and their use of plants, you need to know more about natural resins. Greco-Roman societies were dependent on plant resins for many spices, glues, perfumes, and medicines. Langenheim covers them all and adds important chapters on amber's natural history and trade.

Mann, John. *Murder, Magic, and Medicine*. Oxford: Oxford University Press, 1996.

 The book begins with a brief introduction on how our bodies make and disperse chemical messages. The remainder is an unusually lively account of what happens when molecules made by plants, fungi, and bacteria enter our bodies with, and without, our consent. As a plant chemical often has more than one effect, it is often hard to tell the villains (mandrake, nightshade, aconite, wormwood, coca) from the heroes (foxglove, cinchona, Mexican yam).

Raven, Peter H., Ray F. Evert, and Susan Eichhorn. *Biology of Plants*. 7th ed. New York: W. H. Freeman, 2005.

 This is the standard textbook assigned to most undergraduate classes in plant biology and general botany. I have been using this well-illustrated volume as a source of lecture materials since my Peace Corps days (1974–1977). The latest edition is always the best one to buy, because the authors stay abreast of discoveries and trends in this vast discipline.

Simpson, Beryl B., and Molly C. Ogorzaly. *Economic Botany: Plants in Our World*. 3rd ed. New York: McGraw-Hill Higher Education, 2001.

 How do you know when a plant is domesticated? Where were the great centers of domestication? The authors answer these questions and then present detailed chapters on the history of species used for food, medicine, fibers, alcohol, and so forth. Their analyses of how the contents of chocolate seeds are processed are particularly good. The manufacture of modern, refined candy is a surprisingly recent process.

Stearn, William T., and Peter D. Davis. *Peonies of Greece*. Kifissia, Greece: Goulandris Natural History Museum, 1984.

 Although this work is often treated more as an art book, the authors provide excellent information on Mediterranean peonies in myth and medicine. This is followed by a standard, but beautiful, botanical monograph. Each species is illustrated to show how its leaves and flower vary in nature.

Thompson, John D. *Plant Evolution in the Mediterranean*. Oxford: Oxford University Press, 2005.

 Robert Graves saw a Mediterranean ruled by a triple goddess (maiden, mother, and crone). John Thompson sees plant evolution in the Mediterranean basin as a triple process. It involves climatic changes influencing the length of seasons, ancient and ongoing geological activity, and the long-term impact of humans' agricultural practices and domesticated animals—all of which is very convincing. The book is especially good when it addresses changes in chromosome numbers in wild plants, variation in fragrant oils, and sex expression in the flowers of jasmines, narcissus, daphne, and various mints.

Vaughn, John G., and Catherine A. Geissler. *The New Oxford Book of Food Plants*. New York: Oxford University Press, 1998.

 Here is an opportunity to view some of the least familiar gourmet items and to learn about their classification and countries of origin. Even edible seaweeds get a couple of pages. The beautiful illustrations were drawn and colored by B. E. Nicholson. Your vegetable garden never looked this good.

Botanical Illustration

Baillon, Henri. *Histoire Naturelle des Plantes.* 8 vols. Paris: Librairie Hachette, 1886–1903.

This multivolume series was completed posthumously after Baillon died in 1895. The illustrations emphasize the architecture of flowering branches, individual flowers, and their organs but there are some nice surprises. For example, you will find some simple but clear drawings that show how seeds of *Posidonia* sprout underwater and how the pods of *Lotus* twist as their valves open to release their seeds. When you reach the monocotyledons the artists enjoy depicting leaves and flowering stalks emerging from uprooted and partially dissected bulbs and corms.

Britton, Nathaniel, and Addison Brown. *An Illustrated Flora of the Northern United States, Canada and the British Possessions.* New York: Charles Scribner's Sons, 1913.

Considered a classic by most North American botanists. We still refer to later versions when we want to see the growth form of an unfamiliar plant. I prefer its drawings of water plants to a number of recent books.

Engler, Adolf, and Karl Prantl. *Die Naturlichen Pflanzenfamilien.* 32 vols. Leipzig: Verlag von Wilhelm, 1887–1909.

In some ways, illustrations in this overwhelming series of volumes are superior to those you find in Baillon. Engler and Prantl wanted their artists to draw the mature growth form of plants, so you find more depictions of the growth forms taken by both woody plants and wildflowers. This is an early and respected attempt to use Darwin's theories to trace the evolutionary history of flowers. Drawings reflect an interest in comparing primitive versus advanced organs and structures.

Lindley, John, Joseph Paxton, and Thomas Baines. *Paxton's Flower Garden.* London: Cassell, Petter, Galpin & Co., 1882.

The book began as a series of magazine issues describing rare and choice plants for collectors. The color plates are small but magnificent and reflect Lindley's bias in favor of tropical plants, especially orchids and water lilies.

General Index

Acacallis (princess), 104, 108
Acantha (nymph), 130, 132
acanthus (Acanthaceae), 133, 173
acetic acid, 146
Achilles, 8, 174, 175, 179, 183;
 Neoptolemus (son), 179
Acmena (nymph), 122
aconitine, 161
Acrisius (king of Argos), 148, 153
Adonia (festival), 143
Adonis, 142–144
Adrasteia (ash tree goddess), 71
Aeetes (king of Colchis), 164
aerenchyma (buoyant tissue), 83
Aesop's fables, 101
Africa, 54, 59, 64, 68, 76, 97, 100, 102, 103,
 104, 106, 108, 110, 118, 124, 138, 141, 143,
 151, 165, 177, 180, 182–184, 186, 190, 192;
 Cape of Good Hope, 54, 59, 74,
 177; Cameroon, 151; Libya, 185;
 Madagascar, 64, 70, 92, 106, 108, 110,
 143, 179; Morocco, 39, 61, 75; Rift
 Valley, 131; St. Thomas (African
 island), 52; Tunisia, 31
Agamemnon (king of Mycenae), 52, 171,
 174
Agave (queen of Thebes), 114, 116, 117
Agenor (king), 184
agora (marketplace), 153

Ajax, 174–176
Alciope (nymph), 71, 74; Celmis (son),
 71, 74
Alcmene (queen of Troezen), 156
alcohols, 27
alkaloids, 46, 89, 132; tropane, 146, 156
Alectryon, 130
Alexander the Great, 103
allelopathy, 70
Alpheus (river god), 56
Al-Shebaz, Ihsan, 189, 190
Althaea (queen of Clydon), 145, 147
Amaltheia (mythical goat), 71, 73
amaryllis (Amaryllidaceae), 61
amber, 128, 129; jewelry, 129
ambrosia (food of the gods), 87, 162
America, *see* North America; South
 America
American Indians, 109, 100, 110, 117, 139,
 167, 199; Cree, 199; Chippewa, 109,
 158
amino acids, 89
ammonia and methane, 91
Amphion and Zethus (princes of
 Thebes), 136
Amphitrite (sea nymph), 82
Amphitryon (king of Troezen), 136
Amymone (princess of Argos), 165
Andes, 132, 186

INDEX OF
SCIENTIFIC NAMES

About the Author

Peter Bernhardt is a professor of botany in the Department of Biology at Saint Louis University. He is also a research associate of the Missouri Botanical Garden (St. Louis) and the Royal Botanic Gardens of Sydney (New South Wales, Australia). His research concentrates on the pollination and evolution of flowers.